Coordinating Public and Private Sustainability

This book demonstrates the need to coordinate private and corporate actors with national and global sustainable climate policies, with conventions in the spheres of green energy laws, as well as from the spheres of commercial, trade, and other private law.

While many states have joined together in the Paris Agreements in support of green energy policies, it remains a stark reality that most of the efforts to reduce greenhouse emissions remain with private actors who operate the various industries, vehicles, and vessels that emit the gases in target. The risks of anthropogenic climate change cannot be solved by environmental law alone and will need complementary support from commercial, corporate, and private law. However, aspects of commercial law, securities law, and trade law can be shown to frustrate certain aspects of green energy policies, resulting in damaging "green paradoxes". It raises issues associated with corporate social responsibility and green paradoxes, with international trade laws, and with liability risks for misrepresenting the state of feasible green energy technologies.

The book will be of interest to students and scholars in the fields of energy law, environmental law, and corporate law.

Chair and Professor Roy Andrew Partain is the Director of the Research Centre for Commercial Law at the University of Aberdeen. He is also the Director of its PhD in Law Program as well as the Theme Coordinator for Aberdeen's multiple LLM programs specializing in International Commercial Law, International Trade Law, and Sustainable Development.

Routledge Research in Energy Law and Regulation

Regulation in the European Electricity Sector
Maciej M. Sokolowski

Nuclear Energy Regulation, Risk and The Environment
Abdullah Al Faruque

Local Content Oil and Gas Law in Africa
Lessons from Nigeria and Beyond
Pereowei Subai

Host Government Agreements and the Law in the Energy Sector
The case of Azerbaijan and Turkey
Hakan Sahin

Iraq's Oil and Gas Industry
The Legal and Contractual Framework
Janan Al-Asady

The Development of Iran's Upstream Oil and Gas Industry
The Potential Role of New Concession Contracts
Mahmoud Fard Kardel

Coordinating Public and Private Sustainability
Green Energy Policy, International Trade Law, and Economic Mechanisms
Roy A. Partain

For more information about this series, please visit: www.routledge.com/Routledge-Research-in-Energy-Law-and-Regulation/book-series/RRELR

Coordinating Public and Private Sustainability

Green Energy Policy, International Trade Law, and Economic Mechanisms

Roy A. Partain

Routledge
Taylor & Francis Group
LONDON AND NEW YORK

First published 2020
by Routledge
2 Park Square, Milton Park, Abingdon, Oxon OX14 4RN

and by Routledge
605 Third Avenue, New York, NY 10017

First issued in paperback 2021

Routledge is an imprint of the Taylor & Francis Group, an informa business

Publisher's Note
The publisher has gone to great lengths to ensure the quality of this reprint but points out that some imperfections in the original copies may be apparent.

British Library Cataloguing-in-Publication Data
A catalogue record for this book is available from the British Library

Library of Congress Cataloging-in-Publication Data
Names: Partain, Roy, author.
Title: Coordinating public and private sustainability : green energy policy, international trade law, and economic mechanisms / Prof. Roy A. Partain.
Description: New York : Routledge, 2020. | Series: Routledge research in energy law and regulation | Includes bibliographical references and index.
Identifiers: LCCN 2019043334 (print) | LCCN 2019043335 (ebook) | ISBN 9781138555297 (hardback) | ISBN 9781315149417 (ebook)
Subjects: LCSH: Sustainable development—Law and legislation. | Environmental law, International. | Climatic changes—Law and legislation. | Climatic changes—International cooperation. | Foreign trade regulation. | Greenhouse gases—Law and legislation. | Clean energy.
Classification: LCC K3585 .P37 2020 (print) | LCC K3585 (ebook) | DDC 363.738/746—dc23
LC record available at https://lccn.loc.gov/2019043334
LC ebook record available at https://lccn.loc.gov/2019043335

ISBN 13: 978-1-03-223955-2 (pbk)
ISBN 13: 978-1-138-55529-7 (hbk)

DOI: 10.4324/9781315149417

Typeset in Galliard
by Apex CoVantage, LLC

To Bokhee and Benjamin, for all the right reasons.

Contents

Detailed table of contents

Acknowledgements and notes of appreciation

This project began with a question, could the 'best of best' intents create policy chaos? Apparently, many people were thinking about it, as this book can now testify.

I much appreciate the aid and support I received from my university at the beginning of this project, Soongsil University. I could not have asked for better treatment and support in my research from my colleagues, and I truly could not have asked for a better group of student assistants who always made sure my computer was working and that my printer was loaded with ink and paper.

I remain in great debts to Prof. Dr. Panos Delimatsis, Chair of EU and International Economic Law, and to Prof. Dr. Jonathan Verschuuren, Professor of International and European Environmental Law, for their early encouragement and support of this project.

I would also like to thank the editors and teams behind the journals that accepted earlier stages of this research for their own volumes:

- Roy A. Partain, *Climate Change, Green Paradox Models, and International Trade Laws.* In: Research Handbook on Climate Change and Trade Law. (Panagiotis Delimatsis, ed., Edward Elgar; December, 2016).
- Roy A. Partain, *Is a Green Paradox Spectre Haunting International Climate Change Laws and Conventions?* 33 UCLA J. Envt'l L. & Pol'y 61 (2015).
- Roy A. Partain, *Gored by a Cornucopia: The Risk of Green Paradoxes from Laws and Policies that Incentivize Competitive Energy Innovations*, 3 LSU J. Energy L Resources 433 (2015).
- Roy A. Partain, *Environmental Laws for New and Renewable Energy Could Increase Greenhouse Gas Emissions*, 23 Chungnam L. Rev. 433 (2012).
- Roy A. Partain, *Korea's Green Energy Laws and Methane Hydrates*, 12 J. L. & Pol. Res. 591 (2012).

I would very much like to thank the University of Aberdeen for enabling me the time and support to complete this project. The School of Law has surrounded me with colleagues and students, each of whom have helped me to see bigger and better research questions.

Finally, I would like to thank the wonderful team at Routledge, for enduring me on this long and overdue project.

List of abbreviations

ALARA	As low as reasonably achievable
ASEAN	Association of South East Asian Nations
CCS	Carbon capture and storage
CO_2	Carbon dioxide
DOD	Department of Defense
DOE	Department of Energy
ECSC	European Coal and Steel Community
ECT	Energy Charter Treaty
EOR	Enhanced oil recovery
ERDA	Energy Research and Development Administration
ETR	Effective tax rate
GARCH	Generalized autoregressive conditional heteroskedasticity process
GATS	General Agreement on Trade in Services
GATT	General Agreement on Tariffs and Trade
GHG	Greenhouse gases
IPPC	Intergovernmental Panel on Climate Change
IRC	Internal Revenue Code (26 United States Code)
ITC	Investment tax credits
NAFTA	North America Free Trade Agreement
NASA	National Air and Space Administration
NRC	Nuclear Regulatory Commission
OPEC	Organization of Petroleum Exporting Countries
scf	Standard cubic feet
UNFCCC	United Nations Framework Convention on Climate Change
US	United States
USAF	United States Air Force
USMC	United States Marine Corps
USN	United States Navy
WTO	World Trade Organization

1 Introduction

1.1 Why this book should be read

This book examines how policymakers can better ensure that robust green energy policies are selected and enacted to best ensure the achievement of a sustainable future for all of us and for all future inhabitants on this planet.

The real question, though, is why hasn't this happened already?

There are two hidden problems in that goal, (i) how do policymakers identify which energy policies are robust in reducing greenhouse gas emissions and in reducing the threat of climate change and (ii) how might public rules be drafted and designed to best ensure their success to achieve those public goals of a sustainable and green future, given an already complex legal space of private law, trade law, and other laws in support of energy policies?

In particular, Hans-Werner Sinn challenged this basic agenda for green energy policies, claiming that green energy policies are doomed to fail because the combination of public goals to reduce carbon emissions will motivate private actors to increase their carbon emissions, for reasons discussed in detail over several chapters, resulting in what he labeled as green paradoxes.

So, are green energy policies doomed before they even begin? This book endeavors to suggest that they are not doomed, but that if green energy policies are drafted without considering the economic mechanisms engaged by both the pre-existing legal frameworks and the to-be-implemented green policies, much inefficiency and frustration could result. This book hopes to clarify where certain policy hazards lay and where other pathways may be feasible.

Might private self-interest thwart and frustrate the goals of a sustainable future, as predicted by Sinn? Or, could a 'moon shot' level of investment in diverse green energy projects enable a secure pathway to reduced carbon emissions? What if the situation is actually really complex; can we introduce new legal rules into a complex system of pre-existing legal rules, both public and private, to avoid problems and encourage better pathways?

This book attempts to examine which pathways might be more robust to prevent that frustration of green energy policies by corporate actors in the energy space; which energy goals are more resilient in keeping both corporate interests and public policy aligned to achieve a sustainable future?

This book will explore how economic models have provided arguments on both sides of this debate and how one might proceed to evaluate the claims of 'fitness,' which arguments best match the observed conditions and robustly provide pathways to our policy goals? It will examine a range of the proposed green paradox models to determine if any hold true dangers for policymakers. The book will go on to critically evaluate and sometimes counterargue against the models used in green paradox models.

The book will then evaluate the 'moon shot' approach; can too much green energy policy be a problem in itself? The findings will be that, yes, sometimes too much could be counterproductive for unexpected reasons. But a key finding is that abundant green energy is likely, without certain safeguards, to create competitive pressures for fossil fuels to become available at cheaper prices and likely enable consumers to purchase more fossil fuels and to emit more carbon.

The book will then examine the consequence of uncoordinated energy policies, as currently exist in multiple settings. It will explore the consequences of energy policies developed for purposes of 'national security' and for 'energy security'; that these rule sets operate in both green energy and fossil fuel policy spaces causes additional concern for guiding energy policy to a greener future. This is followed by a similar examination of how international conventions and agreements to ensure energy supplies potentially overlap with green energy policies. Next, the book also explores the dangers to green energy policies created by international trade laws that were designed to aid developing economies but without intent to address green energy policy concerns.

Finally, the book will provide a set of policy recommendations on how to best avoid the uncovered problems while remaining on the path to a sustainable future based on green energy policies – all the while considering the strategic needs and planning of corporate entities to ensure that they too are harmoniously on the same path to a green future.

1.2 The central purpose of this book

Hardin once wrote that inescapable social problems, those without rational solutions, should be considered tragedies in the dramatic sense.[1] Hardin's 'Tragedy of the Commons' was based on the mathematical method known as game theory, that we can examine social problems from a game theoretic perspective to learn and examine the range of potential outcomes from strategic choices. Hardin was concerned that certain social problems, if thusly examined, resulted in failure in all potential outcomes. And on point, he was quite concerned that many environmental problems faced exactly such a situation, that strategic choices made by many diverse parties would lead to sure environmental doom, accompanied by great human suffering.

Sinn presented an argument that would appear to establish that all green energy policies, policies that reduce greenhouse gas emissions, are not only doomed to fail but will also hasten the very evils that they were intended to prevent. This potential green paradox has been analyzed and examined by multiple economists,[2] and surely if there are mechanisms within climate change laws and conventions that give rise to green paradox results, legal researchers, legislators, and climate change policymakers should take caution and consider revamping the existing framework of international climate change conventions and associated domestic policies.

This book suggests that there are both pathways towards and away from green paradoxes, that certain pathways do not result in tragedies in Hardin's sense of inevitability, but that other pathways might indeed be 'tragic' in character and genuinely tragic in consequence.

This book attempts to clarify how policymakers can establish effective green energy policies by illuminating where Scylla and Charybdis lurk, so that we can best navigate to avoid those dangers while remaining on path to our goals.

1.3 On choice of corporate actors and corporate entities

This book does make a simplifying assumption, made *sotto voce*, to focus on corporate actors and similar for-profit group-based entities. This is for several reasons.

The first is that while a human actor, *arguendo*, has a soul, a family, and a place in this world beyond profits and earnings, many legal entities such as corporations are legally bound to prioritize profitability and the creation of net income and positive earnings for their investors and shareholders. Thus, while a human has a wide array of concerns to balance beyond narrow profit-seeking, from ethical and religious views to family and community concerns and private and personal goals that may be wholly non-market-based, a corporate entity is likely to set profitability as one of its key goals, if not the dominant or sole goal, of its raison d'être. This narrow focus, on profitability, facilitates behavioral model-making for policymakers, versus the potential complexity of attempting to plumb and model genuine human behavior.

Second, the vast majority of industrial energy facilities are owned, operated, and stewarded by corporate actors and are not in the direct hands of human investors. Thus, even if one could realistically model a private human's interactions in regard to green energy policies, it might not be sufficiently representative of the task at hand, to guide the whole economy to sustainable pathways of energy policy.

1.4 Readership

This book is perhaps best read by readers who are curious to learn why, if we can recognize the dangers of carbon emissions, have we failed to find a more effective and robust method to guide human activity and industry to achieve a greener alternative? This book is primarily produced with the hope of enlightening readers to understand how the structural elements of green policies interact with other energy policies and with the economic 'logic' rules of profit-seeking enterprises. It is the hope of the author that such readers can come to appreciate the complexity of the situation, to better support robust green energy policies, and to better understand the need to develop these policies in the foreknowledge of how corporate actors can become better integrated and integral to the success of these legal frameworks.

Policymakers and environmentalists will find this a motivating read in that it provides explicit policy recommendations on how to better design environmental rules, particularly rules for green energy policies, that can robustly respond to the challenges presented by the corporate actors active in the various energy industries. It will also highlight how seemingly disjoint areas of law, such as national security or economic development, can come to have substantial impacts on the effectiveness of environmental legal frameworks.

Environmental scholars will find this book of use because it illustrates the advantages, and perils, of relying on economic models to bolster policy arguments. This book is self-evidently aware and informed by the economic analysis of law. The book is equally up front that it is examining law as a type of formal structure, that law can be modeled within game theoretic terms and methods. That the book reveals both benefits and potential disadvantages to such an approach enables it to serve as a guide to 'best use' for these modes of analysis.

1.5 Synopsis and structure

This study presents a review of green paradox models,[3] finds a list of potential sources of green paradox events, and queries if various legal frameworks could enable effective policy responses to those causes of green paradoxes or will those rule sets exacerbate those causes and worsen green paradox events?

This study finds that the result is a mixed bag; specific issues can be seen as beneficial or detrimental, but the combination of those effects is found to be difficult to forecast.

Chapter 2 delivers an introduction and survey to the concepts addressed by the green paradox models. From the UNFCCC targets for the adoption and support of green energy policies, Sinn's early green paradox models are developed. Sinn's theoretical contributions are discussed. His original model of emergent green paradox phenomena is described, and his initial and seminal reliance on Hotelling's model is discussed. Also, his concerns on the inevitability of green paradox problems are reviewed. Similarly, brief explanations of other green paradox models and classifications of green paradox models are provided. A listing of the fundamental types of green paradox models is presented.

Chapter 3 provides introductions and explanatory notes to the four major classes of green paradox models and to one particular integrated class of green paradox models. Throughout the review of the model classes, the central reliance on Hotelling or Dasgupta Heal models is demonstrated. Even when certain models do not directly derive from those two model classes, they often include assumptions that bring their modeling functions in alignment with those two model classes, thus similar results entail.

Chapter 4 investigates the question, are Hotelling and Dasgupta Heal models problematic for the investigation of green paradox models? This study finds that those models might in fact be of concern, especially for legislators and policymakers concerned with the potential effects and side effects of prospective green energy laws. The discussion on Hotelling's model explores the origins and development of his original models. It explains how the models are intended to operate. It provides a detailed listing of Hotelling's central assumptions and demonstrates that Hotelling provided specific caveats on his assumptions and that other evidence can be brought to raise concerns on the applicability of those assumptions to green paradox research. Thereafter, the Dasgupta Heal models are explored with a focus on demonstrating their close affinity with the Hotelling models' assumption, and thus that they would be equally of concern for green paradox modelers. A conclusion is obtained that Hotelling was well aware of the limits of his models, that Dasgupta and Heal extended his models without substantial change to the core assumptions. Thus, the various classes of green paradox models that build on either Hotelling or Dasgupta Heal models also have inherited the same concerns for which Hotelling had previously provided caveats. The chapter concludes that models researching green paradox phenomena built upon either Hotelling models or Dasgupta Heal models need to be provided with precautionary adjustments and caveats for legislators and policymakers.

Chapter 5 shifts the discussion from formalistic economic models to observing the interplay, both planned and unexcepted, from implementing new systems of new legal rules into a functioning complex environment of legal rules, herein the introduction of new green energy policies into a complex set of international trade laws, domestic energy security laws, and international conventions that encourage harmonization across transnational energy markets. The research question is transformed from a specific set of economic models of green paradox results to a broader notion of policy frustration from the complex interplay of uncoordinated energy and other policy frameworks. Might too much of a good thing be a problem for green energy policy?

In Chapter 5, the concept of overstimulating policy response is explored. The concern here is that too many legal frameworks to address energy policy, including policies specifically designed for green energy considerations, could lead to larger carbon emissions. This is not necessarily a green paradox, but there are overlapping areas of concern, that policies not necessarily meant to engage in green energy policies at all do in fact play substantial roles in the effectiveness of those green energy policies, usually through interactions in the marketplace.

Chapter 5 begins with a discussion on the potential for energy efficiency policies to become ineffective; Jevons paradox is discussed, with its Khazzoom-Brookes postulate that establishes that improvements in energy efficiency will increase energy consumption, *ceteris paribus*, due to resultant changes in both supply and demand for energy supplies. The chapter proceeds to introduce issues related to the sharing or 'transfer' of green technologies to better support all nations in their quest for green energy solutions. The chapter also covers the notion of common but differentiated obligations to achieve the goals of climate change prevention.

Chapter 6 examines the role of energy security laws, i.e., those laws that support the secure supply of energy resources against adverse conditions, in driving innovation in energy. Chapter 6 looks to the laws of the United States as an example of such energy security laws. Such targets might include securing petroleum volumes or energy alternatives, such as nuclear energy. Motives for energy security laws might be to protect energy prices from market forces or to support militarized forces. The chapter reviews the vast array of tax incentives and advantages provided to create, support, and subsidize energy policy in the US, finding that the tax code may be the largest provider of active budget support for energy projects in the US.

Chapter 7 inspects two major conventions that address the issues of energy security and international economic stability, the Energy Charter Treaty and the OPEC conventions. The ECT is reviewed both with an eye to its role to provide harmonization and economic opportunities for areas of the former Soviet Union and for its role in ensuring the steady production of hydrocarbons. The ECT's role as a developer and supporter of green energy policies is also critically reviewed. Then OPEC's role as an organization committed to balancing and smoothing global supply and demand for petroleum products is reviewed. Analysis of OPEC's contrarian position on climate change is examined. The potential for these international conventions and organizations to increase carbon emissions is demonstrated.

Chapter 8 considers the role of various international trade conventions in supporting market conditions and free competition conditions. This chapter will examine the WTO/GATT system of agreements and reveal their support of open trade and competitive market conditions. In particular, it explores the duality of supporting exports in primary products, such as petroleum, while also supporting the international trade of products in all energy sectors. A similar review is made of the GATS provisions from an energy services perspective.

Finally, a summary and conclusion are presented in Chapter 9. Green paradox models are well grounded and widely researched within economic literature, their concerns are reasonably valid, and consideration must be made to integrate their policy implications into broader legal analysis. When additional policy considerations, such as energy security policies, are added to the discussion, the potential for increased GHG emissions becomes even more likely. While certain policy pathways can be identified as causing green paradox model results or as avoiding the same, their nexus with international trade law remains both very complex and unclear – much more research in this area is called for.

The research of these models and of their locus within a variety of legal frameworks and economic mechanisms requires the combination of legal requirements and economic models. Further, this present study reviews the concern that certain economic models might be problematic in resolving the validity of early green paradox models due to certain assumptions built into those models when they were originally designed for other research purposes. However, the analysis presented is intended for an audience of legal researchers; mathematical materials are minimized in the presentation and the evidence is presented in a format familiar to lawyers. Hopefully this research will better enable other legal researchers to engage in broader research on the potential impacts of green paradox models on future climate change laws and conventions.

Notes

1 Hardin (1968).
2 *See, e.g.*, van der Werf & Di Maria (2012), 153.
3 While the existing literature is growing, and an extensive survey is provided below at sec. 2.4, it bears reporting that in 2010, the EU's European Research Council provided €2,743,548 in financing to study these green paradox models, providing insight into the seriousness with which these concerns have been taken. Cees Withagen of VU Amsterdam served as the lead researcher on the project, in coordination with Rick van der Ploeg, of Oxford University. More information on that EU-funded project can be located on CORDIS, http://cordis.europa.eu/project/rcn/98935_en.html accessed Aug. 4, 2016; see also additional discussion on their research below at sec. 2.4.2. This present report is not related, financially or otherwise, to their research project.

2 Survey of green paradox models

This chapter provides a review of several dominant classes of green paradox models and attempts to demonstrate their common reliance on the Hotelling models of exhaustible resources or on the closely related Dasgupta Heal models of exhaustible resources with backstop energy resources.

This chapter begins by introducing Sinn's original green paradox concerns and his resultant Hotelling-based carbon tax green paradox models. Sinn's original presentation of the idea of a green paradox is discussed. The preliminary concerns of Sinn are reviewed. Then the original carbon tax green paradox models are described and his other sources of green paradoxes surveyed. Thereafter, Sinn's concerns on the inevitability of green paradox results are presented.

Following the Sinn discussions, reviews are provided of several major classes of green paradox models. Extensive surveys of green paradox models can be found in the literature.[1] A consensus view might be argued to support a four-fold clustering of green paradox models: (i) a class of carbon tax models, (ii) a class of backstop technology subsidy models, (iii) a class of pre-announced policy models, and (iv) a class of international carbon leakage models.[2] Each class of models will be reviewed to demonstrate the extent of their reliance on Hotelling or Dasgupta Heal models.

Finally, a separate model by Michielsen that provides a unifying framework of green paradox discussions is also shown to rely in part on similar economic assumptions to the Hotelling paradigm.

Thus, it will be demonstrated that many, if not most, of the recently published green paradox models rely on the underlying economic assumptions embedded in the earlier models of Hotelling as well as Dasgupta and Heal.

As will be demonstrated below, the green paradox models based on Hotelling models generally found green paradoxes possible, those based on Dasgupta Heal models found them less often, and those based on general equilibrium models were significantly less likely to find green paradoxes. The reasons for this stark and simple result, the dependency on the underlying model form for finding green paradoxes, is reviewed in Chapters 3 and 4.

2.1 The problem of anthropogenic climate change

Before beginning a discussion on Sinn's green paradoxes, it is useful to recall the underlying scientific issue, that of the risks created by anthropogenic carbon emissions to cause climate change.

The scientific community broadly holds that the cause of global climate change is primarily anthropogenic.[3] According to the Intergovernmental Panel on Climate Change (IPPC), a scientific body under the auspices of the United Nations,[4] humanity has the potential to affect the climate of the earth by causing the emissions of GHGs.[5] The effects of those climate changes are broadly seen as hazardous. Climate change legal policies are generally intended to intercept and reverse pre-existing trends of GHG emissions. Climate change impacts human life. The global climate has warmed by 0.85°C,[6] severe weather phenomena have become more frequent and more intense,[7] arctic ice coverage has shrunk,[8] and generally speaking the effects of global climate change have become a part of the regular news.

Thus, the scientific consensus is that the observed changes in global climate have been affected by human activities.[9] The onset of industrialization and the consumption of fossil fuels enabled human activities to substantially alter the global atmosphere via the emission of GHGs.[10] As a result, atmospheric levels of GHGs have greatly increased, with carbon dioxide at 40% and methane at 140% higher levels than existed prior to the onset of industrialization.[11]

To assist in the governance of the dangers posed by global climate change, almost every nation in the world has joined the United Nations Framework Convention on Climate Change (UNFCCC) and its related protocols, conferences, and agreements.[12] While legislators and policymakers sought to prevent the onset of worsening of climate change by the adoption of this convention and subsequent domestic enactments of similar laws, Sinn raised a concern that these green-intended conventions and laws might in fact give rise to paradoxical results that would worsen and accelerate global climate change.[13] The existence, and potential inevitability, of these green paradoxes is of grave concern to policymakers and legislators concerned with preventing climate change.

Anthropogenic climate change is highly associated with carbon emissions; there is a linear relationship – emit more carbon, surface temperatures increase.[14] The dominant sources of carbonaceous emissions are the combustion events of conventional fossil fuel products such as coal, crude oil, and natural gas.[15]

To prevent damage from climate change, these carbon emissions must be properly managed.[16] There are substantial limits to remediation of anthropogenic climate change; once the damage is done to the atmosphere, it is likely to persist. Even with proper management of carbon emissions, much of the pre-existing harms and transformations will remain in place for centuries to come.[17] Worse, the potential to safely store GHGs prior to emissions remains in doubt.[18]

Thus, there is a sense of urgency to arrest carbon emissions before conditions deteriorate. Both international and domestic authorities have developed legal frameworks to control and reduce the threats from anthropogenic climate change.

As anthropogenic climate change is driven primarily by the emission of greenhouse gases, the adopted international conventions and enacted domestic legislations have focused on reducing greenhouse gas emissions. The UNFCCC launched a governance goal to achieve the "stabilization of greenhouse gas concentrations in the atmosphere at a level that would prevent dangerous anthropogenic interference with the climate system."[19]

Nations that have joined under the UNFCCC are required to "formulate, implement, publish, and regularly update ... programs containing measures to mitigate climate change."[20] Those measures are required to focus on reducing emissions and providing for sinks of greenhouse gases.[21] Under the UNFCCC, the regulated greenhouse gases are (i) carbon dioxide, (ii) methane, (iii) nitrous oxide, (iv) hydrofluorocarbons, (v) perfluorocarbons, and (vi) sulphur hexafluoride.[22]

The Kyoto Protocol further spelled out specific obligatory mitigation strategies.[23] Parties are directed, *inter alia*, to (i) enhance energy efficiency;[24] (ii) provide for greenhouse gas sinks and carbon sequestration;[25] (iii) research, promote, develop, and increase the use of new and renewable energy sources;[26] (iv) reduce the various supports and subsidies that enable greenhouse gas emissions;[27] and (v) limit or reduce greenhouse gas emissions.[28] Further, the Kyoto Protocol mandates that certain emission targets be reached by specific deadlines; a similar element is absent in the UNFCCC.[29]

However, as Sinn and others have demonstrated,[30] in certain circumstances, it appears that such legal policies could backfire and thus increase greenhouse gas emissions. Given the importance to prevent anthropogenic climate change, it thus becomes critical for legislators and policymakers to understand if these green paradox concerns are substantial.

The key question is whether current policies can effectively avoid those harms by properly managing GHG emissions, or, are there fundamental problems in the way certain legal frameworks interact, or in the way economic incentives and market structures work, that would frustrate the ability of policymakers to create effective carbon reducing rule sets?

2.2 Sources of green paradox phenomena

The United Nations Framework Convention on Climate Change is the leading international regulatory effort to reduce the threats and hazards from anthropogenic climate change. The UNFCCC primarily focuses on the means of managing the overall levels of GHG emissions to the atmosphere and the means of preventing those emissions. Almost every country in the world has ratified the UNFCCC,[31] and almost as many countries have ratified its Kyoto Protocol.[32] As such, most countries in the world have enacted a variety of domestic regulations to further the goals of the UNFCCC to control and prevent global climate change.

Although the UNFCCC and its Kyoto Protocol serve to reduce GHG emissions and to prevent anthropogenic climate change, questions have arisen as to whether certain green policies could backfire and result in increased GHG emissions. Sinn's seminal paper called these emergent phenomena *green paradoxes.* Researchers have tested Sinn's own original tax-related models of green paradoxes and other potential sources of green paradoxes.[33]

2.3 Sinn's carbon tax green paradox models

2.3.1 Background to models of green paradox policy frustration

This study takes note that a substantial number of emergent green paradox models are based on a small set of economic models originally developed for studying exhaustible resources.[34] Those models, known as Hotelling, Dasgupta Heal, and Heal models, contain modeling assumptions that drive certain behaviors within the models. When those models are utilized to research the effects of green laws and conventions, green paradox results have been observed.

Hotelling first developed his early model on depletion rates in between the two world wars; the policy concerns were questionable pricing by resource owners and allegations of overextraction and wastage of exhaustible resources.[35] He attempted to provide a framework to resolve those and other related policy questions. While his work is seen as seminal today, it was not as commonly cited in its early years. It is worth noting that his models were not exclusively energy resource related but applicable to any exhaustible resource, such as diamonds or precious metals.[36]

In the 1970s, Dasgupta and Heal expanded on Hotelling's model by focusing on depletable energy resources and adding a choice of an alternative energy source.[37] In this manner, they facilitated the energy policy discussions of replacing one fossil fuel with another or with renewable energy resources. However, despite the focus on energy resources and the potential to adopt an energy alternative, their models remained mathematically similar to Hotelling's model and inherited many of the same assumptions.

While the potential causes of green paradox phenomena appear diverse, as discussed later in section 2.4, there are only a couple of economic models underlying most of the discussions. They are the Hotelling model of exhaustible resources and the Dasgupta and Heal backstop technology models.

In a survey of twenty articles discussing green paradox phenomena, van der Werf and Di Maria found thirty-two different models of green paradox phenomena.[38] Within those models, twelve were some form of a Hotelling model and eight were some form of a Dasgupta Heal model.[39] For those models discussing carbon prices and taxes and those models discussing the support of alternative energy technologies, only Hotelling models and Dasgupta Heal models were employed.[40] In addressing the delayed introduction of announced climate change policies, two of the three models reviewed were Hotelling models.[41] It was not until unilateral policy models were explored that Hotelling and Dasgupta Heal models became minority models, accounting for three of fifteen models,[42] but there were also only eleven articles underlying those fifteen models. Thus, the Hotelling model and its derivative Dasgupta Heal models represent at least nineteen of the thirty-two surveyed models; however, most of the remaining models are slight derivatives of Hotelling's original model.[43] Thus many, if not most, of the green paradox models are predicated on a small class of closely related economic models of exhaustible resources.

Given that the majority of green paradox models rely on Hotelling or Dasgupta Heal models and that they share many common underlying modeling assumptions, it merits careful consideration if these models are appropriate for research questions related to green paradoxes. In particular, are they open enough to provide proper inspection of the concern, or are they inherently biased in a manner that might prevent their effective use for green paradox research?

The original rhetorical content of Hotelling's model, including certain key assumptions, was largely adopted by Dasgupta and Heal in their models, and has been imported into a variety of green paradox models.[44] Some of those assumptions potentially pose problems of circular results, e.g., if one assumes full depletion, then full depletion results in the model make the task of evaluating whether green energy policies cause full depletion difficult to separate from the underlying model's assumption of full depletion. These problems create a situation wherein green energy policy analyses predicated on green paradox models might not be as reliable as they might otherwise appear.

2.3.2 Increased carbon emissions from policy mismatch

Sinn explored the problem of anthropogenic climate change as a result of market failure. To evaluate those green policies designed to control carbon emissions, Sinn began with a Hotelling-based model of extraction.[45]

Sinn extended the Hotelling analysis to include a production function that includes land-based capital, such as existing fossil fuels, regular accumulated capital, the carbon-free quality of atmosphere, and time as inputs.[46] The model thus assumes positive and increasing marginal damage to the atmosphere from cumulative fossil fuel use.

Sinn found that there was a singular solution that prevents intertemporal discrimination for this Hotelling model.[47] This unique solution requires a deferral of fossil fuel production; when damage from anthropogenic climate change is taken into account, "a flatter extraction path with less extraction in the present and more in the future is required."[48] The greater the marginal damage to the atmosphere, the greater the reduction in extraction speed is required.

Sinn argued that this deferred production solution is compelling because "it does not involve a value judgment that derives from considerations of intergeneration equity, fairness or sustainability, but follows merely from economic efficiency considerations."[49]

Sinn stated while the world, *sans* climate change, would operate at one equilibrium,[50] the threat of climate change requires a lower-level equilibrium. Nevertheless, Sinn recognized that the world was not following his economic model and its prescribed carbon consumption levels.[51] This was the first problem: the market would continue to overconsume fossil fuels because the costs of climate change were not fully accounted for in market behavior.[52] Climate change could indeed be modeled as a form of market failure.

Sinn identified three major policy issues driving the emergence of the market failures leading to the emergence of global anthropogenic climate change:

- i Intergenerational pricing problems within neoclassical microeconomics;
- ii Equivalent dysfunction of political and economic markets; and
- iii Resource owners' problems of insecure property rights in the resources associated with greenhouse gas emissions.

First, Sinn demonstrated that neoclassical microeconomics failed to provide effective policy recommendations based on the standard model's reliance on modeling multi-generational preferences and utility functions, if known.[53] However, those utility functions and generational preferences are not known in advance of their actual emergence in the future.[54] Thus, the externalities of the carbon emissions could not be appropriately priced and managed by the marketplace due to the lack of complete and accurate information in contemporary time periods.

Second, Sinn posited that policies based on non-market-based ethical considerations would not perform better than the market had already performed; thus, certain political efforts based in 'nirvana ethics' would not be able to cure the market failures.[55] Sinn noted that voters are the same actors as those driving the market; if the actors cannot act clearly in their market transactions, then he asks why should democratic politics result in more clarity regarding the costs of climate change? He answered that similar dysfunction would avail.[56] Thus, Sinn argued, politicians would need to find authority beyond current voters. Could they argue for the needs of future generations, and would politicians be better placed to opine for those future voters than the prospective future ancestors of those future constituents? Again, Sinn argued no, that politicians do not have a claim to superior insight into the values of future voters vis-à-vis those future voters' currently voting prospective ancestors. Essentially, those actors currently in the marketplace and currently voting already took into account the effects of their actions on their future descendants.[57]

Sinn detailed the ethical concerns that certain economists have raised that free market solutions cannot be ethically relied upon because interest rates, and thus discount rates, are likely biased against future generations in over-incentivizing current consumption against long-run welfare growth.[58] Sinn queried to whom the policymaker should turn to solve that dilemma. He argued that if the 'ethical economists' were correct in their concerns then there could be no solution. *Ergo*, the position of 'ethical economists' is either wrong or irrelevant.[59] Moving past 'ethical economists,' Sinn further argued that parents did in fact take their descendants' needs into account as the parents interacted in the market, and thus, government involvement to allow philosophers to advise contrary to those parents would be poor policy.[60]

Sinn proposed that weak assignment of property rights drove part of the market failure. Sinn explored the concern that resource owners often face uncertain property rights to their assets, and the temporal aspect of control led to accelerated depletion of their assets in an attempt to maximize revenues whilst in possession.[61] He focused on the role that states with dictators play in owning fossil fuel resources. Sinn highlighted that their dictators face uncertain terms in office, and that these concerns will imperil otherwise functional markets to overproduce hydrocarbons.[62]

Second, Sinn returned to his property right concerns; policies to deny current fossil fuel resource owners from the benefits of their assets would be defective, because the introduction of additional risk of instantaneous expropriation from resource owners would accelerate the production of fossil fuels even more than the free market would have. Thus, climate change policies should be careful to preserve existing property rights, which in turn means that resource owners should not be faced with temporal limits of production nor should they face other bans on production and resultant profits.

Sinn introduced the idea that the market could respond to green energy policies in ways worse than the previous two results. Sinn cautioned that certain green policies could result in increased greenhouse gas emissions instead of their targeted reductions of the same; this type of unexpected policy backfire he called a 'green paradox.'[63]

2.3.3 Rising carbon taxes could induce green paradox effects

Sinn began his study into green paradoxes by adopting the Hotelling model.[64] Sinn's variant on this model assumed constant marginal costs, but he also assumed that the costs of extraction increased as overall depletion occurred.[65] Sinn also added a tax cost to the extraction costs. Several cases are notable:

- i A constant tax left the production volumes in their original schedule at their original volumes, but with a reduction in price. Overall emissions remain unchanged.[66]
- ii A tax that increased in later periods would require a shift of production from those later expensive periods into earlier periods due to the arbitrage assumed by Hotelling's rule to equate net revenues from all time periods.[67] However, the initial price of the fossil fuel will be reduced in the earlier periods, in contrast to the equilibrium price without a tax.[68]

Sinn's observation was that Hotelling's rule has perverse effects on green energy policies that attempt to reduce emissions by providing negative incentives via carbon taxes. While constant carbon taxes under Hotelling's rule would not reduce production volumes, rising carbon taxes would shift extraction to earlier time periods. This second result was Sinn's primary green paradox.[69] Because the Hotelling model assumed that the fossil fuels would be fully depleted,[70] an increase in production during one time period will cause a corresponding decrease in another; high costs in a later period encourage activity to occur earlier. This gave rise to Sinn's central concern:

> "However, if firms react to a change in demand today by extracting less, they must extract more tomorrow, and *vice versa*, and it is by no means obvious that the demand-reducing measures discussed in Sect. 2 will be able to tilt the extracting path in the right direction."[71]

Thus, Sinn demonstrated that Hotelling's model could be leveraged to demonstrate the existence of green paradoxes;[72] however, those demonstrations should come with Hotelling's caveats. Green paradoxes appear to result from the temporal arbitrage built into the model by its reliance on Hotelling's rule.[73]

Sinn considered two different tax models to validate his green paradox concerns:

i A cash flow carbon tax,[74] and
ii An "ad valorem sales tax on extraction."[75]

He relied on these two carbon tax models to demonstrate that, under a Hotelling model, by providing incentives to avoid fossil fuel production in later time periods, the policies also created countervailing incentives to increase production of fossil fuels in earlier time periods.[76]

> "[T]he resource owners will anticipate extraction ... to compensate for the rising tax rate. Global warming will accelerate."[77] And by 'anticipate,' Sinn clarified that the fossil fuel resource owners "will try to anticipate the price dampening effect by selling more in the present and less in the future."[78]

Thus, those two green tax policies would result in additional anthropogenic emissions of greenhouse gases: "The green paradox implies that such a policy is likely to backfire and create even more harm for the environment by speeding up global warming."[79]

Sinn stated that the green paradox could result from other causes, not merely from carbon taxes, and included these examples of alternative causes of green paradoxes:[80]

i Energy Efficiency: gains in energy efficiency could reduce energy demand from fossil fuels in future time periods;[81]
ii Green Energy: increased supplies from green non-fossil fuel energy sources could reduce energy demand from fossil fuels in future time periods;[82]
iii Non-Green Energy: increased supplies from non-green non-fossil fuel energy sources could reduce energy demand from fossil fuels in future time periods;[83]
iv International Leakage: differing policies between states on abating the causes of climate change.[84]

He stated that the above sources of green paradox could be strengthened by governmental subsidies, by quantity constraints, or by moral persuasion or dissuasion.[85] Additionally, the more the green paradox occurred, and thus the more anthropogenic climate change occurred, the public would increasingly support additional efforts to reinforce those policies, so long as it was contrafactually misunderstood that such policies were reducing emission.[86]

Sinn concluded that "markets unfortunately are unable to find the optimal path" to avoid anthropogenic climate change because they cannot resolve the optimal path between the stocks of carbon pre-combustion and those post-combustion.[87] The problems of incomplete climate change information in fossil fuel pricing and alternative energy pricing, plus the challenges of insecure property rights, lead to the overextraction and overconsumption of fossil fuels.[88] Sinn expected that political efforts to address climate change will either be fiscally wasteful in not accomplishing emission reductions or, worse, will create green paradoxes and worsen the trend against no emission policies at all.[89]

In his conclusion, he offered no new solutions that he had not previously ranked from likely to infeasible.[90] He is left stating, "[t]here is a green paradox."[91] Sinn's sense of frustration rings clear, but it remains largely predicated on the internals of Hotelling's models and should be guided by the caveats noted later in Chapter 4.

2.4 Previous taxonomies of green paradoxes

Sinn set off research into green paradox phenomena when he identified that certain policy measures to combat anthropogenic climate change could backfire and increase GHG emissions.[92] He was also concerned that green paradoxes might contain a positive feedback loop, in that the worse climate change becomes the more the general public would support those measures inadvertently causing increases of emissions.[93] Thus, well-intended policy might set off a paradox of increasing GHG emissions. He summarized the concept thus: "[t]he green paradox implies that such a policy is likely to backfire and create even more harm for the environment by speeding up global warming."[94]

2.4.1 Sinn's original taxonomies of green paradox models

Sinn developed economic models to demonstrate that carbon taxes could drive fossil fuel resource owners, under certain conditions, to produce larger quantities earlier in time; he demonstrated these models with both a cash flow carbon tax[95] and an "ad valorem sales tax on extraction."[96] Sinn identified four other basic sources of potential green paradoxes: (i) gains in energy efficiency;[97](ii) the development of carbon-free new and renewable energy resources;[98] (iii) increased supplies from alternative carbonaceous energy resources;[99] and (iv) international carbon leakage.[100]

Sinn's original green paradox model was a model of increasing carbon taxation, over time, of exhaustible fossil fuel resources.[101] He also anticipated that green paradoxes might emerge from several other common green energy policies: (i) energy efficiency; (ii) green energy; (iii) non-green energy; and (iv) international leakage.[102] Sinn's carbon tax, green energy, non-green energy, and international leakage have become paradigmatic sources of green paradoxes; e.g., van der Werf and Di Maria's survey results, later.[103] But Sinn's concern for energy efficiency has been less addressed within the literature.[104]

2.4.2 *Mainstream taxonomies of green paradox models*

Van der Werf and Di Maria have provided what is perhaps the most complete literature review to date.[105] They suggested that there are several varieties of green paradoxes; the models can be characterized by the types of policy imperfection considered within the models.[106] It can be reasonably summarized that the key underlying issues are policy changes implemented over a period of time, with the later time periods being more difficult for fossil fuel producers. An additional category provides temporal policy problems as implemented across multistate environments. The potential imperfections include (i) when carbon taxes are higher in later time periods;[107] (ii) when green energy alternatives are to be introduced in later time periods;[108] (iii) when policies are not effective until later time periods;[109] and (iv) when some states implement policies later than other states implement green policies.[110] They also listed these same categories with different titling, as (i) carbon price paths; (ii) support alternative energy; (iii) announced policy; and (iv) unilateral policies.[111] In another paper, wherein van der Werf and Di Maria were joined by Lange, they found four similar categories: (i) carbon taxes;[112] (ii) technological backstops (both clean and dirty);[113] (iii) delayed policies (both with and without scarcity);[114] and (iv) international carbon leakage.[115]

A similar taxonomy was developed by van der Ploeg and Withagen.[116] They listed (i) awkwardly coordinated carbon taxes and alternate energy subsidies, a combination of van der Werf and Di Maria's (i) and (ii); (ii) international carbon leakage, which is the same as van der Werf and Di Maria's (iv) earlier; and (iii) alternate energy backstops, which van der Werf and Di Maria included *en passim*. An interesting difference, perhaps, is that van der Ploeg and Withagen see these potential green paradox problems as the result of government failure due to lobbying influences.[117]

2.4.3 *Alternative taxonomies of green paradox models*

While Ritter and Schopf provide a different perspective to support their development of an endogenous cumulative emissions model within a general equilibrium framework, their taxonomy was focused on the underlying mathematical structures of the models in lieu of policy motivations.[118] They found that intertemporal models and intra-regional models are pervasive in the literature.[119] Ritter and Schopf also evaluated the categories of weak and strong green paradoxes.[120]

Michielsen separated green paradoxes from carbon leakages; the first were seen as temporally driven and the second as spatially motivated.[121] Michielsen expected carbon leakage to occur for two reasons: (i) polluters would react by relocating to lax locales; and (ii) the reduction of demand for exhaustible resources by green policy would reduce prices for lax countries, increasing their demand. Green paradoxes, Michielsen explained, were caused by providing incentives to exhaustible resource owners to anticipate green policies by accelerating their extraction activities. Within that framework he included Sinn's carbon taxes and both clean and dirty technological backstops.[122] Michielsen's perspective on these models is fascinating in part because he provides a stronger sense of underlying symmetry across all of the models.[123]

In a more historical method, Fischer and Salant organized the various green paradox models by generations; they identified three generations of green paradox models, each representing increasing sophistication of the underlying models.[124] They see the evolution as essentially refinements on Hotelling models, focused on Hotelling rents.[125] The first generation of green paradox models featured the research efforts of Sinn, Grafton et al., and others.[126] A claimed hallmark was the role of policies to support backstop technologies; policies needed careful balancing to manage cumulative emissions without accelerating near-term emissions.[127] The second generation featured the works of Gerlagh, van der Ploeg, and Withagen and Hoel.[128] These newer models recognized that different extraction costs might avail for different classes of exhaustible resources; this enables carbon taxes and certain subsidies of backstop technologies to become more effective in avoiding green paradox results.[129] Additionally, it was reported that the second-generation models tended to be developed as one-state models, reducing complexity in a way that prevented better investigation into multistate carbon leakage.[130] Finally, the third-generation models were either advancements of Hotelling's model, *a la* Hoel,[131] that could enable multistate analysis or the multistate models of Eichner and Pethig.[132] Somewhat separately, they include the models of Harstad,[133] which enable the governments to acquire and sequester exhaustible resource prior to extraction and combustion, thus obviating the need for taxation or other forms of backstop subsidization.[134] The third-generation models, by enabling multistate models, also enabled the question of whom to tax to become addressable within the models; Hoel's model has the purchasers paying the tax, whereas Harstad's model requires the exhaustible resource producers to pay the tax.[135]

Extending on the green paradox paradigm, arguments have been presented that green paradox model phenomena would be more likely to manifest when consideration of other energy policies are included.[136] As Sinn has argued, the requirements of the UNFCCC and other climate change conventions and domestic enactments are clearly intending to stimulate the production of new and renewable energy technologies that might play a role in emergent green paradox events. Some nations have engaged in energy trade conventions that promote the sustained place of fossil fuels in the marketplace, such as OPEC and the Energy Charter. Other nations, like the US, have chartered domestic legislation to provide for energy security from multiple energy sectors. The coordination of those policies within global trade organizations, such as GATT, can lead to complexity that might support green paradox types of events. Altogether, this broadened approach to Sinn's research agenda found a more certain result of increased GHG emissions beyond the models discussed above.[137]

2.5 Summary and conclusions

This chapter has presented the logic behind Sinn's original formulation of the green paradox hypothesis and of the additional models developed and analyzed by other researchers.

The chapter traces Sinn's concerns back to the policy guidance of the UNFCCC, to reduce carbon emissions to prevent global anthropogenic climate change. Sinn placed Hotelling's model as the foundation of his model and he added a cluster of other operands to complete the green paradox model.

Only when the fossil fuel use was deferred, not prevented or prohibited, was Sinn able to demonstrate a reduction in carbon emissions that did not result in a green paradox. But from a green energy policy perspective, to merely delay carbon emissions is a less attractive option. Sinn's broader result signaled three major policy problems: (i) intergenerational transfer pricing problems, (ii) certain market dysfunctions, and (iii) erosion of property rights leading to subsequent emission problems. These he called green paradoxes, that implementation of green energy policies would result in intergenerational problems, security in property rights issues, and generally destabilize the preexisting trajectory of carbon emissions.

In particular, he worried about models that placed an increasing carbon tax that became more expensive over time, that when combined with other standard economic assumptions, would lead to both cheaper and more abundant fossil fuel supplies becoming available on the market in earlier years, leading to increased consumption and thus increasing the risks from the increased and earlier emissions of carbon from fossil fuels. To repeat from earlier, "The green paradox implies that such a policy is likely to backfire and create even more harm for the environment by speeding up global warming."[138]

Furthermore, Sinn stated that the set of potential green paradox models could be organized into five camps:

- i Imposition of Carbon Taxes: taxes create incentives to use less carbon fuels; results are worsened if the tax rates are rising as time progresses;[139]
- ii Improvements from Energy Efficiency: gains in energy efficiency could reduce energy demand from fossil fuels in future time periods;[140]
- iii Additional Supplies from Green Energy Sources: increased supplies from green non-fossil fuel energy sources could reduce energy demand from fossil fuels in future time periods;[141]
- iv Additional Supplies from Non-Green Energy Sources: increased supplies from non-green non-fossil fuel energy sources could reduce energy demand from fossil fuels in future time periods;[142]
- v International Leakage: differing policies between states on abating the causes of climate change.[143]

While each of these issues, both the earlier green paradox models and the later four, will be taken up in greater depth in later chapters, it is worth noting that much of these effects can be readily recharacterized as a progressively larger supply of energy, a progressively weaker demand for fossil fuels in particular, increasingly weak property rights in fossil fuel capital and resources, unpredictable temporal shifts in demand and pricing, and unpredictable jurisdictional shifts in demand and pricing. While this count of functions more than suffices to potentially enable a chaotic system to determine where the market would clear for fossil fuel purchases, the trio of abundant supplies of competitive goods, weaker demand for fossil fuel products, and a weakening grasp on their legal rights could foreseeably lead to fossil fuel producers reducing their prices to move as much product to recover as much capital as possible before no sales become no longer feasible.

That certainly does not in itself equate to guaranteed increases in sales volumes and thus increases in emissions, for there are certainly goods that fall out of favor at any price, but one suspects that increased volumes of fossil fuels at decreased prices would likely lead to increased purchases, combustion, and carbon emissions. That is, if Sinn's models are correct, that green energy policies would lead to these results.

Next, this chapter reviewed previous efforts to categorize the various models and sources of potential green paradox results. Beginning with van der Werf and Di Maria, they found a meta-theme of two-period policy models, where the second period's policy was worse than the first period's policies for fossil fuel holders or investors, thereby encouraging them to shift their activities forward in time, resulting in an acceleration of greenhouse gas emissions. Next, the categories of van der Ploeg and Withagen were reviewed. Their categories were similar to van der Werf and Di Maria's, but van der Ploeg and Withagen placed greater emphasis on the lobbying influences that result in government failure to develop better policies.[144]

Next, alternative modes of categorizing the green paradox models were examined. Ritter and Schopf looked to the underlying mathematical structures of the models to provide a taxonomy. By so doing, they revealed the existence of 'strong' and 'weak' paradox models, that some paradoxes would have stronger effects than other models. That is to say, not all paradoxes are equally damaging; one might have a policy preference for one set of problems over another set.

Michielsen saw a differentiating issue in temporal models versus spatial models, limiting the notion of green paradoxes to models primarily focusing on temporal policy problems. As stated earlier, one of the key results of Michielsen's research was the demonstration of a strong sense of structural symmetry across all of the models.

Fischer and Salant's taxonomy viewed green paradox models by generations; they identified three generations of green paradox models, each representing increasing sophistication of the underlying models. A key feature of the generations is to include more recent economic models than Sinn's original conception did, such as to include Hoel's models in lieu of Hotelling's.

In a vague sense, this chapter has demonstrated that a range of scholars have found that green paradox models can be substantiated under certain models and given certain assumptions about how those models interface or are substantiated in real life. The green paradox models are clearly based upon non-controversial models from economics, thus the concerns raised by these theorists need to be taken as a serious concern for policymakers and for legislators.

The next chapter, Chapter 3, details how the four basic models work and how Michielsen's models of symmetry hold these models together. The chapter after that, Chapter 4, will evaluate the robustness of those model's assumptions about how they, those same models, interface or are substantiated in real life.

Notes

1 van der Werf & Di Maria (2012), 155; van der Ploeg & Withagen (2013); Ritter & Schopf (2013), Michielsen (2014); Fischer & Salant (2013).

2 van der Werf & Di Maria (2012), 155; van der Ploeg & Withagen (2013); Ritter & Schopf (2013), Michielsen (2014); Fischer & Salant (2013).

3 *See, e.g.*, Intergovernmental Panel on Climate Change [IPCC], Summary for Policymakers, in *Climate Change 2013: The Physical Science Basis, Contribution of Working Group I to the Fifth Assessment Report of the IPCC 17* (Thomas F. Stocker et al. eds., 2013) [hereinafter IPCC Fifth Assessment Report Summary] ("It is *extremely likely* that more than half of the observed increase in global average surface temperature from 1951 to 2010 was caused by the anthropogenic increase in greenhouse gas concentrations and other anthropogenic forcings together."). The IPCC report was co-authored by approximately 830 experts selected from a nomination pool of 3,598 scientists. IPCC, *IPCC Factsheet: How Does the IPCC Select Its Aauthors?* (Aug. 30, 2013), www.ipcc.ch/news_and_events/docs/factsheets/FS_select_authors.pdf. See also, e.g., Nicholas Stern, *Stern Review: The Economics of Climate Change*. Vol. 30, 3 (London: HM Treasury, 2006). "An overwhelming body of scientific evidence indicates that the Earth's climate is rapidly changing, predominantly as a result of increases in greenhouse gases caused by human activities." http://webarchive.nationalarchives.gov.uk/20100407172811/www.hm-treasury.gov.uk/stern_review_report.htm.

4 See "Organization." At the Intergovernmental Panel on Climate Change (IPCC) website. www.ipcc.ch/organization/organization.shtml (last accessed Aug. 4, 2016).

5 While the IPCC is generally acknowledged as the leading politically supported scientific institutional group on climate change science and impacts, it is hardly the only such group finding the existence of anthropogenic climate change and calling for urgent policy actions to address those changes. For example, the Pontifical Academy of Sciences at the Vatican issued a report in 2011 that found, "Warming of the Earth is unequivocal. Most of the observed increase in globally averaged temperature since the mid-20th century is 'very likely' – defined as more than 90% likely – to be the result of the observed increase in anthropogenic greenhouse gas concentrations." Bengtsson et al. (2011), 7. Additionally, they found, "Human-caused changes in the composition of the air and air quality result in more than 2 million premature deaths worldwide every year and threaten water and food security – especially among those 'bottom 3 billion' people who are too poor to avail of the protections made possible by fossil fuel use and industrialization." Bengtsson et al. (2011), 4. As such, the Working Group urged all nations to adopt three policy measures: (i) urgently reduce carbon dioxide emissions; (ii) reduce GHG emissions by up to 50%;

and (iii) begin preparations to adapt for the changes unpreventable by these policy efforts. Bengtsson et al. (2011), 4–5. In support of these policy measures, the Working Group included called for additional renewable energy, enhancements to arboreal carbon sinks, and technological means to reduce atmospheric carbon levels (e.g., CCS). *Id.* As such, their conclusions and policy calls are aligned with those of the IPCC.

6 Stocker & Qin (2013), 3.

7 "It is likely that the frequency of heat waves has increased in large parts of Europe, Asia and Australia. There are likely more land regions where the number of heavy precipitation events has increased than where it has decreased. The frequency or intensity of heavy precipitation events has likely increased in North America and Europe." Stocker & Qin (2013), 3.

8 Arctic ice has shrunk 4% annually since 1979. That date is not suggested as a date of onset of shrinkage but rather as the first year for which reliable data exists against which to compare the coverage of later years. *See* Stocker & Qin (2013), 7.

9 "It is extremely likely that more than half of the observed increase in global average surface temperature from 1951 to 2010 was caused by the anthropogenic increase in greenhouse gas concentrations and other anthropogenic forcings together." Stocker & Qin (2013), 15.

10 "Concentrations of CO_2, CH_4, and N_2O now substantially exceed the highest concentrations recorded in ice cores during the past 800,000 years. The mean rates of increase in atmospheric concentrations over the past century are, with very high confidence, unprecedented in the last 22,000 years." Stocker & Qin (2013), 9.

11 "The atmospheric concentrations of the greenhouse gases carbon dioxide (CO_2), methane (CH_4), and nitrous oxide (N_2O) have all increased since 1750 due to human activity. In 2011 the concentrations of these greenhouse gases were 391 ppm11, 1803 ppb, and 324 ppb, and exceeded the pre-industrial levels by about 40%, 150%, and 20%, respectively." Stocker & Qin (2013), 9.

12 *See* United Nations Framework Convention on Climate Change, May 9, 1992., U.N. Doc. FCCC/Informal/84; GE.05–62220 (E) 200705 [hereinafter UNFCCC], http://unfccc.int/essential_background/convention/items/2627.php. While presented here as primarily two sets of documents, the underlying reality of the UNFCCC is more complex and evolved; a more complete legal story should include details from the Marrakesh Accords of 2001, the 2005 Nairobi Work Program on Adaption, the 2007 Bali Road Map, the 2009 Copenhagen Accord, the 2010 Cancun Agreements, the 2011 Durban Platform for Enhanced Action, the 2012 Doha Amendment to the Kyoto Protocol, and most recently the 2013 Warsaw Outcomes. This study needs only the basic common predicates underlying all of the these efforts, and thus will limit its discussions to the earlier UNFCCC and the Kyoto Protocol.

13 Sinn (2008), 377–381.

14 "Cumulative total emissions of CO_2 and global mean surface temperature response are approximately linearly related (see Figure SPM.10)." Stocker & Qin (2013), 25.

15 The two worst offenders are CO_2 and CH_4; they are five-fold and eight-fold more impactful than the next worse source of concern as ranked by total emitted mass. *See* Figure SPM.5, Stocker & Qin (2013), 12.

16 "A lower warming target, or a higher likelihood of remaining below a specific warming target, will require lower cumulative CO_2 emissions." Stocker & Qin (2013), 25.

17 "A large fraction of anthropogenic climate change resulting from CO_2 emissions is irreversible on a multi-century to millennial time scale, except in the case of

a large net removal of CO_2 from the atmosphere over a sustained period." Stocker & Qin (2013), 26.

18 Carbon capture and sequestration (CCS) is referred to as carbon dioxide removal (CDR) by the IPCC reports. "CDR methods have biogeochemical and technological limitations to their potential on a global scale. There is insufficient knowledge to quantify how much CO_2 emissions could be partially offset by CDR on a century timescale." Stocker & Qin (2013), 27.

19 UNFCCC, *supra* note 9, art. 2. While both the UNFCCC and the Kyoto Protocol have extensive language on the support of climate science and scientific monitoring, these topics do not appear to have substantial bearing on the green paradox concerns, so they have been omitted from the current review framework.

20 UNFCCC, art. 4 § 1(b).

21 UNFCCC, art. 4 § 1(b).

22 Kyoto Protocol, *supra* note 10, annex A. This list is not set in stone, as the 2012 Doha Amendment would add nitrogen trifluoride to that listing. *See* United Nations Framework Convention on Climate Change Conference, Doha, Qatar, Amendment to the Kyoto Protocol, U.N. Doc. C.N.718.2012.TREATIES-XXVII.7.c, Art. 1, Annex A (Dec. 8, 2012) [hereinafter Doha Amendment], https://treaties.un.org/doc/Publication/CN/2012/CN.718.2012-Eng.pdf.

23 Kyoto Protocol, art. 2, § 1(a).

24 Kyoto Protocol, art. 2, § 1(a)(i).

25 Kyoto Protocol, art. 2, § 1(a)(ii), (iv).

26 Kyoto Protocol, art. 2, § 1(a)(iv).

27 Kyoto Protocol, art. 2, § 1(a)(v). This concerns the green paradox research directly in that by reducing the tax credits or deductions available to energy producers, the requirement effectively requires a net increase on carbon-related taxes. Depending on how those changes are implemented, they could fit well within established areas of green paradox concerns. *See infra* in section 2.3.3.

28 Kyoto Protocol, art. 2 § 1(a)(vii)–(viii).

29 Kyoto Protocol, art. 3 § 1. The targets are to be attained by 2012. *Id.* The Doha Amendment to the Kyoto Protocol would extend that timeline to 2020 and deepen the emission cuts to be achieved. *See* Doha Amendment, art. 1.C.

30 *See infra*, at sections 2.2 and 2.3.

31 195 countries had ratified the United Nations Framework Convention on Climate Change (UNFCCC) as of March 24, 2014; contrast that total against the 193 members of the United Nations. *See* "First steps to a safer future: Introducing the United Nations Framework Convention on Climate Change." UNFCCC website, https://unfccc.int/essential_background/convention/items/6036.php (last accessed Aug. 4, 2016). *See* also "Member States of the United Nations." UN website: www.un.org/en/members/ (last accessed Aug. 4, 2016).

32 192 nations and regional organizations have ratified the Kyoto Protocol. *See* "Status of Ratification of the Kyoto Protocol." UNFCCC website, https://unfccc.int/kyoto_protocol/status_of_ratification/items/2613.php (last accessed Aug. 4, 2016).

33 See a literature review of green paradox research at section 3.1.

34 *See infra* at sections 4.3, 4.4, and 4.5.

35 As Hotelling noted, one side assumed intentional underproduction and the other side assumed overproduction of exhaustible resources. Hotelling (1931), 138.

36 Hotelling (1931), 152.

37 *See generally* Dasgupta & Heal (1974), 5–6; see also Heal (1976), 372–377 (with special attention to Equations 4, 5, and 10).

38 van der Werf & Di Maria (2012), 156–158.

39 van der Werf & Di Maria (2012), 156–158. Van der Werf and Di Maria refer to the models as Heal models due to the underlying citations to Heal's 1976 article. For the purposes of this article, we have chosen to label these models as Dasgupta Heal models due to Heal's reliance on the earlier paper. *See infra* sections 4.4 and 4.5.

40 van der Werf & Di Maria (2012), 156–157.

41 van der Werf & Di Maria (2012), 157.

42 van der Werf & Di Maria (2012), 157–158.

43 van der Werf & Di Maria (2012), 156–158. Clearly, not all of the models were founded upon Hotelling or Dasgupta Heal models.

44 *See infra* Chapter 3.

45 Sinn (2008), 367.

46 Sinn (2008), 372 eq. 8 (listing Equation 8 as $Y=f(K,R,S,t)$, where S is the atmosphere quality and $f_s>0$, $f_{ss}<0$). In Sinn's Equation 8, K is ordinary capital and R is the resource capital. Sinn (2008), 367 (identifying these two variables in the context of Equation 2). For more discussion on Hotelling's models, *see infra* sections 4.1 and 4.2.

47 Sinn (2008), 372 eq. 9. For more discussion on Hotelling's models, *see infra* Chapter 4.1 and 4.2.

48 Sinn (2008), 373.

49 Sinn (2008). However, it is a fair critique to mention that the model assumed that production was reduced by climate change, by the conditions required of S, f_s, and f_{ss}; there is no alternative result possible within the initial conditions as set by Sinn. While there is great consensus on the scientific impacts of climate change, there is much less certainty on the future net productivity or welfare results. The author's current study is on the effectiveness of legal policy to achieve its stated ends; the potential welfare results of those laws is left for separate research.

50 Sinn (2008), 374 eq. 11 (listing Equation 11, which generally models all four behaviors discussed in this book). *See also* Sinn (2008), 375 fig. 1 (providing a graphical depiction of the four variants of the model).

51 Sinn (2008), 373 ("The problem is that society does not respect this rule.").

52 Sinn's discovery of emergent green paradox phenomena, and their potential inevitability, would be the second problem. Sinn (2008), 377.

53 Sinn sets up the intergenerational paradigm in the first paragraph of Part 3. "To understand the market failure, an intertemporal analysis is needed that concentrates on the wealth society bequests to future generations." Sinn (2008), 366. The main thrust of his intergenerational model is presented within "Neoclassical optimism." Sinn (2008), 368–369.

54 Sinn (2008), 368 ("Equation (4) describes an optimal portfolio mix between man-made and natural capital to be bequeathed to future generations . . . Equation (4) does not, however, indicate how much the present generation should bequeath and what level of consumption relative to the consumption of future generations would be efficient or fair."). Sinn's comments reflect the difficulty of intertemporal models when institutional shifts in preferences are to be expected but unforeseeable in character.

55 Sinn (2008), 369–370 (reflecting the author's disdain of the sustainable economic development perspectives of Anand, Page, Sen, Solow, and Stern). That is, political actions such as the adoption of climate-related laws or international legal conventions such as the UNFCCC would fail unless they receive the popular support of their underlying democracies. As Sinn warns, if politicians took actions in contrast to democratic support, "it would leave the firm ground of methodological individualism and get stuck in the muddy waters of Nirvana ethics." Sinn (2008), 370.

56 Sinn (2008), 369–370.
57 Sinn (2008), 370.
58 Sinn (2008), 368–369.
59 Sinn (2008), 369. Sinn argued that if the common citizen is errant in his understanding of climate change and the related discount rate issues, then any democratic leader chosen by an electorate of such voters would perform no more accurately than those who elected her into office. *Id.* ("These politicians will not find any mistakes in the intertemporal allocation pattern of markets and will, therefore, not take any countervailing policy actions.")
60 Sinn (2008), 370 (commenting that to follow the logical implication that individuals were not reliable for economic decision-making would ultimately undermine the functional concept underlaying basic economics). Perhaps some middle ground might be reasonably sought between Sinn's "pure" neoclassical models and the new behavioral models of economic decision-making. So long as the resultant empirical models of decision-making are rational and predictable, it does not matter if the actor herself is rational *per se.*
61 Sinn (2008), 370–371.
62 Sinn (2008), 371 (noting that at least 70% of both crude oil and natural gas reserves were held by the dictators of the Gulf states, Venezuela, and the territories of the former Soviet Union). Additionally, from those areas he listed six dictators or monopolists by name, three of whom have been assassinated and two more of whom have been exiled since the article was written in 2008, reinforcing the validity of their short tenure as resource owners. *Id.*
63 Sinn (2008), 375 fig. 1. In some ways, the idea of the green paradox is an exaggerated form of the instantaneous expropriation concern, in that resource owners suddenly find themselves at potential loss of their profits from their property rights under carbon taxation.
64 Sinn (2008), 377–380 (presenting models for green policy paradoxes). The price of exhaustible resources is controlled by a relationship referred to as Hotelling's rule. *Id.* at 370 eq. 7, 381 (listing Equation 7 and later defining it as a modified version of the Hotelling rule). For discussions on Hotelling's model of exhaustible, *see infra* sections 4.1 and 4.2.
65 Sinn (2008), 366, where Sinn sets the costs of unit extraction as $g'(S)<0$, wherein S is the total remaining stock of fossil fuel. As S were to be depleted and reduced, the costs g would increase. Similar assumptions can be found within Part 4's "simplified interpretation," *id.*, 374. Sinn did include technical modeling that assumed eventual complete depletion of the reserves both with and without carbon taxes. *See* Cairns (2014), the assumption of full depletion enabled the result of higher fossil fuel production under a carbon tax.
66 Cairns (2014), 80 eq. 2; *see also id.* at 79–80 (defining the constants and variables).
67 Cairns (2014), 80 eq. 3.
68 Cairns (2014), 80.
69 For more discussion on Sinn's green paradox as motivating this study, *see infra* section 9.1.
70 The original model assumes that full depletion will occur. The model can be modified to recognize less than full resource depletion, but the *ex ante* determined replacement limit will continue to be fully depleted. Thus, the temporal problem of Hotelling models is endemic to the model. *See infra* sections 4.2 and 4.3.3.
71 Sinn (2008), 377 (emphasis added).
72 Sinn (2008), 377–380. Hotelling's model made finding a green paradox too readily feasible; this analysis suggests that researchers might seek alternative foundations for investigating green paradox phenomena.

73 For a discussion of Hotelling's assumptions, *see infra* section 4.2.

74 Sinn (2008), 377 eq. 13.

75 Sinn (2008), 378 eq. 14. Such an extraction tax is more routinely referred to as a severance tax or a production tax. Sales taxes are generally imposed downstream of the wellhead at arm's length sales points; a common location is the lease edge transfer point at the LACT meter. Property taxes called "ad valorem" are imposed as real estate taxes against the value of minerals; they exclude the value of the land surface.

76 Sinn (2008), 378. Sinn analogized to a closed-loop piston system: "If only one piston is pressed down, the others go up. If, however, all pistons are pressed equally, none of them moves." *Id.* In the event of green energy policies that provide disincentives to produce fossil fuels in later periods, that later period is the piston pressed down causing the earlier period pistons of fossil fuel extraction to go up, as it were. *Id.*

77 Sinn (2008), 380.

78 Sinn (2008), 381.

79 Sinn (2008), 380.

80 Sinn (2008), 381. Cases (ii) and (iii) listed later are the original concepts from Dasgupta and Heal's backstop models and underlay a class of green paradox models. *See* Dasgupta & Heal (1974), 3–4 and at 18–19 (Dasgupta & Heal called renewable resources "reproducible inputs," *id.* at 4, and "synthetic substitutes," *id.* at 18, as contrary to 'exhaustible resources.' They included solar energy and nuclear fusion as such reproducible inputs, *id.* at 18.); Heal (1976), 371–372. (Heal's model focused on resources that had both cheaper yet exhaustible sources and more expensive but effectively inexhaustible sources. He cited Nordhaus's study on oil from conventional reservoirs and from shale oil reservoirs as an example of such a resource, *id.* at 371–372.) Case (iv) is the area known as international carbon leakage. It generally appears that both Sinn and subsequent models have focused primarily on the Dasgupta and Heal proviso that backstops might be both highly substitutable and displacing to the original fossil fuel. However, there is room to consider the case of poor substitutes or of slow adoption of a substitute backstop that might allow the newly surplus energy supplies from fossil fuels to price compete with the oncoming backstop energy source.

81 Sinn (2008), 364 and at 381. Both his first sense of efficiency (lighter cars, housing insulation) and fifth sense (e.g., improved engine design) from efficiency gains, as well as the energy recovery systems such as biomass and regenerative vehicle brakes on hybrid cars, fit in this category. *Id.*

82 Sinn (2008), 364 and at 381. Renewable green energy sources such as wind, water, and solar voltaics are in this category. *Id.*

83 Sinn (2008), 376, 381. Herein Sinn suggested nuclear fusion as connected with supporting some form of a hydrogen economy. *Id.*

84 Sinn (2008), 377. Sinn foresaw the idea of international leakage, where one country moves ahead with green energy policies and as a result of such efforts countries without green policies in place could afford to consume more fossil fuels. *Id.* ("One country's green policies just help the other country buy energy at lower producer prices.").

85 Sinn (2008), 381.

86 Sinn (2008), 381. ("[A]s the world becomes warmer and more and more people become afraid of the greenhouse effect, public support for such measures will rise so that the demand-reducing effect caused by government interventions is likely to become stronger and stronger.").

87 Sinn (2008), 388.
88 Sinn (2008), 388.
89 Sinn (2008), 388.
90 Sinn (2008), 388–389.
91 Sinn (2008), 388.
92 Sinn (2008), 360.
93 Sinn (2008), 381.
94 Sinn (2008), 380.
95 *See* Equation 13. Sinn (2008), 377.
96 *See* Equation 14. Sinn (2008), 378.
97 In this category fits both his first sense of efficiency (lighter cars, housing insulation) and fifth sense (e.g., improved engine design) from efficiency gains, as well as the energy recovery systems such as biomass and regenerative vehicle brakes on hybrid cars. Sinn (2008), 364 and 381.
98 In this category are renewable green energy sources such as wind, water, and solar voltaics. Sinn (2008), 364 and 381.
99 Herein Sinn suggested nuclear fusion as connected with supporting some form of a hydrogen economy. Sinn (2008), 364 and 381.
100 Sinn foresaw the idea of international leakage, that if one country moved ahead with green energy policies that such efforts could afford more fossil fuels to be consumed by those countries without green policies in place. "One country's green policies just help the other country buy energy at lower producer prices." Sinn (2008), 377.
101 Sinn (2008), 377–381.
102 Many green paradox models, including most of Sinn's models, rely extensively on models developed by Hotelling and extended by Dasgupta and Heal. Those models might be poorly suited for the verification of green paradox models. For a more complete discussion on Sinn's and other Hotelling-based economic models of green paradoxes, *see* Chapters 3 and 4.
103 Sinn's green energy can be linked to green technological backstops and his non-green energy can similarly be linked to dirty technological backstops. *See* discussions later, *en passim*, on the potential to replace certain exhaustible resources by either clean/green technologies or by other forms of exhaustible resources; they are commonly discussed in the green paradox literature. Economic models of such backstops originated with Dasgupta & Heal (1974). *See also* Heal (1976).
104 An interesting historical note could connect this current energy crisis back to the original coal depletion concerns of Georgian England and the Jevon's Paradox that connected energy efficiency to higher levels of energy consumption. See the discussion on Jevons paradox, *infra* section 5.2.
105 van der Werf & Di Maria (2012).
106 van der Werf & Di Maria (2012), 155.
107 van der Werf & Di Maria (2012), 160, citing to Gerlagh (2011), 79–102; Michael Hoel, The Green Paradox and Greenhouse Gas Reducing Investments 5(4) *International Review of Environmental and Resource Economics* 353–379 (2011); and Hoel (2012), for models of exogenously imposed carbon taxes on exhaustible resources.
108 van der Werf & Di Maria (2012), 156, citing to, e.g., Gerlagh (2011), M. Hoel & S. Jensen (2012), and to Grafton, Kompas, & Long (2012).
109 van der Werf & Di Maria (2012), 156, citing to, e.g., Di Maria, Smulders, & van der Werf (2012), 104–119; and Thomas Eichner and R. Pethig, Carbon Leakage, the Green Paradox, and Perfect Future Markets 52(3) *International Economic Review* 767–805 (2011).

110 van der Werf & Di Maria (2012), 157–158, citing to, e.g., Burniaux & Oliveira Martins (2012), 473–495; Harstad (2012), 77–115; and Eichner & Pethig (2011).
111 *See* Table 1. van der Werf & Di Maria (2012), 155–159.
112 van der Werf & Di Maria (2012), 3, citing to both of Hoel's 2011 articles.
113 van der Werf & Di Maria (2012), 3, citing to Gerlagh (2011), 79–102, for models of clean backstop technologies and then to van der Ploeg & Withagen (2012) 342–363; and to Grafton, Kompas, & Van Long (2012), for models of dirty backstop technologies.
114 van der Werf & Di Maria (2012), 3, citing to Eichner & Pethig (2011), and Di Maria, Smulders, & van der Werf (2012).
115 van der Werf & Di Maria (2012), 3.
116 van der Ploeg & Withagen (2013), 1–2.
117 van der Ploeg & Withagen (2013), 1.
118 Ritter & Schopf (2013), 1–4.
119 *See* van der Werf & Di Maria (2012), *en passim.*
120 Ritter & Schopf (2013), 2–3.
121 Michielsen (2014), 2.
122 Michielsen (2014), 2.
123 See section 3.5 for a more complete discussion of Michielsen's models.
124 Fischer & Salant (2013), 2–5.
125 Fischer & Salant (2013), 3.
126 The featured models were published in the 2008–2011 time frame. Fischer & Salant (2013), 2–3.
127 Fischer and Salant identify a reliance on forced full depletion as a central assumption to these first-generation models. Fischer & Salant (2013), 3.
128 The featured models were published in the 2011–2012 time frame. Fischer & Salant (2013), 2–3.
129 While not stated in their description on first-generation models, it is implied that the earlier models treated all exhaustible resources as having identical costs of extraction. Fischer & Salant (2013), 3.
130 They cite Hoel as a representative critic of those models. Fischer & Salant (2013), 3, citing to Michael Hoel, The Supply Side of CO_2 with Country Heterogeneity', 846–865.
131 Michael Hoel, 'The Supply Side of CO_2 with Country Heterogeneity.' 846–865.
132 Fischer & Salant (2013), 4.
133 Harstad (2012).
134 Fischer & Salant (2013), 4.
135 Fischer and Salant describe the second-generation models as lacking this capability. Fischer & Salant (2013), 4.
136 See Part 2 of this book, *infra* Chapters 5, 6, 7, and 8.
137 In particular *see infra* at sections 4.6 and 8.3.
138 Sinn (2008), 377–380.
139 Cairns (2014), 80.
140 Sinn (2008), 364 and at 381. Both his first sense of efficiency (lighter cars, housing insulation) and fifth sense (e.g., improved engine design) from efficiency gains, as well as the energy recovery systems such as biomass and regenerative vehicle brakes on hybrid cars, fit in this category. *Id.*
141 Sinn (2008), 364 and at 381. Renewable green energy sources such as wind, water, and solar voltaics are in this category. *Id.*
142 Sinn (2008), 376 and at 381. Herein Sinn suggested nuclear fusion as connected with supporting some form of a hydrogen economy. *Id.*

143 Sinn (2008), 377. Sinn foresaw the idea of international leakage, where one country moves ahead with green energy policies and as a result of such efforts countries without green policies in place could afford to consume more fossil fuels. *Id.* ("One country's green policies just help the other country buy energy at lower producer prices.").

144 van der Ploeg & Withagen (2013), 1.

3 Internal mechanisms of green paradox models

This chapter delves into the details of the green paradox models, to unveil how they work and upon what assumptions they are founded. The goal of this chapter is to find a key cluster of assumptions that can be critically examined for robustness; this is done to help answer the question, are the models of green paradox phenomena reliable for policymakers?

While the popularized phrase is most often stated in the singular case, as 'green paradox', the literature reveals that there are multiple identified sources of emergent green paradoxes. In conclusions, a listing of commonly investigated potential causes of green paradoxes can be presented:

- Carbon taxes that increase over time; this increase could also be of a quantum or discrete nature;
- Emergence of new and renewable energy resource alternatives that effectively displace and replace traditional fossil fuels, but the transition occurs within a sufficient temporally delayed period;
- Emergence of non-traditional 'dirty' energy resource alternatives that effectively displace and replace traditional fossil fuels, but the transition occurs within a sufficient temporally delayed period;
- Uneven development of climate protection regimes across the globe with some countries enacting and enforcing such regulations and other countries less so;
- Deferred enactment of green policies; it is generally assumed that such delay is sufficient for actors to rationally respond to changing their strategic behaviors;[1]
- Unique to Sinn, energy efficiency was raised as potential source of concern;
- Coordination problems between discordant energy innovation measures.

Beyond the original presentations of these models, which existed within a theoretical economic space, herein the perspective of the potential interaction with international trade laws has been added to explore the legal complexity and impact on rights as originally suggested by Sinn.

The models are categorized into four camps, plus one:

- i Models of rising carbon taxes;
- ii Models of backstop technologies;
- iii Models of delayed policy implementation;
- iv Models of 'international' carbon leakage; and
- v Michielsen's integrated model of both intertemporal and interspatial carbon leakages.

Each of these models is formally explored and revealed to illuminate what makes them work and how each model can result in a green paradox. Special attention is paid to the critical components necessary to enable those green paradox outcomes, in order to support the analyses in the next chapter, Chapter 4, wherein the potential problems of these modeling assumptions are examined in detail.

3.1 Models of rising carbon taxes

The policy concept within this class of models is that authorities would apply some form of a carbon tax or fee upon either the extractors or combustors of fossil fuels to provide the economic incentive to reduce the usage of fossil fuels.[2]

Exemplar models of this form of green paradox include Gerlagh,[3] Hoel,[4] and Habermacher.[5] These models were built on earlier suggestions to have a temporally increasing carbon tax to phase out the usage of fossil fuels.[6] Van der Werf and Di Maria provided a taxonomy of this model class.[7] They reviewed both Hotelling and Dasgupta Heal versions of the models.[8]

Van der Werf and Di Maria's Hotelling model begins with a roster of assumptions about the depletion decisions of the operator. The model includes an 'extraction path' or depletion function of a stock resource,[9] an exogenously determined price for the fossil fuel per unit,[10] a tax on the carbon emissions set to match a unit usage of fossil fuel,[11] and an increasing cost of production for the fossil fuel:[12]

- i The interest rate, r,[13] is determined exogenously.[14] This implies that they obtain capital from fully competitive capital markets, and that their internal sources of capital, if existent, are not competitive with r.
- ii The resource owners are assumed to be price takers.[15] This assumption is standard for fully competitive markets with competitive vendors of perfectly substitutable goods; the price of the resource is governed by Hotelling's rule.
- iii The resource owners optimize intertemporal profits by choosing an extraction path over time, but the model assumes/requires full depletion by the final time period.[16]
- iv The model assumes that the cost of extracting units of fossil fuel increases over time as more cumulative extraction occurs;[17] i.e., the more that has already been extracted, the more expensive it will be to extract the next unit.[18]

v A perfectly substitutable alternative green energy source exists, known as a 'backstop technology.'[19] It has a predetermined price, b. The model assumes that when the price of the fossil fuel exceeds b, the consumers will no longer purchase the fossil fuel at all.[20]

vi The resource owners and operators will always be able to sell every unit of produced fossil fuel, because the model assumes that the market will continue to completely clear even as the price of the fossil fuel approaches infinity.[21]

As to these assumptions, the model operates by assuming that from time zero until the end time, the whole reservoir of fossil fuel will be depleted.[22] This provides an interesting revelation, in that the model is essentially assuming that the returns to the producer grow at the interest rate, r.[23] This condition is called the Hotelling rule, and it means that the decision maker is temporally indifferent as to when fossil fuels are produced. This is because the profits from all time periods are effectively increased at the same rate as the discount factor of net present value calculations.[24] Van der Ploeg and Withagen refer to the centrality of the Hotelling rule in establishing the green paradox models; they deny that extraction costs are relevant considerations for when crude oil is produced and that the asset value of the reserves is what determines when crude oil is extracted.[25]

Since a Hotelling model requires the complete depletion of the resource,[26] and because the model invokes the Hotelling rule, taxes on later year production and sales will provide an incentive to reschedule those volumes to years without those taxes, i.e., to earlier years.[27] Because the Hotelling model assumes complete depletion, a carbon tax or fee can only reschedule the production and sales of those fossil fuels; it cannot reduce their production.[28] If the carbon tax, τ, grows at the same rate as r, then no rescheduling is effected because the tax is essentially the same at all time periods.[29] If the growth of the tax rate exceeds the interest rate, then the rescheduling to the earlier time period will occur.[30] While not in van der Werf and Di Maria's model, the equation holds the interesting policy point that if the tax starts high, but then drops, producers can foresee that result and will then increase production of fossil fuels in later time periods.[31]

Van der Werf and Di Maria argued that when the carbon tax is rising, a green paradox will result because the producers will optimize their production volumes to be sold prior to the switch over to alternate green energy sources. They also argued that a green paradox would not occur if the tax grew equal to or less than the interest rate.[32] However, this result would hold under any Hotelling model that faces a shortened production time frame, regardless of causation, due to the requirement of full extraction, as mentioned previously. Thus, whenever the fossil fuel producer reasonably anticipated that the imposition of a carbon tax would suffice to price the fossil fuel higher than the alternative, the producer would be forced by the model to extract the fossil fuel prior to that point in time. Thus, relying on standard Hotelling models will result in green paradoxes, so long as the carbon tax creates an earlier endpoint of the time frame.

The Dasgupta Heal model is introduced to enable the producer to decide to cease extraction prior to complete depletion by contrasting the cost of extraction against the price of an alternative energy technology.[33] As the model builds upon the Hotelling model, similar concerns as discussed previously are inherited, and to that extent their discussion is not repeated hereunder.

For green paradox discussions, the Dasgupta Heal model has two unique effects. First, the model provides a point in time when fossil fuel will no longer be extracted due to its comparatively high costs. Second, the model enables some amount of fossil fuel to remain. These changes could reduce the artificiality of the Hotelling results with a forced temporal shift to earlier periods simply because the model requires complete depletion.

The Dasgupta Heal model assumes a 'backstop' green energy alternative; any introduced carbon tax will effect a reduction in the price that will terminate fossil fuel extraction.[34] The model creates a trigger that the fossil fuel ceases to be extracted when the costs of extraction, after a certain amount of depletion, reaches the same price as the alternative green energy source.[35] If a carbon tax is added to the price of fossil fuel extraction, then the cost of extraction plus the carbon tax needs to remain under the price of the alternative energy source. Equivalently stated, the cost of extraction needs to remain below the price of the alternative reduced by an equivalent value to the carbon tax.[36]

The model provides that the carbon tax effectively reduces the total amount to be extracted; it also affects when that extraction occurs. If the carbon tax rises more slowly than the interest rate, then the carbon tax is more expensive in earlier periods and extraction shifts to later time periods. This also lowers net emissions; thus, no green paradox results.[37] This is also true when the carbon tax rises equally with the interest rate; again, no green paradox.[38] However, when the carbon tax rises quicker than the interest rate, making future extraction more expensive than current, then a green paradox will result.[39] In that case, time-frame fossil fuel extractions remain reduced.[40]

A two-period Dasgupta Heal model with endogenous investment in the alternative green energy source revealed that the behavior of the extraction costs determined if a green paradox resulted or not.[41] If the costs of extraction rose sufficiently fast enough, then a green paradox could result. Otherwise, under flat or decreasing extraction costs there were no resulting green paradox results.[42]

So, the Dasgupta Heal models provide less opportunity for a green paradox than the Hotelling models allowed, above within the current section. This would primarily appear to be due to the modification to the Dasgupta Heal models to allow incomplete depletion, whereas their Hotelling models required full depletion of the reserves. Thus, when presented with either economic incentives or shorter time frames, the Hotelling models required time-shifting the production schedules to the earlier time frames and ensured a green paradox for earlier time periods. The Dasgupta Heal models are not as readily green paradox yielding, in that only when certain conditions avail can green paradox results occur, especially so when modified as noted earlier. A green paradox could occur under a Dasgupta Heal model only when the cost of extraction increases in later periods, due to either carbon taxes or higher costs of extraction due to depletion.

But much depends on the time value of money as measured in the interest rate versus other changing cost factors. It is perhaps not odd to find that if future costs are too high, then business owners will attempt to make more profit in earlier time periods. If the overall effect of carbon taxes is to make future production of fossil fuels 'more costly,' then perhaps it would be reasonable to expect that fossil fuel producers would attempt to produce more in the earlier periods.

3.2 Models of backstop technologies

The policy concept within this class of models is that authorities would apply some form of a subsidy to stimulate the development and feasibility of alternative green energy sources to provide the economic incentives to reduce the usage of fossil fuels.[43] Exemplar models of this form of green paradox include van de Ploeg and Withagen,[44] Gerlagh,[45] Grafton et al.,[46] Hoel,[47] Hoel and Jensen,[48] and Strand.[49] Not everyone agrees that these models are distinct from the previously examined carbon tax models,[50] in that taxes and subsidies can be seen as two means to the same economic policy ends.[51]

The models assume economic support in the form of government-provided subsidies to reduce the effective price of alternative green energy sources.[52] Again, the Hotelling and Dasgupta Heal models are the dominant templates for research.[53]

The first major assumption of the subsidy model, under a Hotelling depletion model, is that the final price of depleted units will equal the price of the backstop technology of the alternate energy source.[54] It follows that the lower the effective price of the substitute, the earlier that fossil fuels will be priced out of the market;[55] thus the policy becomes how to lower that price, *b*. However, under the Hotelling depletion model, the resource owner would need to accelerate the production of the fossil fuel to meet that new alternative energy price.[56] That reaction would lead to both additional volumes of fossil fuels production at each time period and also to reduced prices for those increased volumes of fossil fuels.[57] A green paradox is sure to occur. The stronger the subsidy effect on the alternative energy source, the stronger the resultant green paradox.[58] A similar model was extended to consider the role of increasing extraction costs and of damages from cumulative carbon emissions.[59] That model found that the marginal cost of the backstop technology was determinative in whether the fossil fuel fields were fully depleted due to the green policy of subsidizing the backstop technology. As might be expected, the Hotelling depletion model found that the field would be fully depleted, but the Dasgupta Heal model found that the field would not be fully depleted; thus the Hotelling model provided an assured green paradox, but the Dasgupta Heal model was dependent on the marginal costs of the backstop technology in creating a green paradox.

A form of international leakage can be seen within this context, if two countries set subsidies that effectively create different backstop prices, *bs*, for their domestic consumers.[60] In that case, one country will be delayed in the switch to the backstop and additional fossil fuel will be extracted alongside additional carbon emissions; a green paradox will result.[61]

When the Hotelling model is modified to enable incomplete depletion and competition between the fossil fuel and the backstop technology,[62] there are interesting results.[63] The optimal carbon tax would not be an exponentially rising tax but a carbon tax growing at a slower rate than the interest rate.[64] This is to encourage the delay of production by making near-term volumes effectively more costly to produce than later period production volumes.[65]

But that model then analyzes the next best policy if carbon taxes are not feasible; however, the analyses are welfare driven, not emission volumes driven.[66] It discovers that there are two cases: (i) when fossil fuels are cheaper than the backstop and (ii) when the backstop is cheaper than fossil fuels.[67]

- i *When the backstops are more expensive*, the model suggests optimal policy would be to increase the price of the backstop by taxing it.[68]
- ii *When fossil fuels are more expensive*, the model suggests optimal policy would be to decrease the price of the backstop by subsidizing it.[69] The lower the backstop cost, the greater the potential for incomplete depletion of the fossil fuel reserves.[70]

These policy results reflect a green welfare function,[71] not an overall emissions concern, so the findings are not determinative, directly, of the incidence of green paradoxes. The overall result is that initial conditions are critical and complicated; green paradoxes may result under certain conditions. But overall, the Hotelling paradigm of full depletion-causing models to suggest green paradoxes remains a concern.

3.3 Models of delayed implementation after green policy announcements

The types of models presented hereunder are models that study the behavior of exhaustible resource producers if the actors, be they producers or consumers, learn of upcoming policies prior to the implementation of those policies.

> "In reality, most environmental policies (or even government policies in general) do not come as a surprise. Coming to an agreement (within a government, or between different governments) and administrative procedures cost time."[72]

In those scenarios, the producer has at least one time period without the implementation of the new policy, but with awareness that such policy will be implemented in a later time period; thus, the producer can make strategic use of that knowledge to ensure maximum profits. The first two models are Hotelling models with forced full depletion. The producers are limited in the time periods within which to complete depletion, so they accelerate and increase emissions in the term prior to the implementation of the policies. The other model presented demonstrates that the environmental policies have impacts on consumption and cause a reaction to accumulate capital to prevent reduced consumption. This savings strategy in turn accelerates demand for fossil fuels due to their capital efficiency, even without the Hotelling assumption of forced full depletion.

Van der Werf and Di Maria found that the dominant model type used in this line of research was the Hotelling model of exhaustible resources.[73] Di Maria et al. relied on a Hotelling model,[74] and Eichner and Pethig's general equilibrium model was an extension of the Hotelling framework.[75]

Di Maria et al. provided a time before and after the imposition of a carbon tax. In effect, they studied a particular form of a rising carbon tax, one that had a period of zero tax rate.[76] The carbon tax acts as a constraint against production, and making the Hotelling assumption of forced full depletion, the model derives that production will be rescheduled to an unconstrained time period. If the tax rate is rising as in this model, then emissions will be accelerated causing a green paradox.[77]

Eichner and Pethig's general equilibrium model relied on a three-state Hotelling model that included two time periods.[78] This model broke out the regions into a fossil fuel exporting state, a state with enforced green policies, and a state lax in green policy enforcement.[79] Again, the models make the Hotelling assumption of forced full depletion.[80] Also, the green policies are only imposed in the second time period.[81] So, although Eichner and Pethig set their model in a general equilibrium setting, instead of the partial equilibrium setting of Di Maria et al., the overall result is the creation of a policy incentive to produce more carbon-emitting fuels in an earlier time period because of *de jure* limits to production in the later time period.[82]

Smulders et al. took a different approach in avoiding the exhaustible resource model.[83] They explicitly did not assume forced full depletion, what they refer to as the "scarcity condition."[84] Instead, they looked to the scarcity of capital and of the decisions leading to its accumulation.[85] By taking this approach they shifted the focus from energy supply to energy demand.[86] Their model demonstrates that when capital accumulation can offset limited energy supplies, and when consumers can react to accumulate capital to prevent loss of future consumption opportunities, a green paradox will result from the increased savings in the near term.[87] It is direct because consumers do not want to experience a decline in energy consumption that fossil fuel consumption will increase in the near term.[88] What appears to be driving this model, deeper than the capital efficiencies of different energy supplies or their intertemporal elasticities of substitution, is that the consumers are facing a shortage of time to accumulate capital, which is derived from the cheaper fossil fuel.[89]

3.4 Models of international carbon leakage

International carbon leakage can be broadly summed up as the idea that if fossil fuels are not used in one location, then they might be used elsewhere. The concern of an emissions-increasing green paradox as a result of the relocation of that usage is a secondary level of analysis separate from the original leakage analysis. Leakages occur because of economic incentives to relocate the usage of fossil fuels; there are multiple potential incentives discussed in the literature.

Van der Werf and Di Maria identify five basic channels of carbon leakage.[90]

First, the *marginal damages* channel encompasses the concept that while emissions abatement might be unilaterally undertaken, the benefits of that abatement will accrue to everyone globally since it is the total amount emitted to the whole atmosphere that determines climate change hazards.[91] One country underwrites the benefits of all, thus creating the opportunity for many to free ride those unilaterally paid costs. Assuming that countries set their marginal costs of abatement equal to their marginal benefits of reduced climate change hazards, Hoel has found that the spillover benefits from a unilateral reduction in emissions will impact the marginal analysis of other countries.[92] Nevertheless, when countries behave uncooperatively, Hoel found that overall emissions were reduced. Thus, the marginal damages channel was not likely to result in green paradox phenomena.[93]

Second, the *energy market* channel captures the effect of a unilateral reduction in emissions on the global market for conventional fossil fuels.[94] For example, if one country reduces its purchases of conventional fossil fuels, more quantity will remain on the market for others to purchase. The results depend on price elasticities of demand and cross-price elasticities of demand.[95] Of the four models reviewed, three of the four were Hotelling or Dasgupta Heal models; the remaining model was a static adjusted general equilibria model (AGE).[96] The two Hotelling models found possibilities of green paradox phenomena, which is no surprise.[97] The Dasgupta Heal model introduced a new policy option: states could acquire reserves-in-place and decide to sequester the reserves permanently and prevent the carbon from ever being emitted.[98] Thus, the results of the energy market channel models depended heavily on the underlying models of exhaustive resource utilization; those that found substantial likelihood of green paradoxes were likely to be based on Hotelling models.

Third, the *terms of trade effect* channel is similar to the previous *energy market* channel, except that it examines the spillover consequences for products made or transported using fossil fuel inputs.[99] The policy concern is that while a country might ban the use of fossil fuels in its own jurisdiction, its citizens might import products from countries without that policy and defeat the policy's purposes.[100] A key concern is the substitutability of the goods between countries and the incidence of transport costs.[101] Paltsev reported finding it very difficult to identify green paradoxes even with high substitutability, while Burniaux and Oliviera Martins found negative leakage (i.e., net emission reductions) from products with low substitutability.[102] A variety of studies have been undertaken; negative leakage is generally seen as more likely than positive leakage, and much more likely than the possibility of green paradoxes.[103]

Fourth, the *international trade in factors of production* channel – which perhaps should have been called the *international capital* channel – examines the movement of capital when some countries constrain the use of fossil fuels and other countries do not.[104] The primary concern is that capital might move to follow ease of use and flow to those countries with more lax green policies. It is also important to note that the surveyed models are the same models surveyed for the *terms of trade effect* channel; thus, the lack of a green paradox finding is extended to these models.[105]

Finally, the *technology change/technology spillover* channel is presented;[106] however, this is a more hopeful topic than the worrisome lines of research explored earlier. The *technology change/technology spillover* channel explores the potential for unilateral action on green energy policies to spill over into other countries. In this scenario, technology to reduce emissions becomes distributed across countries that did not invest in the costs of developing it.[107] Practically every surveyed model revealed negative carbon leakage, which one would assume would be the outcome.[108]

Thus, international carbon leakage models provide an interesting result: less evidence of increased emissions from green policies. Furthermore, the relationship between economic model foundations and green paradox research results was substantial: Hotelling models yielded green paradoxes, Dasgupta Heal models could yield green paradoxes, and the other models yielded evidence contrary to the presence of green paradoxes. The importance of the affinity for Hotelling models and the findings of green paradox phenomena appear to hold for this class of international carbon leakage models.

3.5 Michielsen's integrated model of intertemporal and interspatial leakages

While most articles accommodate various causes of green paradoxes with different mathematical presentations, Michielsen presents a singular model that can accommodate both intertemporal and interspatial concerns, as well as various backstop technologies.[109] Michielsen refers to intertemporal concerns as instances of green paradoxes, but labels the spatial concerns as carbon leakage.[110] He identifies two potential causes of green paradoxes: (i) carbon taxes that increase over time and (ii) the future development of backstop technologies.[111] He then expands the backstops category in two dimensions for a total of four possibilities; there are cheap and expensive backstops, and there are clean and dirty backstops.[112] He identifies two potential causes of carbon leakages: (i) the relocation of dirty industries from countries with effective green policies to those states lacking effective policies and (ii) the application of green policies in one set of countries that could cause the price of carbon-emitting fuels to fall and increase the demand for them in countries without effective green policies in place.[113]

Michielsen's basic model makes several notable assumptions:

- i The existence of an exhaustible resource, a clean backstop, and a dirty backstop,[114]
- ii The exhaustible resource has zero costs of production, but the backstops have constant marginal costs,[115]
- iii The resource owners will always fully deplete their exhaustible resource,[116]

iv Reliance on Hotelling's rule for intertemporal valuations,[117] and
v The energy resources are imperfect substitutes for each other.[118]

He also assumes that the prices of the exhaustible resource will be the same in both countries for his interspatial model.[119]

Michielsen's analysis of rising carbon taxes finds that Sinn's carbon-pricing green paradox occurs if the demand for the dirty backstop is inelastic with regards to the exhaustible resource in both time periods. This inelasticity means that the tax effectively reduces the price of the exhaustible resource in the earlier time period *vis-à-vis* the later period.[120] If the exhaustible resource and the dirty backstop are very close substitutes in both time periods, Michielsen finds that the carbon tax raises the price of the exhaustible resource in both time periods and increases emissions in the earlier period.[121] However, should demand for the dirty backstop be elastic in the later period, then the effect of the carbon tax is to reduce prices in both time periods and to reduce emissions in the earlier time period. No green paradox results in this situation.[122]

When Michielsen expands his analysis of carbon taxes to an interspatial setting, he reports that the calculations are practically identical to those of the intertemporal model.[123] As such, carbon leakages result in green paradoxes in the same two cases as in the intertemporal settings. These carbon leakages are controlled primarily by the degree of product substitutability and demand inelasticity, with the proviso that the time periods are restated as the two locations.

Michielsen's analysis of backstop technology provides for ready reference against the clean backstops of Dasgupta and Heal and against the dirty backstops of Heal.[124] Michielsen makes the assumption that once a backstop technology is available in one country, the technology would readily become available in all countries. This assumption eliminates the need to develop an interspatial analysis of backstop technologies.[125] In developing his intertemporal model of backstop technologies, Michielsen renews his assumption of full depletion of the exhaustible resource.[126] He finds the potential for a green paradox more likely under a backstop scenario than under the earlier carbon-pricing models.[127] However, the complexities of backstop models are nontrivial. For example, a drop in the price of the exhaustible resource in the earlier period, caused by its increased production, will reduce demand for a close substitute dirty backstop; thus, overall emissions will potentially result in some cross-netting to reduce overall impact.

Michielsen demonstrates that the more perfectly the clean backstop serves as a substitute for the exhaustible resource, the stronger the likelihood that a green paradox will result.[128] He evaluates the scenario when the clean and dirty backstops are perfect substitutes for each other and finds several results:[129]

Green paradoxes were obtained:

i When the clean is cheaper than the dirty backstop in both periods, then the dirty backstop is never used and exhaustible resource owners accelerate production and cause a green paradox.

ii When the clean is *ex ante* cheaper than the dirty backstop in the second period, then subsidies will reduce reliance of the dirty backstop in the earlier period and increase depletion speed of the exhaustible resource.

iii When the dirty backstop and the exhaustible resource are perfect substitutes, as conventional crude oil and shale oil are, a green paradox results when the price of crude oil in the later period is lower than its dirty backstop.[130]

But green paradoxes did not occur:

iv When the dirty backstop is cheaper in both periods, and if subsidies fail to alter that condition, then no effective change in emissions would occur.

In summary, Michielsen found a wide variety of scenarios wherein intertemporal and interspatial green paradoxes could occur, especially with the existence of backstop technologies that are the primary hopes of most green energy policies. Those findings are predicated on Michielsen's use of certain Hotelling assumptions, such as full depletion and Hotelling's rule, even though his model does differ from a traditional Hotelling model.

3.6 Summary and conclusions

This chapter has examined the basic models of green paradoxes to reveal how they work, across five different approaches to the basic models and their assumptions. Special attention has been put to discovering the critical ingredients of the models that are necessary or central to the creation of counterproductive increases in carbon emissions, the green paradox results. It is hoped that the reader now has a functional understanding of the models and is ready for a set of critical analyses raising doubts on the reliability of some aspects of these models, undertaken in the next chapter.

Gerlagh,[131] Hoel,[132] and Habermacher[133] presented earlier versions of the rising carbon tax models. Van der Werf and Di Maria reviewed both Hotelling and Dasgupta Heal versions of these models and suggested a taxonomy of these models.[134] At the core of these models is perhaps the easiest to intuit version of the green paradox models, that if the costs of carbon production or consumption will become substantially more expensive in a later time period(s), then usage might time-shift to the cheaper earlier time periods. Critically, these models rely heavily on the effects modeled by Hotelling and Dasgupta Heal models of exhaustible resources.

Next, the chapter presented analyses on the backstop technology models, that the use of carbon will become displaced in the market by comparatively advantaged technologies at a later or second time period. Models in this grouping include models from van de Ploeg and Withagen,[135] Gerlagh,[136] Grafton et al.,[137] Hoel,[138] Hoel and Jensen,[139] and Strand.[140] In many ways, these models are functionally similar to the increasing tax models, in that the fossil fuel producer/user is given strong incentives to move fossil fuel use to an earlier time period. In another way, the subsidies to the alternative energy sources is a mirror reverse of the increasing taxes applied against carbonaceous fuels in the prior set of models. And again, the Hotelling and Dasgupta Heal models are at the heart of these backstop technology models, again relying on Hotelling's ideas of full depletion, same as before in tax-based models.

Third, in what might be better described as the 'rational response to delayed bad news' model, the models of delayed policy implementation provide a scenario wherein the government deliberates and decides on green policies but takes time to bring the policies into effect, creating a 'pre-policy' period and a 'difficult policy' period for the carbon fuel producer/user to strategically consider in deciding when to act on carbon activities. Most of the models, again, relied on Hotelling's model, however, Smulders et al. went a different path and examined this concept from a demand side instead of a supply side, like the other models did. Smulders et al. focused on capital accumulation by the consumers, which in turn became impacted by the later-period higher cost of fossil fuels.

The leakage models focus on where carbon utilization is shifted either temporally or spatially. There is, of course, some debate about whether both of these models are green paradox models or only the temporal leakage is, but the core issue in these models is that policy impact is limited to a time period or a jurisdictional area and that limitation causes the policy to not be effective. Clearly these types of problems could arise from many types of structural issues, but van der Werf and Di Maria identify five basic channels of carbon leakage from the proposed green paradox models:[141]

- i The *marginal damages* channel warns that while emissions reductions might be unilaterally undertaken, the benefits will accrue globally, thus creating opportunity for many to free ride those unilaterally paid costs.
- ii The *energy market* channel captures the effect of a unilateral reduction in emissions on the global market for conventional fossil fuels.
- iii The *terms of trade effect* channel examines the spillover consequences for products made or transported using fossil fuel inputs; that while a country might ban the use of fossil fuels in its own jurisdiction, its citizens might import products from countries without that policy and defeat the policy's purposes.
- iv The *international trade in factors of production* channel models the movement of capital when some countries constrain the use of fossil fuels and other countries do not, that capital might move to those countries with more lax green policies.
- v The *technology change/technology spillover* channel explores the potential for unilateral action on green energy policies to spill over into other countries, distributing that technology to free-riding countries that did not invest in the costs of developing it.

Yet, again, deeply embedded in most of these models we find the Hotelling model at the core.

Fourth, Michielsen's models are fascinating in that they cover the field of the previous four models and reveal deep structural similarities across the models. In particular, he found that the intertemporal models and the interspatial models created the same effects in policy frustration. He also demonstrated that the better the technological backstop is, the worse the green paradox effects will be. In many ways, his models both confirmed the 'family-ness' of the models and confirmed that, if certain assumptions are correct, that the green paradox results forecast by Sinn would indeed occur. Yet, again, we find Hotelling's models at the core of the arguments.

This chapter has studied and broken out the main models of the green paradox theory; it has detailed the key assumptions of each model and revealed the similar clusters of assumptions across all five model clusters. With this result, we can now move forward to test the robustness of those assumptions: are enough of these assumptions defensible to enable the models to function as designed, or will too many of the assumptions be falsified or at least left in substantial doubt, requiring the models to be questioned as to their reliability for policy formation purposes? These issues are to be addressed in the next chapter, Chapter 4.

Notes

1 *Arguendo*, it could be said that the previous four concerns are all variants of this delayed policy concern.
2 van der Werf & Di Maria (2012), 160. The discussion on this model will be lengthier than other models, because many of the model's assumptions and behaviors are similar to the other models and thus can be explained once hereunder. Also, this model is the dominant green paradox model, as it was the original proposal by Sinn, *see* discussion *supra* at section 2.3.3.
3 *See* Gerlagh (2011).
4 *See* Michael Hoel (1991). *See also* Hoel, *The Green Paradox and Greenhouse Gas Reducing Investments* (2011).
5 *See* Habermacher & Kirchgässner (2011).
6 *See generally* Nordhaus (1994) (providing a non-green paradox model of temporally increasing carbon taxation).
7 *See* van der Werf & Di Maria (2012), 160–165.
8 van der Werf & Di Maria (2012), 160–165.
9 van der Werf & Di Maria (2012), 160. *See, e.g.*, equations (1.a) through (1.e) for the assumptions of the model's extraction path.
10 van der Werf & Di Maria (2012), 160. "Resource-owners are price takers."
11 van der Werf & Di Maria (2012), 160. "$\tau(t)$ is the carbon emissions tax (the units are set such that one unit of resources use generates one unit of emissions)."
12 van der Werf & Di Maria (2012), 160–161. "$c(X(t))$ is the unit extraction, which we allow to be an increasing function of the amount of cumulative extraction $X(t)$."
13 From the author's personal experience, many operators in practice have cheaper, internal sources of capital than the exogenously determined r. Their investment decisions are not driven by external r but by other competitive investments, as measured in terms of opportunities lost given limited resources in other sectors than financial capital. Hurdle rates often exceed 15% or higher, in great excess of market levels of r.
14 van der Werf & Di Maria (2012), 160.

15 *See* van der Werf & Di Maria (2012), 160; *see also infra* section 4.3.1 (discussing Hotelling's assumption on free markets).
16 *See* van der Werf & Di Maria (2012), 160–161; *see also infra* section 4.3.5 (discussing Hotelling's assumption on flexible rescheduling of production).
17 *See* van der Werf & Di Maria (2012), 160–161; *see also infra* section 4.3.6 (discussing Hotelling's assumption on rising costs of extraction).
18 van der Werf & Di Maria (2012), 160–161; *see also* van der Ploeg & Withagen, *Relevance of Green Paradoxes*, *supra* note 39, 2–3 (discussing why extraction costs might become "more costly as less accessible reserves have to be explored").
19 van der Werf & Di Maria (2012), 161; *see also infra* section 4.4 (discussing Hotelling's foreshadowing of Dasgupta and Heal's backstop alternative energy models).
20 van der Werf & Di Maria (2012), 161; *see also* van der Ploeg & Withagen, *Relevance of Green Paradoxes*, *supra* note 39, 2–3 (discussing backstops and dirty backstops).
21 van der Werf & Di Maria (2012), 161. *See also infra* section 4.3.1 (discussing Hotelling's caveats on the potential for energy resource markets to not clear, i.e., that the producers might not be able to sell all of their produced volumes).
22 *See* van der Werf & Di Maria (2012), 161 (defining Equation 2).
23 *See* van der Werf & Di Maria (2012), 161 (defining Equation 3).
24 *See* van der Werf & Di Maria (2012), 161 (defining Equation 3). The net present value calculation creates a discount from later revenues by application of ((revenue/$(1-r)^n$) where n is the number of future time periods. Hotelling rule suggests that the revenues numbers increase in synchronization with r over time, so the net result of time passage is null.
25 van der Ploeg & Withagen (2013), 2 ("Extraction costs do not change the picture in an essential way.").
26 *See also infra* section 4.3.2.
27 van der Werf & Di Maria (2012), 161–162.
28 van der Werf & Di Maria (2012), 161.
29 van der Werf & Di Maria (2012), 162.
30 van der Werf & Di Maria (2012), 162.
31 van der Werf & Di Maria (2012), 162 (defining Equation 5).
32 van der Werf & Di Maria (2012), 162. The actual reference is to a "weak green paradox," which they defined as an increase in greenhouse gas emissions. *Id.* They contrasted that against a notion of "strong green paradox," which finds a decrease in welfare as a result of that increase in greenhouse gas emissions. *Id.*, 155. For the purposes of this book, green paradox refers solely to the phenomenon of increasing anthropogenic greenhouse gases as a result of legislation and other legal conventions that attempt to reduce such emissions. This book addresses the effects of positive law, potential adverse results, and potential fixes.
33 van der Werf & Di Maria (2012), 162.
34 van der Werf & Di Maria (2012), 163.
35 van der Werf & Di Maria (2012), 162.
36 van der Werf & Di Maria (2012), 163 (defining Equation 7).
37 van der Werf & Di Maria (2012), 163.
38 van der Werf & Di Maria (2012), 163.
39 van der Werf & Di Maria (2012), 163–164.
40 van der Werf & Di Maria (2012), 163.
41 van der Werf & Di Maria (2012), 164.
42 van der Werf & Di Maria (2012), 164.
43 van der Werf & Di Maria (2012), 165–166.
44 *See* van der Ploeg & Withagen (2012).
45 *See* Gerlagh (2011).
46 *See* Grafton, Kompas, & Long (2012).

47 *See* Michael Hoel, *The Supply Side of CO_2 with Country Heterogeneity* (2011).
48 *See* Hoel & Jensen (2012).
49 Jon Strand, *Technology Treaties and Fossil-Fuels Extraction*, 28 ENERGY J. 129 (2007).
50 *See* van der Ploeg & Withagen, 2013, 2–3 (intertwining the two classes of models). The differences are recentralized on the Hotelling "full depletion in all cases" models versus the Heal "costly extraction" models. The argument provided is that Hotelling models provide sure green paradoxes, but that Heal models are less likely to produce green paradoxes. *Id.*
51 To tax the producer of A or to subsidize the producer of B would provide much of the same effect, in that A becomes more expensive than B to producers.
52 *See* van der Werf & Di Maria (2012), 165–166.
53 van der Werf & Di Maria (2012), 166–173.
54 van der Werf & Di Maria (2012), 166–167. The value of the unit fossil fuel price will equal the price of the alternate energy substitute; the fossil fuel price being based on a price from the initial time period as affected by cumulative depletion under the Hotelling rule resulting in increasing costs of extraction. That is, $p(0)e^{rt}=b$. *See id.* For a discussion of the impact of choosing the function e^{rt}, *see infra* section 4.3.3 (critiquing the Hotelling model of depletion).
55 van der Werf & Di Maria (2012), 167.
56 van der Werf & Di Maria (2012), 167.
57 van der Werf & Di Maria (2012), 167.
58 van der Werf & Di Maria (2012), 167. This is a functional result that follows from the earlier observation that any policy that provides an earlier end to the potential production time frame will result in all of the potential production volumes being produced earlier. It is an artifact of the Hotelling assumption of complete depletion based on Hotelling's rule.
59 van der Werf & Di Maria (2012), 167 (describing and discussing the model used in van der Ploeg & Withagen (2012)).
60 van der Werf & Di Maria (2012), 168 (describing and discussing the model used in Hoel, *Supply Side of CO_2* (2011)).
61 van der Werf & Di Maria (2012), 168 (describing and discussing the model used in Hoel, *Supply Side of CO_2*, *supra* note 129).
62 *See, e.g.*, van der Ploeg & Withagen (2012), 346. The authors use Equation 3(a) for their modified Hotelling model and Equation 3(c) for the potential depletion boundary condition. *Id.* Under Equation 3(a), while depletion might be incomplete, the total expected depletion is foreseeable and thus the operator can reschedule production volumes just as they would under simpler Hotelling models; policy effectively creates smaller depletable stocks. *See id.*
63 van der Ploeg & Withagen (2012), 345–346, 351–353.
64 van der Ploeg & Withagen (2012), 351.
65 van der Ploeg & Withagen (2012), 351 (stating Proposition 5).
66 van der Ploeg & Withagen (2012), 351, 351–353.
67 van der Ploeg & Withagen (2012), 351, 351–353.
68 "The higher the tax and the cost of the backstop, the smaller is the initial rate of fossil fuel extraction and the later exhaustion of fossil fuel reserves takes place." van der Ploeg & Withagen (2012), 351, 352–353, 361.
69 van der Ploeg & Withagen (2012), 351. *See* Proposition 6, "With the functional forms given in (6) full exhaustion takes longer (T larger) if the initial fossil fuel stock S_0 is high, the cost of the backstop net of the subsidy $b - \sigma$ is high, the maximal marginal extraction costs g is high and the choke price for fuel a is low. In case of partial exhaustion, the transition occurs slower if a, g or s are marginally lower and S_0 and b marginally higher."
70 van der Ploeg & Withagen (2012), 353.

71 van der Ploeg & Withagen (2012), 353.
72 van der Werf & Di Maria (2012), 174.
73 van der Werf & Di Maria (2012), 157 table 1.
74 van der Werf & Di Maria (2012), 174 (discussing the model used in Di Maria, Smulders, & van der Werf (2012)).
75 van der Werf & Di Maria (2012), 175 (discussing the model used in Eichner & Pethig (2011)).
76 van der Werf & Di Maria (2012), 175 (citing Di Maria, Smulders, & van der Werf (2012)).
77 van der Werf & Di Maria (2012), 174–175 (citing Di Maria, Smulders, & van der Werf (2012)).
78 van der Werf & Di Maria (2012), 175 (citing Eichner & Pethig (2011)).
79 van der Werf & Di Maria (2012), 175.
80 van der Werf & Di Maria (2012), 175 (discussing the model used in Eichner & Pethig (2011)). "As in the Hotelling model introduced in Section 2, the entire resource stock will get exhausted over time."
81 van der Werf & Di Maria (2012), 175 (citing Eichner & Pethig (2011)).
82 van der Werf & Di Maria (2012), 175 (citing Eichner & Pethig (2011)).
83 van der Werf & Di Maria (2012), 176 (citing Smulders et al. (2012).
84 Smulders et al. (2012), 365 ("[W]e abstract from scarcity of energy resources, i.e., there is no stock of energy resources that owners are eager to deplete. While the papers cited above all rely on the scarcity of the polluting input to generate the paradoxical announcement effect, we show that scarcity is not required.").
85 Smulders et al. (2012), 365. ("The build-up of capital is time-consuming so that investment behavior is forward looking. When the climate policy is announced, investment responds and the change in capacity affects energy demand before the climate policy is implemented. The existing literature typically assumes the resource stock to be the only predetermined stock variable.").
86 Smulders et al. (2012), 365. ("We thus pay attention also to the dynamics at the energy demand side, rather than focusing on the supply side.").
87 Smulders et al. (2012), 372 (describing Proposition 3).
88 Smulders et al. (2012), 371–372.
89 Smulders et al. (2012), 366–367. Equation 2.1 establishes the production function as predicated on energy, Equation 2.2 makes solar and fossil fuels perfect substitutes, and Proposition 1(i) establishes the fossil fuel economy so long as the marginal costs of fossil fuel are less than those of solar energy. *Id.* The authors also make the assumption that the initial economy without a carbon tax relies on fossil fuels, because "otherwise, no intervention is needed." *Id.* at 371.
90 van der Werf & Di Maria (2012), 179.
91 van der Werf & Di Maria (2012), 179–180.
92 van der Werf & Di Maria (2012), 180 (discussing Hoel (1991)).
93 van der Werf & Di Maria (2012), 180 (discussing Hoel (1991)).
94 van der Werf & Di Maria (2012), 180–181.
95 van der Werf & Di Maria (2012), 181. However, if the fundamental supply function is inelastic with regards to price, at least in the short run, then the volumes available for consumption will not be increased and thus carbon emissions would not increase. This is potentially the case when fossil fuels are constrained by transportation and distribution systems that might need long lead times to be expanded. An additional concern could be the lead time to explore and initiate production from new wells or fields. For most fields in production, these are routine constraints as the fields were designed to market as much product as

could be extracted; thus, there is not much upward slack designed into their systems.

96 van der Werf & Di Maria (2012), 181–183. A more updated look at an AGE model is provided below in the discussion on the Michielsen article. *See infra* section 3.5.

97 van der Werf & Di Maria (2012), 181–182.

98 van der Werf & Di Maria (2012), 183 (discussing the model used by Harstad (2012)). However, the Harstad model does not answer what the former resource owner would do with the capital received for the reserves; one wonders if the former owners might not seek out new fields to sell in-place.

99 van der Werf & Di Maria (2012), 183–185. Products may be made directly from fossil fuels, as in plastic components, or the fossil fuels may be used only indirectly in the manufacturing and/or transportation of the product, as in transported foodstuffs.

100 van der Werf & Di Maria (2012), 183–184.

101 van der Werf & Di Maria (2012), 184.

102 van der Werf & Di Maria (2012), 184 (discussing Paltsev (2001), and Burniaux & Oliveira Martins (2012)).

103 van der Werf & Di Maria (2012), 184–185. Most of these models were some form of general equilibrium models.

104 van der Werf & Di Maria (2012), 185.

105 van der Werf & Di Maria (2012), 185–186. As earlier, the finding of negative leakages is fairly consistent within this class of models.

106 van der Werf & Di Maria (2012), 186.

107 van der Werf & Di Maria (2012), 186–187.

108 van der Werf & Di Maria (2012), 186–187.

109 Michielsen (2014), 88.

110 Michielsen (2014), 88.

111 Michielsen (2014), 87.

112 Michielsen (2014), 87 n. 1, 88.

113 Michielsen (2014), 98.

114 Michielsen (2014), 88. “Consider a model with three types of energy: an exhaustible resource, a dirty backstop and a clean backstop.”

115 Michielsen (2014), “The backstops are inexhaustible, supplied competitively and have constant marginal costs. Though the word ‘backstop’ is sometimes used to denote a perfect substitute for an exhaustible resource, we explicitly allow for imperfect substitutability. The exhaustible resource is supplied competitively by a group of energy exporters and costless to extract.”

116 Michielsen (2014), “For the energy exporters, it is always optimal to fully exhaust the fossil resource stock *S*.”

117 Michielsen (2014), 89 (providing an instance of Hotelling’s rule in Equation 4).

118 Michielsen (2014), 89 (identifying assumptions A1, A2, and A3 and explaining how they show that energy types are imperfect substitutes).

119 Michielsen (2014), 90.

120 Michielsen (2014), 92; *see also id.* at 91 (providing the full theoretical results in Proposition 2).

121 Michielsen (2014), 91.

122 Michielsen (2014), 91.

123 Michielsen (2014). at 98. “Our model can be used to analyze spatial rather than intertemporal carbon leakage by relabeling ‘period 2’ as a climate-conscious country, ‘period 1’ as a non-abating country and setting the interest rate to zero.”

124 *See infra* sections 4.4 and 4.5.

125 Michielsen (2014), 98–100, "The model does not explicitly incorporate industry relocation effects but shows how unilateral carbon taxes affect world market fossil fuel prices and thereby emissions in non-abating countries." This assumption is readily challenged; simply because a patent might be readily viewed in every country does not equal the claim that each country has equal access to capital or other critical matters of infrastructure to equally implement the backstop technologies. E.g., nuclear fission technology is by no means novel but remains in the effective control of a fairly small number of manufacturers and operators. Similarly, windmills are technologically ancient, yet modern, innovations, and manufacturing capacities are similarly constrained. The limited capacity of each state to handle sophisticated integration of technologies is reflected in the economic theory of economic complexity and its economic complexity index (ECI). *See generally* Hidalgo & Hausmann (2009).
126 Michielsen (2014) at 93.
127 Michielsen (2014) at 92 ("As opposed to the case of a future carbon tax, exhaustible resource owners always bring extraction forward when clean alternatives become cheaper in the future.").
128 Michielsen (2014) at 93. Also, *vice versa*, owners of exhaustible resources are "protected" by imperfect substitutes and thus green paradox results can be avoided. *Id.*
129 Michielsen (2014) at 93 (identifying Equation 13 and discussing its theoretical treatment).
130 Michielsen (2014) at 93–94 (identifying and discussing Corollary 3).
131 *See* Gerlagh (2011).
132 *See* Hoel (1991); *see also* Michael Hoel, The Green Paradox and Greenhouse Gas Reducing Investments (2011).
133 *See* Habermacher & Kirchgässner (2011).
134 van der Werf & Di Maria (2012), 160–165.
135 *See* van der Ploeg & Withagen (2012).
136 *See* Gerlagh (2011).
137 *See* Grafton, Kompas, & Long (2012).
138 *See* Hoel, *The Supply Side of CO_2 with Country Heterogeneity* (2011).
139 *See* Hoel & Jensen (2012).
140 Jon Strand, *Technology Treaties and Fossil-Fuels Extraction*, 28 ENERGY J. 129 (2007).
141 van der Werf & Di Maria (2012), 179.

4 Misplaced reliance on economic models of exhaustible resources

The level of reliance that so many green paradox models have on either Hotelling or Dasgupta Heal models has been demonstrated by the discussion in Chapter 3. This chapter attempts to determine if that reliance on the Hotelling and Dasgupta Heal models is well founded.

First, the background to the origin of Hotelling's model is provided to yield insight into the function and purpose of the model. Next, the study will explain the working of the model. The focus will then turn to the assumptions of the model, the caveats that Hotelling provided against those assumptions, and other concerns related to those assumptions. It will be demonstrated that reliance on a Hotelling model for green paradox studies might not be well founded.

Second, this chapter will provide a brief introduction to the origins of the Dasgupta Heal backstop models. The reliance of the Dasgupta Heal models on the original Hotelling models will be demonstrated. Similar to the previous discussion, this analysis will demonstrate that reliance on Dasgupta Heal models for green paradox studies might not be well founded. This conclusion will be equally valid for both dirty backstop models and green energy backstop models.

After Hotelling's model of exhaustible resources, backstop technology models are probably the second most common set of models discussed in green paradox research. The backstop models analyze the optimal production path of an exhaustible resource when there is a substitutable alternative energy technology available, known as a "backstop." There are two basic sets of models: those with green energy technologies and those with carbon-emitting technologies.

Partha Dasgupta and Geoffrey Heal created these models in the 1970s;[1] the models were developed in response to concerns that exhaustion of fossil fuels could limit economic growth.[2] One model evaluated then-unconventional fossil fuels as a backstop technology, while another model evaluated nuclear energy as a backstop technology choice.[3]

Both models are generalizations of Hotelling's model of exhaustible resources.[4] Thus, many of the concerns on Hotelling's model apply equally to Dasgupta Heal models.[5] Both models make the same mathematical assumptions as in Hotelling's original model: that forced full depletion will occur within the time of the models.[6] Thus, while the models are well regarded for other applications within resource economics, the following analysis will demonstrate that the use of Dasgupta

Heal models within green paradox settings might be less than optimal for resolving critical research questions.

4.1 Background of Hotelling's models

Harold Hotelling wrote "The Economics of Exhaustible Resources" in 1931 due to calls for the regulation of "minerals, forests, and other exhaustible assets."[7] At that time, there were concerns that some actors were rushing to harvest exhaustible resources and causing a surplus of supply, a collapse of pricing, and great resource waste in many cases.[8] These particular concerns gave cause to the nascent conservation movement and led to calls for the government to protect exhaustible natural resources by limiting the periods and quantities of extraction.[9]

On the other hand, Hotelling also published his article in response to concerns that other actors were colluding to prevent production and to force high prices onto the public.[10] In previous years, this collusion had led to the development of anti-monopoly laws, as famously applied to Standard Oil. In his article, however, Hotelling made reference to a more contemporary case from California wherein several post-break-up Standard Oil affiliates allegedly conspired to limit production and protect prices.[11]

There was clamor for laws to limit production, to encourage production, to impose taxes and royalties, and to provide legal guidance on mineral ownership.[12] Thus, either the resource owners and operators were overproducing, wasting, and losing welfare through excessively cheap prices, or the resource owners and operators were colluding to prevent extraction and refining to limit supply and ensure higher prices. He referred to these two complaints as the "Scylla and Charybdis between which public policy must be steered."[13]

Before he could assist in the determination of reasonable policy, he needed to build a theoretical device. Hotelling was particularly concerned with the need to handle infinities and the importance of the "calculus of variations."[14] Thus, much of his model was innovative both in its treatment of exhaustible resources and in its adoption of calculus prior to Samuelson's text.[15] Because of those factors, his model has been seminal and heavily relied upon.[16]

Given the theoretical challenges Hotelling was working against,[17] he developed a clean, clear, but perhaps very narrow, model of an exhaustible resource. But this was no accident; Hotelling repeatedly qualified the use of his model and advised its careful use: "However, there are in extractive industries *discrepancies from our assumed conditions* leading to particularly wasteful forms of exploitation which might well be regulated in the public interest."[18] This is an example of Hotelling's caveats: that his model differed from realistic decision processes, and also that his model was designed more as a tool to formulate policy that could change the way industries operated in the real world.

His models were not intended as scientific demonstrations of how things actually worked at the time; rather, the models were predictions of how industries might behave under ideal conditions. Hotelling was also trying to develop a policy perspective based on public welfare; he assumed that eventually the resource would become fully exhausted.[19] Thus, while Hotelling's model of exhaustible resources is without peer, the user must carefully determine if that vehicle is the correct one to use to accommodate theoretical needs.[20]

4.2 Hotelling's model: optimal depletion pathways

Hotelling begins his model by controlling for the prices of the resource over time by relying upon Bernoulli's model of compound interest and the price of the first mineral extracted, p_0.[21] Hotelling assumes that minerals will be removed in order of the cheapest first, from a supply of the resource in place, a.[22] From these assumptions, he predicts that the quantity to be produced or extracted at any time t is controlled by the price receivable.[23] If the moment of final, and thus full, depletion can be named T, then the total amount to be depleted can be solved as the sum of depletions from time 0 to time T; which he solved with an integral against p_0, t and the interest rate.[24]

After extending the model to include social utility and welfare, Hotelling finds that under ideal conditions the pricing structures and interest rates result in similar production schedules for both free competition and optimal-welfare depletion rates.[25] He qualified, however, that the model should not be read to support laissez-faire conservation policies for fossil fuel resources, because the overall complexity and uncertainty of fossil fuel markets might result in behaviors contrary to the forecasted results: "there are in extractive industries discrepancies from our assumed conditions."[26] This was the focal point of his research: to identify if conservation policies might be required to attain the socially optimal level of production. Hotelling found that while the model said no regulation would be necessary in free competition scenarios, it was nonetheless necessary to qualify these findings and ultimately argue in favor of regulation.[27]

Hotelling also provided a monopolistic model that resulted in a finding that monopolies over exhaustible resources would lead to slower depletion of those resources than under the free competition model. This model also resulted in suboptimal welfare since monopolies would over-conserve the exhaustible resource.[28]

Hotelling's rule on exhaustible resource prices can be presented simply as the idea that the net price of a fossil fuel should increase consistent with the interest rate; the particular assumptions and their consequences are discussed in the next section.[29] More specifically, Hotelling's rule states that when the market is in equilibrium, the net price of a fossil fuel, i.e., the sales price less marginal costs and marginal taxes, should rise at the same rate as the interest rate; the net price of a fossil fuel should increase in relation to the interest rate, but remain temporally equivalent across all time periods.[30]

Hotelling assumed that the costs of extracting resources increased as the resources are depleted.[31] He compared the fossil fuel price at time t less the extraction costs at time t, as discounted by the interest rate up to that time t against a similar composite value at time s.[32] If these two values were not the same, then production volumes could, and should, be temporally shifted until net revenue is maximized across all time periods. Once that occurs, that consistent value is the temporally consistent net price for the fossil fuel; that value reflects a full and appropriate time discounting.[33]

The model is often expanded to reflect both the current level of extraction and the total remaining available reserves of fossil fuel in order to facilitate use in econometric studies.[34] The costs of extraction in such a model are said to depend on both matters.[35] Some theorists have preferred a simpler model, one that reduces complexity by assuming a constant marginal cost of extraction.[36]

Sinn's original green paradox focused on carbon taxes.[37] Hotelling addressed two forms of taxes on exhaustible resources;[38] if those resources were coal or oil then they would have been carbon taxes.

Hotelling demonstrated that unanticipated taxes on the capital value of a mine would have "no effect other than to transfer to the government treasury a part of the mine-owner's income."[39] However, he also demonstrated that an anticipated capital value tax would have an effect, an effect equivalent to the mine owner facing a higher interest rate and, thus, a higher discount rate.[40] Higher interest rates and discount rates favor earlier production; thus, due to Hotelling's equivalency of capital taxes to interest rates, higher capital taxes would mandate earlier production.

In practice, certain versions of carbon taxes, called severance taxes, are currently levied against extractors or producers. Hotelling found that an announced, constant-level severance tax led to conservation over a longer period of time.[41] But, Hotelling also found that the severance tax lowered prices,[42] so long as the demand function was downward sloping, i.e., that consumers would want more of the commodity when prices are low, and less when its prices are high.[43] Hotelling also demonstrated that the majority of the tax incidence would fall on the owner of the resource.[44] Because of the treble welfare benefits – a slower rate of production for a longer period,[45] a reduction in prices, and the incidence falling on the resource owner – Hotelling deemed severance taxes to be a "good tax."[46]

However, Hotelling emphasized that even a small severance tax was likely to reduce overall welfare for the community.[47] In contrast to the capital tax, which expedited production and depletion, severance taxes could be used to control and delay production and depletion.

In conclusion, Hotelling developed models to explain ideal forms of behavior for exhaustible resources in competitive and monopolistic settings. He determined that certain carbon taxes could defer production and reduce prices.[48]

But he readily conceded that many of his modeling assumptions were contrary to reality, or were readily contrary to current industrial realities of carbon-rich exhaustible resources.

Finally, he spent his final pages warning how complex reality actually was, and that realistic models would suffer greatly from complexity and chaos in the modern mathematical sense of those two words. These issues will be explored in greater depth in the following sections.

4.3 Caveats on Hotelling's depletion models

In Chapter 3, the importance of the Hotelling and Dasgupta Heal models and their internal assumptions were made evident. The previous discussion demonstrated the function of Hotelling's model to discern optimal depletion pathways, especially under certain tax policies. At the center of these two discussions were the internal assumptions of Hotelling's original models; the following provides a list of these significant modeling assumptions. After introducing each assumption, a discussion is provided of Hotelling's own caveats on the assumption and of realities that directly conflict with these assumptions, even though they were likely well known to him at the time.

4.3.1 Assumption of free market/monopoly conditions

Hotelling first modeled the depletion of an exhaustible resource with an assumption of free competition, and then separately with assumptions of monopoly.[49]

Despite his development of models based on either purely competitive market economic assumptions or purely monopolistic economic assumptions, Hotelling closed his paper by commenting that exhaustible resource markets were *neither* competitive, as his basic model assumed, *nor* monopolistic; instead, these markets faced a small number of resource owners that were neither competitive nor monopolistic.[50] Additionally, Hotelling explicitly recognized that the free competition conditions assumed in his models did not exist in real life.[51]

Hotelling found that commonplace economic concepts predicated on traditional supply and demand analysis might fail since the pricing space of exhaustible resources is often complex. He admitted that his own previous research suggested that more than one price might simultaneously exist in such a market; thus, the market for exhaustible energy resources might not face a "clearing market."[52] Lacking the game theoretic tools that developed decades later, Hotelling nevertheless described a game with *m* competitors each with *n* mines producing competitive (i.e., perfect substitutes) resources.[53] He provided a rough proof that such conditions should result in higher than equilibrium prices and lower than demanded quantity of production than at equilibrium.[54]

However, Hotelling warned of "indeterminateness" existing in the economic space of exhaustible resource producers when the numbers of producers are few and in competition: "When the supplies of the complementary goods are exhaustible, the same indeterminateness exists."[55] Additionally, he wrote, "[t]hese affrays give an example of the instability of competition when variations of price with location as well as time complicate commerce in an exhaustible asset."[56]

Hotelling argued that the market price of crude oil products is complex and indeterminate, fitting no particular abstract model; modelers need to take caution that their models are either sophisticated enough or provide sufficient caveats, as Hotelling did, that policy advice must be cautiously administered.

4.3.2 Complete information on reserves and depletion schedules

Hotelling assumed that the resource owners and operators possessed complete information on the size and extent of their resources, future prices, feasible technology paths, and every other relevant consideration. "We have tacitly assumed all of the conditions fully known."[57]

It goes without saying that this was not the case in his time nor in ours. But the evidence is clearly building against the paradigm of a "stock" concept of exhaustible fossil fuels:

> Although the total resource of hydrocarbons in the Earth's crust for all practical purposes is fixed, the fraction reported as reserves is dynamic ... The continuous additions to reserves might seem reassuring, but historical data suggest that they rather increase the unpredictability and conceal the true prospect of future production capacity.[58]

Hotelling also assumed for his model that the full resource base is known and will be fully depleted by the resource owner and operator.[59] Hotelling referred to both a "total supply of the substance,"[60] which he denoted as *a*, and an "upper limit *T* being the time of final exhaustion."[61]

This system of known depletion leads to a logical paradigm that the owner faces a fixed stock of resource that could be produced in any of *n* time periods, but the lack of production in one time period forces the production to other time periods.[62] If production cannot come later, then it must come now; that is the heart of most green paradox models, in that incentives are found that discourage later-period production with resultant increases to current or near-term production.

Yet, Hotelling admitted that (i) the volume of resource would be unknown *ex ante*; (ii) that time would reveal additional data on the size of the resource; (iii) that time would reveal additional information as to the quality and utility of the resource; and (iv) that the economic value of the resource might vary over time. Thus, most of his critical assumptions for his models of exhaustible resource were functionally not seen in his research into market conditions. As he stated,

> The problems of exhaustible resources involve the time in another way besides bringing on exhaustion and higher prices, namely, as *bringing increased information*, both as to the *physical extent* and *condition* of the resource and as to the *economic phenomena attending its extraction and sale*.[63] In the most elementary discussions of exchange, as in bartering nuts for apples, as well as in discussions of duopoly, a time element is always introduced to show a gradual approach to equilibrium or a breaking away from it. Such time effects are equally or in even greater measure involved in exploiting irreplaceable assets, entangling with the secular tendencies peculiar to this class of goods.[64]

In another caveat, Hotelling noted that the demand curve determines if complete exhaustion would ever be completed; thus, he left room for incomplete depletion within a less-than-infinite horizon of time.[65] The determining issue was whether the demand was linear, which would fully deplete, or exponential, which would continue to deplete forever at decreasing rates.[66]

Hotelling also foresaw the potential impact of technological backstops, foreshadowing Dasgupta and Heal's models,[67] which Hotelling said could, *ceteris paribus*, greatly reduce the demand for the exhaustible commodity.[68] It only follows logically that Hotelling would have also foreseen that realistic conditions could set the demand price for the exhaustible resource below its costs of extraction and thus terminated its extraction.[69] It can now be also safely asserted that many coal and crude oil deposits are abandoned long before their technical reserves are depleted.[70] Some authorities offer programs to encourage the 'adoption' of abandoned wells to return them to production.[71] Such programs are necessary because resource owners will cease production when their marginal costs of lifting exceed their expected marginal revenues; oil can become too costly to extract in certain circumstances.[72]

Overall, one of the central tenets of Hotelling's model, that of foreseeable or predictable depletion paths, was extensively caveated by Hotelling himself and reasonably should be handled with caution by other modelers.

4.3.3 Conflagration of full depletion and profit maximization

Hotelling makes a complicated assumption, combining several ideas: resource owners will maximize the net revenues from each unit of exhaustible resource,[73] while also fully depleting their assets.[74] His main control against full depletion was a concern for whether the time frame was finite or infinite, not *per se* if fully depleted or not.[75]

Hotelling did take notice of the vast wastage occurring when markets are in formation or when unclear property rights encourage overproduction.[76] Thus, he did recognize that the resource owners were not fully aligned with profit maximization, at least not as reflected in his model based on free competition.

Further, in the introduction to his 1931 article, he referred to artificial conspiracies to limit the volumes of production to achieve lower prices in the market.[77] He also spent extensive efforts developing theories of monopolies and duopolies which might delay production over infinite horizons.[78]

However, these deviations from his initial assumption are to be expected, as in classical microeconomics, a producer will increase production so long as marginal revenues are in excess of marginal costs to do so, and the producer will attempt to not go beyond the point wherein its marginal costs and revenues are equivalent. Thus, it is reasonable to expect that certain circumstances could lead to cessation of extraction and production if the marginal costs of a fossil fuel were sufficiently high *vis-à-vis* their marginal revenues.[79] Models reflecting this have been developed; Levhari and Liviatan modified a Hotelling model to accommodate incomplete depletion or the possibility that production would terminate with positive reserves left in the ground.[80]

Thus, while the idea of full depletion might be motivated by the idea of maximizing sales volumes, it would be constrained by marginal analysis to less than complete depletion.

4.3.4 Hotelling's rule part i – compound interest and value of resource

Hotelling relied on Bernoulli's model of compound interest; it served as the foundation of the so-called Hotelling's rule. His rule modeled that an initial price p_0, given t years, with interest rate γ, will achieve the final value of $p_0e^{\gamma t}$.[81] And in reverse, that the discount effect can be rendered by $p_0 = p_te^{-\gamma t}$.[82] Hotelling also assumed for his model that the units of exhaustible resource are of equal utility and value at each and every time period into which they might be produced.[83]

Industrial practitioners generally disavow the relevance, accuracy, or utility of Hotelling's rule to determine the values of petroleum resources.[84] Adelman and Watkins found that long-run net oil prices ran apposite to Hotelling's model.[85] Gaudet did not argue for the invalidation of Hotelling's rule, but he did find that in a century's worth of data, the trends found were "certainly not" those forecasted by Hotelling's rule.[86] Most modelers who want to rely on Hotelling's rule need to add many additional data streams to provide better model fit, which is frankly a frustration to the *raison d'etre* of the rule.[87] Halvorsen and Smith found that there were extensive difficulties in employing econometric models to test the accuracy of Hotelling's rule due to a lack of appropriate *in situ* mineral value pricing data;[88] however, to the extent of available data they found that the "empirical implications of the theory of exhaustible resources are strongly rejected."[89]

Gronwald demonstrated that when oil prices are tested on a GARCH model, oil prices did not display upward trends as expected by Hotelling and peak oil models, but rather displayed a flat trend line with much turbulence.[90] "[O]il prices do not exhibit a stable and predictable behavior,"[91] but they are "marked by 'discontinuous' shifts."[92] He summarized that if combined with Holland's model of price-determined scarcity for oil, these GARCH results revealed a non-scarce supply of petroleum over time.[93] Gronwald found this difference from Hotelling's assumptions problematic for Sinn's green paradox models.[94]

Were the assumptions on intertemporal pricing and 'Hotelling's rule' on how intertemporal rates were to be determined well founded? It appears not. The centrality of Hotelling's rule itself to affect prices has been studied. The intertemporal arbitrage, centering on the discount rate, appears to be less central to fossil fuel pricing than other factors such as technological change, revisions to reservoir scale, and market structure.[95] Additionally, there is nothing *per se* about Hotelling's rule that is uniquely fossil fuel *cum* exhaustible resource motivated; rather, the same rule could apply to a wholesale vendor trying to clear a warehouse prior to a next period inventory tax.[96] It is merely a rational model on profit optimization, with additional constraints added for depleting or depreciating a stock of capital or inventory.[97]

In establishing his theory of resource value, Hotelling committed a *faux pas*, from a postmodern perspective, in declaring that valuable metals are better used for industrial purposes than artistic or other less obviously productive means.[98] He defended his position, stating that utility is better defined by goods that serve the poor,[99] yet provides no welfare theorem or function to back up that rhetorical comment. This was potential for an artful dodge to Sinn's 'ethical economists' query as to in which generation the greater value of the resource lies;[100] but it forces a mathematical result that utility cannot be of more or less value for different cultures and different stages of technologies.[101]

Additionally, many resource owners, such as the owners represented by OPEC, are generally held to have some ability to affect short-term market volumes and derivatively crude oil prices. Similar assumptions were held in Hotelling's era, as per the concerns on the oil trusts restricting production to support higher prices; Hotelling said much the same, "[a] large producing company can very commonly affect the price by varying its rate of marketing."[102]

In short, Hotelling's basic assumptions on pricing and valuation for exhaustible resources might not be applicable to all forms of exhaustible resources and were specifically caveated for fossil fuels by Hotelling himself. Further, Even Hotelling gave credit to the idea that the producers could manipulate the prices of the resources, further challenging the influence of Hotelling's rule for fossil fuels from exhaustible resources.

4.3.5 Hotelling's rule part ii – flexible schedule of extraction

Hotelling wrote that "it is a matter of indifference to the owner of a mine whether he receives for a unit of his production a price p_0 now or a price $p_0e^{\gamma t}$ after time t,"[103] establishing that mineral owners are functionally indifferent to when minerals are extracted, except for the price borne by the market at the time of the sale. Also, production could be disrupted and delayed, without consequences within the model. This presents the rhetorical result that fossil fuel producers could freely reschedule production volumes to accommodate, or be responsive to, effects caused by green energy policies.[104]

Was Hotelling correct that producers could flexibly reschedule production? No, basic geophysics prevents that in most oil and gas fields. The intertemporal flexibility assumed by the Hotelling model is also questionable. Field production volumes might not be readily reschedulable;[105] both physical engineering problems and institutional legal constraints limit flexibility to reschedule production to optimal periods.[106]

Exploration and development are also time-consuming; they might take years to implement once a financial investment decision is made. In contradiction to the assumption of Hotelling's rule temporal arbitrage to seek λ, intertemporal rescheduling is not readily available at all times, and production volumes might be locked in for a material period of time. Once production capacity is installed, generally, a field is allowed to produce for a long period and enter into natural decline before, if ever, additional capital commitments are made to provide for secondary or tertiary recovery.[107] When natural decline is modeled against the price of the fossil fuel over time, it can be demonstrated that the resultant price is lower than that forecast by Hotelling's rule.[108] Additionally, this analysis reveals that physical conditions determine the extraction path and that physical motive to expel the crude oil and natural gas is another critical exhaustible resource.[109] Generally speaking, oil and gas fields begin at close to peak capacity, for both the wells and their infrastructure, and that substantially additional production volumes are not possible without substantial additional investments in additional wells and pipelines.[110] "Output can be reduced but not increased."[111] Production will not be readily increasable. In other circumstances, "output can be reduced,"[112] but there are substantial risks to overall resource recovery if a field is substantially choked or delayed in production. The wells are fed crude oil and natural gas by the motive energy of subterranean pressures and potentially subterranean gases, including methane.[113] The subterranean pressures and motives that drive well performance could be lost or reabsorbed in the reservoir zone if stabilized too long. Thus, physical engineering concerns prevent the free rescheduling of production volumes once a field is initiated into production; thus, Hotelling's rule will be frustrated and price paths will deviate from the expected pathways.

The economics that underwrote recognition of commercially viable reserves in one time period might be lacking in latter time periods, and thus a well might be abandoned and plugged while substantial technologically producible volumes remain in place in the reservoir. Additionally, there are physical limits to the temporal rescheduling of petroleum production; volumes can be permanently lost if certain production rates are not maintained. The path of depletion might not be flexible but rigid. Thus, the strategic potential to reschedule fossil fuel production to address green energy policies might be more constrained than Hotelling's model might otherwise suggest.

4.3.6 Rising extraction costs

Hotelling assumed that the costs of extraction go from cheap to expensive; "[t]hey will be removed and used in order of accessibility, the most cheaply available first."[114] "The cost of extraction increases as the mine goes deeper."[115]

While this modeling assumption might be reasonable for some types of mining or foresting,[116] it is usually not correct for crude oil and natural gas.[117] Even where the "most cheaply available first" assumption could be used in crude oil,[118] the facts would be that of a wildcat operator that produces to a local storage tank *sans* pipeline transport to distribution networks.[119] E.g., natural gas frustrates this particular assumption of Hotelling's model because it is not well transported without extensive pipelines and thus requires large *ex ante* investments.[120] In-field exploratory and development costs are massive, whereas later investments and subsequent costs are much smaller, leading the fields to evidence costs similar in character to those of the model of natural monopolies.

Was Hotelling correct about the costs of extraction rising over time? Probably not, but the devil is in the details of defining costs over long time periods. The cost functions of Hotelling's model of exhaustible resource are not reflective of actual fossil fuel conditions, at least not for crude oil and conventional natural gas.[121]

Actual fossil fuel projects face large initial fixed cost investment commitments – most oil and gas fields are essentially *natural monopolies* in producing fossil fuels. Thus the assumption of $C(0,Q) = 0$ is almost never accurate; their initial costs are never zero but materially substantial.[122] Hotelling even commented on the unique cost structure of oil capital costs in alignment with this observation.[123] Costs of extraction do not necessarily increase; they may well decrease over cumulative production volumes. The ongoing field costs are generally a small fraction of the carried fixed costs, thus the marginal costs are often substantially below the average costs of production.[124] Marginal costs may be dropping, as capital investments decline over time and operational expenses would not be expected to increase at rates higher than the drop in marginal capital investments.[125] It is therefore reasonable to question if the assumptions of increasing costs of extraction, as cumulative volumes increase, are generally correct for crude oil and natural gas, again, especially considering that many fields operate as natural monopolies.

The assumption on increasing costs of extraction as cumulative volumes increase is met by several concerns. Many fields display the economics of natural monopolies, in that high capital costs are required *a priori* to initial production and that average costs and marginal costs decrease as production increases; ultimately costs may rise near the fields' end-of-life years, but that might be decades out for many fields in production and beyond the timing concerns raised by Sinn.[126]

4.3.7 Secure property rights

Hotelling assumed full and secure property rights in his model.

However, Hotelling acknowledged that insecure property rights could motivate wasteful behaviors. This foreshadowed Sinn's similar concerns, discussed in Chapter 2. "Each owner must drill and get the precious oil quickly, for otherwise his neighbors will get it all."[127]

In summary, while Hotelling's model provided useful insight into the specific questions he was researching, extensions of his models should be careful to take into account his own caveats on his models and to ensure that the underlying assumptions of his models do not frustrate the current goals of a modeler. Further, to the extent that earlier discussion revealed that many green paradox models have relied on Hotelling models, these concerns need revisiting to ensure that the models and their policy impacts are well protected from Hotelling's own concerns.

4.4 Caveats on Dasgupta and Heal's 1974 green energy backstop model

Dasgupta and Heal first investigated the idea of a green technology backstop for an economy with nearly depleted fossil fuel reserves during the oil shocks of the 1970s.[128] They evaluated a model, and several of its variants, which assumed that future technological developments would enable a clean renewable alternative to fossil fuels.[129]

The basic Dasgupta Heal model assumes that the conventional fossil fuel would fully deplete while reaching the price of the backstop technology, which would then be produced indefinitely.[130] The fossil fuel and its green energy backstop are assumed to be perfect substitutes within the model for simplicity; this assumption enables a perfect singular switch from fossil fuel to green energy at the right pricing point.[131] Heal later modified that family of models to consider what would today be called dirty backstops.[132] Most of the green paradox papers that rely on a Dasgupta Heal model refer to this later article and not to the green energy backstop paper.[133]

The Dasgupta Heal models rely on extensive use of Hotelling's rule for the valuation of intertemporal net profits and resource valuation.[134] Both the simple generalization presented at § 0.3 and the production model presented at § 1.2 involved forced full depletion of the primary fossil fuel prior to the switch to a backstop technology.[135] These *ex ante* conditions bind the owner to completely produce the reserve volumes during the execution of the model. Thus an event which reduces or increases the production in one period will need be offset in another period.[136] The resultant rescheduling of fossil fuel production is therefore not a result of policy incentives but of *a priori* modeling conditions.

Dasgupta and Heal did present a model within § 2 that does not *ex ante* force full depletion of the resource stocks.[137] But, it counterbalanced that modeling benefit by excluding the role of policy in creating changes to the arrival of technology.[138] Thus, the impact of policy matters is *per se* beyond the model and thus potentially frustrates the use of this model for other green paradox models.

Dasgupta and Heal addressed technological change and uncertainty not by providing endogenous means but by providing mathematical substitutions that depend upon correctly identifying the random mathematical process that controls when, dare *if*, the future green technology would arrive.[139] As stated in their concluding remarks, "in this paper we have supposed that the random variable is *uninfluenced by policy*; that is, that the acquisition of knowledge is costless."[140] Yet that random variable is the single determinant of the existence of green technology within the model. Thus, it might be difficult to rely on Dasgupta and Heal's technological change version of their model to analyze the effects of environmental policy on carbon-emitting exhaustible resource production.

But even if one could make certain adjustments to include policy effects within their technological change mode, there would be another significant obstacle to overcome. Dasgupta and Heal suggested that the assumption of higher discount rates could be used to offset the randomness of future uncertainty on the feasibility of green energy backstops; however, "it is generally recognized that it leads to errors."[141] To avoid those errors, their model would require some extreme market conditions. Both the capital markets and the resource markets need to reflect zero valuations to prevent market errors.[142] Thus, to the extent that one was able to overcome the previous difficulties, one would need to be able to demonstrate that the effects of a green paradox under this particular form were capable of being distinguished from both the effects of incorrectly anticipating the probability function's distribution and of relying on higher discount rates to offset the issues of the probability function.[143]

In closure, Dasgupta and Heal's models assumed many aspects of Hotelling's models and as such should retain the caveats attending his efforts. Further, their models introduced new concerns that might potentially frustrate research into green paradox phenomena.

4.5 Caveats on Heal's 1976 dirty energy backstop model

Heal developed a backstop model wherein an alternative fossil fuel was employed as the backstop, in lieu of green energy alternatives. He described his dirty backstop model as an analysis of "the optimal strategy for consuming a resource whose total availability is infinite, but whose cost of extraction is an increasing function of the total already extracted."[144] He broke down crude oil into two segments, volumes from conventional crude oil and volumes derived from shale oil.[145] The first resource faces increasing extraction costs and the second constant extraction costs.[146] Just as within Dasgupta Heal (1974),[147] Heal relied on Hotelling's rule to provide intertemporal stability of net profits.[148] By providing a ceiling to the price of crude oil, being limited by the constant extraction costs of shale oil, Heal demonstrates an argument that crude oil prices should begin higher than equilibrium prices and drop towards their marginal extraction costs over time.[149]

The central problem with the model is that it is designed to first deplete a certain *ex ante* determined stock of its conventional crude oil before the model would switch to continuous production of petroleum from shale oil rocks. The ultimate question of how much conventional crude oil to produce is preset exogenously.[150] The model assumes that there is a specific volume of conventional crude oil that can be extracted before the costs of extraction reach the costs of producing from shale oil.[151] That volume of conventional crude oil, *z-bar*, is unchangeable within the model; there is no endogenous mechanism to adjust it.[152] While this is not a forced full depletion *a la* Hotelling, it is essentially the same mathematical form and will result in a similar effect: policies to alter the timing of the switch to the backstop will not affect the total volumes of conventional crude oil to be produced; those volumes will simply be accelerated or delayed, not reduced. The model receives the price of the backstop exogenously,[153] as it does the resultant quantities of accumulated production from conventional crude oil,[154] but it would be reasonable to assume that lower backstop prices imply fewer produced volumes; a green paradox model would need to provide the necessary mechanisms.

In conclusion, the Heal models for dirty backstops strongly follow the models developed earlier by Dasgupta and Heal, and thus contain many of the same concerns for green paradox modelers as for those models.

4.6 Conclusions

Concerns have been raised that certain international conventions and domestic legislations driven by green policies to mitigate anthropogenic climate change could backfire by increasing greenhouse gas emissions. Researchers have developed economic models to analyze if and when such green paradox phenomena might be obtained from green energy policies. This chapter has examined the core assumptions of those models and found material concerns with those models and their implementations.

Most of the current models that demonstrate potential green paradoxes rely on economic models originating in studies on the optimal depletion of exhaustible resources. One common class of models used in green paradox research is the Hotelling model of exhaustible resources. The Dasgupta Heal classes of models, of exhaustible resources with technological backstops, are another common class of models found in green paradox research. The Dasgupta Heal models are in large part extensions of the Hotelling models, and to that extent, contain many of the same theoretical building blocks that lead to the concerns uncovered in this chapter.

The Hotelling and Dasgupta Heal models share certain economic modeling assumptions that induce certain behaviors; this book has investigated the fitness of those model classes for research into the potential emergence of green paradox phenomena. This research has revealed that these model classes are problematic and might be poor foundations for this line of research.

These findings are in alignment with the findings of other researchers. Gronwald said his findings that Hotelling's rule did not forecast oil prices well "create[d] additional concerns regarding the adequacy of Hotelling-type models for oil price modeling purposes ... that researchers and politicians alike should be aware of the behavior of the price of oil when designing and evaluating climate policies."[155]

This chapter has questioned the ability of certain green paradox models to accurately determine where such phenomena might arise, and thus it questions the ability of these models to accurately inform lawmakers and policy setters of the consequences of their legislative actions. In particular, researchers building models, to investigate green paradoxes, that build on top of the Hotelling or Dasgupta Heal models of exhaustible resources should be aware of the caveats provided by Hotelling himself, that the models should not be used without complementary reference to the real-world conditions and complexities of mining.

The previous two chapters and this chapter demonstrated that a wide variety of green paradox models do materially rely on the Hotelling and Dasgupta Heal models. Sinn's original model of carbon taxes inducing green paradox results was itself an extension of Hotelling's model. It had been shown that four major classes of green paradox models primarily relied on the same two classes of exhaustible resource models.

There did appear to be a sliding scale in implementation;

i Models based on Hotelling routinely found green paradoxes;
ii Dasgupta Heal models found paradoxes less often; and
iii Models based on exhaustible resources models other than those two classes found few green paradoxes.

The evidence of affinity between underlying model choice and green paradox findings was demonstrated.

Next, an investigation into the underlying models of Hotelling and Dasgupta and Heal was undertaken. An extensive discussion was drawn on Hotelling's research program, his economic model of exhaustible resources, and of the central assumption within his model. A detailed review of those assumptions, of his caveats to them, and of other relevant information on the accuracy of those assumptions was presented. It was found that Hotelling operated his model with caution and extensive caveats; he found the pricing space of exhaustible resources, particularly of fossil fuels, to be complex and indeterminate and thus difficult to model accurately. The green energy backstop models of Dasgupta and Heal and the dirty backstop models of Heal were demonstrated to have built upon and extended Hotelling's models without substantial change to his models, underlying assumptions. As such, use of their models' inherits the same need for caution and caveat as Hotelling's models would.

Thus, it was demonstrated that Hotelling's models require cautious use and should include caveats unless sufficiently modified.[156] It was demonstrated that Dasgupta and Heal extended Hotelling's models while retaining the bulk of his models' assumptions. Thereafter, modelers of green paradox research have built upon those foundations and incorporated the assumptions of the Hotelling or Dasgupta Heal models without substantial alteration.

This direct inheritance of assumptions leads to certain problems. The correlation of underlying model choice to the research results of green paradox emergence has been shown to be substantial; caution should be employed in the interpretation of choice of economic model by legislators and policymakers. Also, many of the assumptions of Hotelling's models were shown to need caveats or perhaps be revised in light of countervailing realities or practices. As such, Hotelling's models and those models based upon Hotelling's models might not readily provide certainty with regards to the emergent risks of green paradoxes.

If new laws or policies might substantially effect environmental concerns, many states and federal systems require review of those laws and policies for their environmental impact prior to their enactment and adoption; e.g., within the EU, the SEA Directive is applicable.[157] To the extent that Sinn's concerns of a green paradox suggest review of impending laws or policies, caution should be employed to ensure that the underlying models are not solely reliant on Hotelling or Dasgupta Heal models. Conversely, if the models do rely on those economic models, the models should have proper caveats and cautions made clear to the non-economist readers of the reports.

It is not the intent of this monograph to suggest that green paradoxes cannot occur; this research is in earnest pursuit of how to more rigorously ascertain their existence.[158]

The findings of this chapter do, however,

i sugeest that more attention might be warranted in examining the underlying models in understanding why green paradoxes might be found and ii encourage the inclusion of a broader range of resource models, beyond Hotelling and Dasgupta Heal models, to evaluate the potential emergence of green paradox risks.

This chapter has fundamentally challenged the mathematical models employed in the study of green paradoxes, based on the original caveats provided by Hotelling himself. Furthermore, this chapter has illuminated that policy cannot be properly determined without broader engagement with the scientific and engineering details of the situation; similarly, the legal contexts and legal environments of the markets and activities must be equally brought into consideration in the development of optimal policy.

The next sequence of chapters will examine precisely that–the legal environment of the activities that potentially lead to increased greenhouse gas emissions and to phenomena of green paradoxes. Those chapters will reveal that in certain cases, green energy policies could lead to increased carbon emissions, if adopted without sufficient coordination and displacement of other energy or environmental policies.

Notes

1 Heal has updated substantial context to their efforts:

> The first discussion of renewables in the economics literature was in the post-1973 oil shock era, when we rediscovered and refined Hotelling's work on resource depletion. We invented the phrase "backstop technology," a technology that would eventually replace exhaustible resources with an energy source continuing forever. Partha Dasgupta and I used the idea in our work extending Hotelling's analysis (Dasgupta & Heal 1973), William Nordhaus worked with this idea in his book on the efficient allocation of energy resources (Nordhaus 1973), and so did many others. In fact, a quick search for "backstop technology" on Google Scholar produced 8,540 references. No one modeled the backstop explicitly, but clearly it was not a fossil fuel that we had in mind.

Heal (2010), 140.

2 *See* Dasgupta & Heal (1974), 3; *see also* Heal (1976), 371.

3 *See* Dasgupta & Heal (1974) (discussing unconventional fossil fuels); Heal (1976) (discussing nuclear energy alternatives). Because both the Dasgupta Heal paper and the Heal paper utilize essentially the same models, and because the jointly authored paper came first, and because the latter tome repeated the joint effort, this present tome refers to both of the underlying models as the Dasgupta Heal models.

4 *See* Dasgupta & Heal (1974), 5 ("What we review here is a slight generalization of the well-known 'cake-eating' problem analyzed first by Hotelling and later by Gale."); *see also* Heal (1976), 373 ("Except for the conditions of the supply of the resource, the model is much as in Dasgupta Heal (1974).").

5 *See infra* sections 4.4 and 4.5.

6 While one of the Dasgupta Heal models did not make the forced full depletion assumption, it did remove the potential for policy to affect the onset or pricing of the green backstop technology. Thus, that model too is problematic for application within green paradox settings.

7 Hotelling (1931), 137; see also Devarajan & Fisher (1981) (providing a full discussion on the historical setting and impacts of Hotelling's modeling on

exhaustible resources and listing Hotelling's main two goals as to assess conservation arguments and to improve on the then-current static models).

8 Hotelling (1931), 137.
9 Hotelling (1931), 137.
10 Hotelling (1931), 138.
11 Hotelling (1931), 138.
12 Hotelling (1931), 138; *see also id.* at 143–144.
13 Hotelling (1931), 138.
14 Hotelling (1931), 140.
15 Hotelling (1931), 140; *see also* Samuelson (1947).
16 In 2019, a search on Google Scholar documented over 6,100 citations to Hotelling's study on the economics of exhaustible resources. For the number and listing of citing papers, visit http://scholar.google.com/scholar?cites=15133507373036129912&as_sdt=5,31&sciodt=0,31&hl=en.
17 This is referring to both the need to innovate a theoretical model and the need to provide mathematical tools to prevent his paper from being rejected.
18 Hotelling (1931), 143–144 (emphasis added).
19 Hotelling (1931), 141–142 (Hotelling refers to the condition as "final exhaustion"). *See also id.* at 157–158 (Hotelling developed conditions for the socially optimal course to final exhaustion). Levhari and Liviatan explicitly found that (i) "Hotelling assumed that the output of the well or mine is reduced to zero at the terminal point," and (ii) "Hotelling assumed that the firm always continues to produce up to the point where the resource is completely exhausted." Levhari & Liviatan (1977), 178. Other versions of Hotelling's models do exist. *See, e.g.*, van Veldhuizen & Sonnemans (2014). Van Veldhuizen and Sonnemans found that Hotelling model variants included models that account for exploration or technical innovation, enable non-profit-maximizing goals, and allow for less competitive conditions within general Hotelling settings. *Id.* at 5–6. They also found that other models explored divergent behaviors of marginal cost curves, especially the impacts of technological innovation or new resource discovery on short-term marginal costs declines. *Id.*
20 *See also* Slade & Thille (2009), 256 (surveying the "large empirical literature that tests and applies the Hotelling model"). Slade and Thille found that (i) circumstances of imperfect competition, (ii) distortionary taxation, (iii) risk aversion, and (iv) incomplete assignment of property rights could lead to frustration of the Hotelling models. *Id.*
21 *See infra* section 4.3.4.
22 Hotelling (1931), 141.
23 Hotelling (1931), 141.
24 Hotelling (1931), 141.
25 Hotelling (1931), 143.
26 Hotelling (1931), 143–145.
27 Hotelling (1931), 143–146.
28 Hotelling (1931), 152.
29 Cairns (2014), 78; *see also id.*, 79 eq. 1.
30 Cairns (2014), 78.
31 Cairns (2014), 79.
32 Cairns (2014), 79.
33 Cairns (2014), 79.
34 Cairns (2014), 79.
35 Cairns (2014), 79.
36 Cairns (2014), 79.
37 Sinn (2008), 377; *see also supra* section 3.1.

38 Hotelling (1931), 164.
39 Hotelling (1931), 164.
40 Hotelling (1931), 164 (demonstrating through mathematical equations that the exponent of the exponential function becomes the sum of the interest rate and the tax rate).
41 Hotelling (1931), 166 (identifying through formulae Hotelling's precise statement on the extension of the production period). Also, 'conservation' in this instance meant reduced levels of production versus otherwise uncontrolled production rates. *Id.* at 165.
42 Hotelling (1931), 166–167 (showing Hotelling's precise statement of the severance tax's reducing effect on prices).
43 Hotelling (1931), 167.
44 Hotelling (1931), 166–167.
45 *See, e.g.*, Levhari & Liviatan (1977). Levhari and Liviatan found that when incomplete exhaustion was available to the producer, contrary to Hotelling's assumption of full exhaustion, then the results of a severance tax on the rate or duration of depletion were potentially indeterminate. *Id.*, 191–192. They also found that Hotelling's results were unique to the conditions of *ex ante* determined complete exhaustion. *Id.* Such a result might also change Sinn's findings of a green paradox under carbon taxation. *See supra* sections 3.1 and 9.1.3.
46 Hotelling (1931), 167.
47 Hotelling (1931), 168–169.
48 Hotelling (1931), 168–169. This determination was made despite potential adversity to social welfare *sans* consideration of climate change impacts.
49 Hotelling (1931), 140, 146.
50 Hotelling (1931), 171–175. It is unfair to label his models as unrealistic, as they were designed with other purposes in mind. But it is clear from Hotelling's direct caveat that modelers cannot directly export the results of those models to practical policy without further precautions to ensure that the results still hold applicable in realistic settings.
51 Hotelling (1931), 145–146 ("[A] different reason for caution in deducing a laissez faire policy from the theoretical maximizing of V under 'free' competition is that the actual conditions, even when competition exists, are likely to be far removed from the ideal state we have been postulating."). Herein, V denoted utility over the total time of depletion, thus the maximization of utility derived from the full depletion of the resource. *See id.* at 142.
52 Hotelling (1931), 171–172 (referring to Hotelling (1929)).
53 Hotelling (1931), 171–172.
54 Hotelling (1931), 173. This is so primarily because there is sound strategy for the resource owner to raise his prices to wait to sell when all of his volumes can be sold at a higher price due to the exhaustion of his competitors. *Id.*
55 Hotelling (1931), 174 (referring to the indeterminate results of a competitively set pair of monopolists selling complementary goods). The mathematical discussion begins within a discussion on duopoly. *See id.*, 171–173.
56 Hotelling (1931), 175.
57 Hotelling (1931), 144.
58 Jakobsson, Bentley, Söderbergh, & Aleklett (2012), 861.
59 Levhari & Liviatan, *supra* at note 234, 178. *See also* Hotelling (1031), 141–143. E.g., while the precise relationship depended on the underlying demand function, Hotelling provided a demonstration on how the initial resource base, a, could be derived from knowledge of the initial price, p_0, and the time of final exhaustion, T; *see id.* at 142. Watkins disputed this paradigm of a stock of an exhaustible resource, preferring to analogize reserves as inventory produced

by other means. *See* Watkins (2006), 510. The controversy of "stock" versus "flow" was surveyed recently by Jakobsson et al. *See* Jakobsson, Bentley, Söderbergh, & Aleklett (2012), 861.

60 Hotelling (1931), 141.

61 Hotelling (1931), 141. (describing Equation 3, wherein Hotelling derives T by setting the search conditions as the final price, $p_0e^{\gamma t}$, and the final depletion volume, $q = 0$, which is null, to determine T from supply function, $q = f(p,t)$). Also, "T gives the time of complete exhaustion." *Id.* at 142.

62 *See, e.g.*, Stiglitz (1976) (providing the description of a two-period production choice, now or later).

63 Adelman has argued that the fundamental paradigm of economists tracking reserves as if they were well-known entities is problematic at its core, that rather the paradigm assumption should be changed from fixed stocks of exhaustible resources to that of "flows from unknown resources into a reserve inventory." Adelman (1990), 2. He has provided such a model; at its core is a capital arbitrage or option decision to invest in new field search costs or of costs to add capacity at currently known fields. *Id.* at 3, 5–6.

64 Hotelling (1931), 174–175 (emphasis added).

65 Hotelling (1931), 142.

66 Hotelling (1931), 142.

67 Hotelling (1931), 153–154 ("[T]he progress of science might lead to the gradual introduction of new substitutes for the commodity in question, tending to make g negative."). The commodity could be exhaustible coal or oil, and g denoted a sense of complementarity character for a good. *Id.* at 154–155.

68 Hotelling (1931), 154 (presenting a linear version of the demand function that integrated the role of the potential backstop).

69 Hotelling did not develop that potential result of a backstop as its "gradual introduction" was likely assumed beyond the time frame within which he was attempting to address the laws on resource waste and resource taxation.

70 Potentially Hotelling reserved a caveat for this issue, in that he did not require the value of quantity to be produced to be a continuous function of time. *See id.* at 147 (stating that "we do not restrict q to be a continuous function of t, though p will be a continuous function of q," wherein q is quantity to be produced, p its market price, and t time); *see also id.* at 151 (providing the caveat that "the rate of production may suffer discontinuities in spite of the demand function having a continuous derivative, these breaks will always occur during actual production, never at the end.").

71 *See, e.g.*, Idle and Orphan Well Program, Cal. Dep't of Conservation, www.conservation.ca.gov/dog/idle_well/Pages/idle_well.aspx (last visited Nov. 8, 2014) (describing California's "adopt a well" program to adopt abandoned oil wells that have remaining producible volumes but were previously plugged and abandoned); 2014 Orphan Well List, *Cal. Dep't of Conservation*, ftp://ftp.consrv.ca.gov/pub/oil/orphan/Current%20Orphan%20List.pdf (last visited Nov. 8, 2014) (providing a list of adoptable oil wells); Two Severance Tax Incentives Extended the Two-Year Inactive Well Incentive for Oil Wells and Gas Wells and the High-Cost Gas Incentive, *R.R. Comm'n of Tex.*, www.rrc.state.tx.us/oil-gas/publications-and-notices/notices-to-industry/notices-to-industry-1994-1999/two-severance-tax-incentives/ (last updated May 21, 2014) (outlining Texas's tax incentive to achieve similar results from two-year inactive wells).

72 While crude oil reserves are positive value assets, the costs to extract, transport, and market are nontrivial and might sum to prevent the exploitation of the reserves. "It is more likely, as is true of many cases in the real world, that the firm will stop producing at a stage where 'reserves' still exist but under conditions which make further extraction too costly." Levhari & Liviatan, *supra* at

note 19, 178. *See, e.g.*, IRC § 451, wherein a tax credit is provided for those oil wells whose costs might exceed their limited revenues due to their fallen and thus 'marginal' levels of production during periods of low market prices for crude oil. Indeed, the concept of reserves itself recognizes the role of commercial feasibility in the role of production; if reservoir volumes cannot be produced commercially, i.e., profitably, then they do not qualify as "reserves." *See, e.g.*, "Reserves are estimated remaining quantities of oil and gas and related substances anticipated to be economically producible, as of a given date, by application of development projects to known accumulations. In addition, there must exist, or there must be a reasonable expectation that there will exist, the legal right to produce or a revenue interest in the production, installed means of delivering oil and gas or related substances to market, and all permits and financing required to implement the project." 17 CFR 210.4–10(1)(26). *See also* Hotelling (1931), 142 (analyzing the depletion path under free competition).

73 "We shall assume always that the owner of an exhaustible supply wishes to make the present value of all his future profits a maximum." Hotelling (1931), 140.

74 Hotelling (1931), 140–142 (identifying modeling assumptions from the discussion on free competition).

75 Hotelling (1931), 142. Hotelling provided two formulae in response; "if $q = a - \beta p$, all will be exhausted in a finite time." *Id.* In general terms, if the price at price at near-depletion is expected to be very high, then the period of depletion becomes longer in duration; but in most cases full depletion would face a finite time frame. *Id.*

76 Hotelling (1931), 144 ("[G]reat volumes of natural gas and oil are lost because of the suddenness of development makes adequate storage impossible.").

77 Hotelling (1931), 138.

78 Hotelling (1931), 146, 171 (discussing the potential "remarkable" intricacies of "bargaining, bluff, and bluster" that can become engaged in semi-monopolistic settings, all of which could lead to fields not being properly or fully depleted for long or permanent periods).

79 *See, e.g.*, Jakobsson, Bentley, Söderbergh, & Aleklett, 862–863 (discussing marginal and average costs of production).

80 *See* Levhari & Liviatan (1977), 178–179 (naming their model as one of incomplete exhaustion).

81 Hotelling (1931), 140. Much of Hotelling's rule is actually just the assumption of temporally equivalency via Bernoulli's compounded interest formula, that resources from all time periods were of equal value. Given economies of changing technological functions, as we see in the real world, there are many ways in which this assumption might not hold true for exhaustible resources over medium-term to long-term time frames.

82 Hotelling (1931), 140.

83 Hotelling (1931), 140. Hotelling saw value as the integral of utility over a time period. *See id.* at 143.

84 *See, e.g.*, Cairns, *supra* note 60, 80 (observing that "[p]ractitioners, whose conscious, rational decisions are supposed to implement the rule, flatly and (to this author's knowledge unanimously) deny its relevance.").

85 *See* Adelman & Watkins (2008), 5–6; (finding that "there is no such thing" as the assumed premise of full depletion within a time frame of two periods).

86 Gaudet (2007), 1037.

87 Gaudet (2007), 1037; *see also* van der Ploeg & Withagen, *supra* note 39, 2 (providing the caveats necessary to make Hotelling's rule functional).

88 *See* Halvorsen & Smith (1991), 126–128.

89 Halvorsen & Smith (1991), 137.

90 *See* Gronwald (2012), 1314–1316. An autoregressive conditional heteroskedasticity (ARCH) model tracks a time series of data that is expected to have error

rates that themselves may contain structure or probabilistic characteristics. A generalized autoregressive conditional heteroskedasticity model (GARCH) is an ARCH model with an error rate determined by a autoregressive moving average (ARMA) model.

91 Gronwald (2012), 1314.
92 Gronwald (2012), 1316.
93 Gronwald (2012), 1316.
94 Gronwald (2012), 1316.
95 Cairns (2014), 80.
96 Cairns (2014), 80.
97 Cairns (2014), 80.
98 Hotelling (1931), 145.
99 Hotelling (1931), 145 (stating that utility and happiness "depends on the distribution of wealth, and is greater if the products of the mine benefit chiefly the poor.").
100 Sinn (2008), 369–370.
101 For example, most climate law researchers hope for an era where hydrocarbons have no economic utility as a fuel due to superior market choices in the same way that no one continues to hunt whales for lamp fuel today. Perhaps whales are just as valuable as they ever were, but it would an awkward economic argument to suggest that they are as economically central to market pricing as they once were. Similarly, it might be errant that all exhaustible resources retain their identical value across all time periods.
102 Hotelling (1931), 146. Marketing referred to the volumes sold, and not to advertising.
103 Hotelling (1931), 140.
104 The most direct reference to interruptions in production occurs in Hotelling's discussion on retardation of production levels under monopolies. *See* Hotelling (1931), 151–152. He employs the phrasing "may suffer discontinuities," which sounds more like functional problems than aspirational arbitrage delays in production. *Id.* at 151.
105 Jakobsson, Bentley, Söderbergh, & Aleklett (2012), 864–865 (discussing the industry term *maximum efficient rate*, the physically most efficient rate to produce the largest volume of resource given its particular circumstances, and its impact on production decisions). Ion efficient recovery could risk permanent loss of resource. *Id.*
106 Cairns (2014), 81–82 ("In sum, any time at any producing property in the oil industry, output is constrained by a technological/geological constraint.").
107 Cairns (2014), 81.
108 Cairns (2014), 81–82.
109 Cairns (2014), 81–82.
110 From the author's personal experience, fields are generally left with some safety margins to enable surge production. However, generally operators are legally required to ensure production levels at best commercial practices for the resource owners.
111 Cairns (2014), 82.
112 Cairns (2014), 82.
113 Cairns (2014), 81.
114 Hotelling (1931), 141.
115 Hotelling (1931), 152.
116 Hotelling mixed his metaphors, but relied heavily on mines and mining, which are quite different in engineering and development costs from oil and gas wells. Hotelling (1931), 152. The quote above is made in conjunction to gold and diamonds. *Id.*

117 One imagines that a coal operator retrieves those volumes first at hand by digging; or similarly within a gold mine a main vein would be worked first. But crude oil and natural gas require very large investments in development before the first produced volumes can be extracted; because of the high ratio of fixed costs to operating costs, the average cost of production drops as more volumes are produced.

118 Hotelling (1931), 141.

119 The stand-alone wildcatter modes of production were more common at the time of Hotelling's writing, but they were already on their way to extinction. Today, such operations are extremely rare; wildcatters are now focused on the exploration and early development phases that do not require the massive fixed cost investments that development and production entail. Where one does find such stand-alone wells is usually in old fields with levels of production so low that gathering pipes is not considered repair-worthy, thus a switch to local storage tanks is desired.

120 As such, the first produced metric cube of natural gas is arguably the 'most costly' metric cube produced.

121 Cairns (2014), 81.

122 Cairns (2014), 81. Exploration is costly, drilling and development is costly, and the infrastructure to sustain ongoing operations is costly to install (as a separate category from actual ongoing maintenance costs); all these costs are sunk costs prior to the first volume of production.

123 *See* Hotelling (1931), 164. The production functions of petroleum production are said to be derived from uniquely high fixed costs prior to first production.

124 Levhari & Liviatan (1977), 182–183 (noting that the role of marginal costs on depletion pathway decisions is covered within the exposition of the incomplete exhaustion model).

125 At some point, the field has virtually no field costs other than depreciation of existing capital investment and minor operational expenses, followed by plugging and abandoning.

126 Increasing prices might assume later volumes are *per se* on a diminishing returns function and thus would face higher marginal costs, but real-world cost structure can display natural monopoly trends of declining marginal costs over production runs.

127 Hotelling (1931), 144.

128 *See* Dasgupta & Heal (1974), 6, 13, 19 (referring to Cases A and B, where Case A has a positive stock of exhaustible resource and Case B has fully depleted its stock of the same).

129 Dasgupta & Heal (1974), 18 (describing a technology that could render "essential," i.e., without substitutes, fossil fuels into "inessential" substitute goods, listing solar energy and nuclear fusion as examples of such technologies).

130 Dasgupta & Heal (1974), 7 (detailing in Proposition 2 the depletion of the resource until time *T* and the use of the backstop after time *T*).

131 Dasgupta & Heal (1974), 19. Dasgupta and Heal do provide support for the idea that their model could be extended to imperfect substitutes and for modeling a switch that enables an overlapping time period. *See id.* (discussing the likelihood that the durable commodity and exhaustive resource energy sources are perfect substitutes and concluding, "In fact there is every reason to suppose that [they are] not.").

132 *See* Heal (1976), 371 (referring to William D. Nordhaus's economic models on the development of shale oil as an example of a potential backstop technology for crude oil that might be in functionally unlimited supply albeit more costly than crude oil prior to its depletion).

133 For further discussion on Heal's dirty backstop, *see infra* sections 4.4. and 4.5.

134 *See generally* Dasgupta & Heal (1974).
135 Dasgupta & Heal (1974), 6, 12–13.
136 Dasgupta and Heal did take note of a mathematical alternative, that if the resource stock was not to reach a fully depletable state, that certain other conditions would need apply that would result in the original resource stock having been effectively infinite in scale. *See id.* at 6. While Dasgupta and Heal did not continue that intellectual thread, a similar thread has been analyzed by Stürmer and Schwerhoff. *See* Stürmer & Schwerhoff (2012).
137 Dasgupta & Heal (1974), 19–20 (presenting the main model in Equations 2.1, 2.2, and 2.3, with the prophylactic conditions to prevent "being caught short with none of the exhaustible resource before the substitute is discovered" at Equations 2.4 and 2.5).
138 Dasgupta & Heal (1974), 19. The arrival of the green energy technology that will serve as the backstop to crude oil consumption is predicated upon a probability function, ω_t, that yields a singular random event between the beginning and the closure of the model's timeline. *See id.* at 19–20.
139 Dasgupta & Heal (1974), 23 (providing a discussion on what impacts different forms of probability, for example a Poisson distribution or a log normal distribution, might have on the model's probability function, ω_t); *id.* at 23 (providing a method for enveloping the probability function, if one could be certain enough of the underlying probability function, as demonstrated at Proposition 12).
140 Dasgupta & Heal (1974), 27 (emphasis added).
141 Dasgupta & Heal (1974), 27.
142 Dasgupta & Heal (1974), 22–23, 27.
143 Dasgupta and Heal revisited this topic in 2004, stating:

> The presence of nonlinearities compounds the importance of uncertainty. The biophysical impacts associated with the loss of natural capital can be highly nonlinear: these impacts may be small over a considerable range, and then become immense once a critical threshold is reached. Crossing the threshold leads to a "bifurcation," a situation where the characteristics of the natural system change fundamentally.

Arrow, Dasgupta, Goulder, Daily, Ehrlich, Heal, Levin, Mäler, Schneider, Starrett, & Walker (2004), 168.
144 Heal (1976), 371–372.
145 Heal (1976), 373 eq. 2.
146 Heal (1976), 373 fig. 1 (illustrating the rising costs to extract crude oil which are eventually cut off by the ceiling of constant extraction costs for producing shale oil). Heal presented no evidence that shale oil would actually have such an extraction costs function, which is a substantial deviation from the traditional Hotelling assumption of rising extraction costs for all exhaustible resources. *See id.*
147 Heal (1976), 373.
148 Heal (1976), 375 eq. 10.
149 Heal (1976), 372–373. By doing so, Heal was able to argue that oil prices were functioning well in contrast to claims by other economists that then-current prices of crude oil might have suggested monopolistic over-conservation of crude oil to inflate prices and obtain monopoly profits. *Id.* (referring to previous research on that topic).
150 Heal (1976), 373 fig. 1 (depicting the switching event); see also *id.* at 373 eq. 2 (presenting the two-phase cost of extraction formulae).
151 Heal (1976), 373 eq. 2 (defining the boundaries of z, the volume of conventional oil to be produced before the cost structures of shale oil [denoted as β] permanently cause the switch to shale oil).

152 Heal (1976), 374 (dismissing the potential of a different volume, stating, "The alternative is that cumulative extraction over the entire horizon does not exceed *z-bar*: conditions sufficient to rule this out are self-evident.").
153 Heal (1976), 373 (defining in Equation 2 the transition price as β).
154 Heal (1976), 373 (defining in Equation 2 final accumulated production of conventional crude oil as *z-bar*).
155 Gronwald (2012), 1316.
156 However appealing the logic of the Hotelling model of exhaustible resources might have been for some energy researchers, other voices have seen it in less favorable lights – particularly those researching conventional crude oil and natural gas markets. Ironically, those critiquing Hotelling's models are often but detailing the caveats that Hotelling himself made in his own papers.
157 *See* Council Directive 2001/42 of the European Parliament and of the Council of 27 June 2001 on the Assessment of the Effects of Certain Plans and Programmes on the Environment, 2001 O.J. (L 197) 30, 30–37 (EC), http://eur-lex.europa.eu/legal-content/EN/TXT/PDF/?uri=CELEX:32001L0042&from=EN.
158 *See, e.g., supra* section 2.4.3 (discussing the existence of certain green paradox models that are not predicated on Hotelling or Dasgupta Heal models); Adelman (1990), 1, 5–7 (providing an alternative model of petroleum depletion that does adopt the majority of Hotelling's assumptions, particularly rejecting the concept that there is "an exhaustible fixed stock of oil to divide between two [or more] time periods" [citation and quotation marks omitted]).

5 Complexity in energy policies can lead to greater emissions

5.1 Introduction to uncoordinated energy policies

The 1992 United Nations Framework Convention on Climate Change (UNFCCC; "the Convention") is the leading international regulatory effort to reduce the threats and hazards from anthropogenic climate change. The UNFCCC primarily focuses on the means of managing the overall levels of greenhouse gas emissions released into the atmosphere and the means of preventing those emissions. Almost every country in the world has ratified the UNFCCC,[1] and almost as many countries have ratified its Kyoto Protocol.[2] As such, most countries in the world have enacted a variety of domestic regulations to further the goals of the UNFCCC to control and prevent global climate change.

The UNFCCC and the Kyoto Protocol establish certain policy goals to coordinate global efforts to reduce the impact of anthropogenic greenhouse gas emissions. However, as examined in previous chapters, questions have arisen as to whether certain green policies could backfire and result in increased greenhouse gas emissions; these concerns are called green paradoxes.[3]

Broadly summarized, the concern over green paradoxes is that asynchronous implementation of climate change policies across multiple jurisdictions could be dysfunctional; these sets of problems were originally known as carbon leakage problems. A similar concern arose in review of proposed rising carbon taxes;[4] under certain circumstances, temporal issues in green climate policy implementation could lead to increased greenhouse gas emissions.[5] These risks, however, are not limited to the economic sphere of interest, but are also interactive with the legal rules and policies surrounding these activities.

The combination of diverse energy policies and legal frameworks for diverse energy policy goals by diverse stakeholders could lead to increased energy supplies that, when combined with international trade laws that notably support primary product exports such as fossil fuels, could encourage increased emissions of greenhouse gases. *Ergo*, if the present legal measures are left as-is, with diverse and poorly coordinated goals and greenhouse gas emissions, there is a foreseeable risk that the hazards from anthropogenic climate change could be worsened by higher levels of emissions, even if green energy laws were successful in their own goals of stimulating innovation in green energy production and supply.

This part of the book investigates a complementary line of research to the first part of the book: whether naïve implementation of the UNFCCC regulatory goals to provide innovation in new and renewable energy sources, *sans* complementary coordination with other measures to provide innovations in other energy technologies, could result in increased greenhouse gas emissions.

And yes, these next chapters will find that such an implementation could indeed result in increased greenhouse gas emissions;[6] because while some of the measures support innovation in green energy sources, other legal measures support innovation in fossil fuels and other non-green sources of fuels. This is a portfolio of policies likely to result in oversupply in the long run, which is likely to result in price competition in green, fossil, and non-green energy supplies, increasing the likelihood that lower-priced fossil fuels will be consumed and carbon gas emitted to the atmosphere.

Chapter 5 will analyze the UNFCCC and its associated agreements such as the Kyoto Protocol. The analysis presented suggests that such international conventions created to limit the risks of anthropogenic climate change do drive innovation in new and renewable energy supplies. Such innovations are intended to provide increased volumes of energy supplies at affordable prices in order to displace carbon-emitting energy supplies, thus preventing anthropogenic sources of climate risk. However, the key conclusion is that these legal efforts would increase energy supplies if successful.

Chapter 6 examines the role of energy security laws, i.e., those laws that support the secure supply of energy resources against adverse conditions, in driving innovation in energy. Such targets might include securing petroleum volumes or energy alternatives, such as nuclear energy. Motives for energy security laws might be to protect energy prices from market forces or to support militarized forces. Chapter 6 looks to the laws of the United States as an example of such energy security laws.

Chapter 7 inspects select international agreements and concludes that these particular agreements sustain or encourage the development of fossil fuels, including petroleum, coal, and natural gas.

Chapter 8 considers the role of various international trade conventions in supporting market conditions and free competition conditions. This chapter will examine the WTO/GATT system of agreements and reveal their support of open trade and competitive market conditions.

Chapter 9 integrates the previous chapters into a finding of a potential green paradox event: the combined results of multiple legal policies to encourage energy innovations could result in increased energy supplies that would price compete, potentially resulting in increased greenhouse gas emissions, *ergo*, a green paradox.

5.2 Jevons paradox and similar effects of energy efficiency gains

A discussion is due to Sinn's listing of energy efficiency as a source of green paradox models, because their role and impact within green paradox models might be apparent from a *prima facie* review.

The UNFCCC and related regulatory efforts have sections that promote the adoption of energy-efficient technologies as a complementary strategy to encouraging renewable and carbon-free energy sources. The basic concept is that if engines and machines needed less energy, then less conventional fossil fuels would need to be consumed. However, as William Stanley Jevons first wrote nearly two centuries ago, energy efficiency does not necessarily lead to a reduction in energy demand and may well encourage increased energy demand.[7] If so, gains in energy efficiency could lead to increased GHGs.

There are several motivations for the traditional Jevons paradox and the related theories of 'rebound effects';[8] hereunder are several quick sketches of known related microeconomic models.

First, one needs to be aware of the inelasticity of demand; if a market is able to absorb all of the energy provided to it at high prices, then it will likely absorb greater supplies of energy at lower prices. Thus, a displacement in energy use due to a decreased technological need does not prevent that displaced energy supply from being consumed, thus leading to increased GHG emissions.

Second, efficiency gains can create a virtual increase in supply. Considered from a unitized perspective:[9] assume a task originally took two parts of energy to complete and then was made more efficient to require only one part of energy; although the overall supply of energy was left unchanged, the user of the machine will observe twice as much supply *vis-à-vis* their operational needs. From the perspective of the consumer, energy efficiency would make the supply of energy appear increased. Greater energy supplies could lead to increased GHG emissions.

Third, reducing the necessary energy for any particular task brings that task in range of more numerous populated but smaller energy budgets; energy efficiency puts more tasks in range of more people.[10] By enabling more people to consume energy, it is possible that energy efficiency can lead to additional economic activity and potentially economic growth.[11]

Greening, Greene, and Difiglio proposed a four-part typology to separate the various mechanisms responsible for the effects postulated by Khazzoom-Brookes.[12] The Khazzoom-Brookes postulate states that improvements in energy efficiency will increase energy consumption, *ceteris paribus*.[13] As the postulate assumes no change in energy prices, the quantity demanded necessarily reflects a new demand function for energy after the achievement of energy efficiency. Greening, Greene, and Difiglio recognized the four mechanisms as (i) direct rebound effects; (ii) secondary fuel usage effects; (iii) energy market clearing mechanism effects; and (iv) transformational effects.[14]

For consumers, this can enable two different results. First, the consumer may face substitution effects; the lower prices from energy efficiency gains incentivize consumers to switch to those energy products needed by the efficient products.[15] Similarly, firms will find it optimal to displace more costly inputs with similar inputs, if the inputs are sufficiently substitutable.[16] Firms with normal production functions will then make those substitutions and increase their overall energy consumption.[17] Second, the consumer may face income effects; lower energy prices enable the consumer to relatively experience higher income levels and thus to explore alternative higher levels of demand.[18]

In conclusion, as discussed later,[19] energy efficiency and the Jevons paradox present market results that appear to function much as competitive product to fossil fuel products at the same time that energy efficiency lowers energy prices and creates an effectively larger energy supply. Energy efficiency is particularly complex in its green paradox model implications, and much research remains needed in clarifying how climate policy interacts with energy efficiency in affecting GHG emissions.

5.3 Pathways for climate change mitigation technology

The objective of the UNFCCC is the "stabilization of greenhouse gas concentrations in the atmosphere at a level that would prevent dangerous anthropogenic interference with the climate system."[20] Greenhouse gases are defined by their behavior, as gaseous constituents of the atmosphere that absorb and re-emit infrared radiation, regardless of source;[21] the only *per se* greenhouse gas mentioned in the UNFCCC is carbon dioxide.[22]

The UNFCCC requires the parties to "formulate, implement, publish, and regularly update ... programmes containing measures to mitigate climate change."[23] Those measures are required to focus on reducing emissions of and providing sinks for greenhouse gases.[24] The Kyoto Protocol spelled out specific obligatory mitigation strategies.[25] Parties are to

- i enhance energy efficiency,[26]
- ii provide for greenhouse gas sinks and carbon sequestration,[27]
- iii research, promote, develop, and increase the use of new and renewable energy sources,[28]
- iv reduce the various supports and subsidies that enable greenhouse gas emissions, such as tax breaks for crude oil production, and[29]
- v limit or reduce greenhouse gas emissions, including methane emissions.[30]

The Kyoto Protocol improves on the UNFCCC's definition of greenhouse gases by providing a list of *per se* greenhouse gases:

- i Carbon dioxide;
- ii Methane (commonly known as 'natural gas');
- iii Nitrous oxide;
- iv Hydrofluorocarbons;
- v Perfluorocarbons; and
- vi Sulphur hexafluoride.[31]
- vii The Doha Amendment added nitrogen trifluoride to that listing.[32]

Technological innovations are required to accomplish energy efficiency goals, the development of greenhouse sinks and carbon sequestration, and the potential development of new and renewable energy sources.

Further, the Kyoto Protocol mandates that certain emission targets be reached by specific deadlines – an element that is absent in the UNFCCC.[33]

5.3.1 Technology sharing or 'transfer'

The parties to the UNFCCC are required to develop, apply, and transfer the technologies that can enable them to meet the prior requirements to manage greenhouse gases.[34] Developed parties have specific historical advantages, and thus have the duty to support developing parties in accomplishing their obligations and the broader goals of climate change mitigation.[35] The Annex II parties are to provide financial resources to better enable the developing parties acquire and implement climate change mitigation technologies; this includes "all practicable steps to promote, facilitate and finance."[36] Similar requirements are found within the Kyoto Protocol.[37]

The Kyoto Protocol has several mechanisms to better ensure the transfer of climate change abatement technologies. The first among these is the "financial mechanism."[38] The financial mechanism enables the transfer of funds from developed parties to developing parties to finance the acquisition and operation of green technologies. An example of the financial mechanism is the Green Climate Fund to be operated from Incheon, South Korea. Second, the Kyoto Protocol calls for a "clean development mechanism," which would enable developed parties to engage in green climate projects in a developing party's jurisdiction and enable both parties to benefit from the generation of emission accounting rules.[39] Finally, the Kyoto Protocol enables emission account unit trading in order for parties to pursue economically efficient pathways of mitigating climate change.[40] Thus, the ultimate diffusion of climate change abetting technologies is mandated by the Kyoto Protocol and economically supported by its parties.

A third mechanism is the "technology mechanism." At the Conference of the Parties in Doha, Qatar 2012, Decision 14/CP.18 authorized the implementation and initiation of the Climate Technology Centre and Network under the United Nations Environment Programme; this action followed from Decision 1/CP.16.[41] Thus, the technology mechanism is now operational.

5.3.2 Common but differentiated obligations

While all parties remain obligated to the obligations of the Convention, developing parties are permitted certain differences in implementation from the developed parties. This issue plays a substantial role in when and how emission targets might be achieved; indeed, as discussed later in this chapter, the Organization of Petroleum Exporting Countries (OPEC) has taken a very specific stand on this issue in particular.

Developing parties are allowed to set their standards with reference to the attainment efforts of the developed parties.[42] Economies in transition are given wider berth.[43] A variety of countries are given pre-emptive understanding to their special needs and concerns; included on the list are countries that will be especially harmed by climate change and countries that rely heavily on revenues from fossil fuels and energy-intensive products.[44] Additionally, the

Convention recognizes that the least developed parties will need specific forms of assistance.[45]

The UNFCCC has approximately 200 parties, but certain Annex I and II parties bear more burdens than do other parties. Annex I parties are primarily European countries plus Russia, Japan, the United States, Canada, Australia, and New Zealand. Annex II is the same list minus the parties who were formerly a part of the Soviet Union. Annex II is *de facto* a list of developed parties, who are held financially responsible for assisting developing parties. Annex I parties assumed obligations to adopt national policies to mitigate climate change.[46] Additionally, Annex I parties are also required to coordinate economic and administrative policies with each other to enable climate change mitigation.[47] The rest of the parties, especially those developing parties, are not explicitly obligated to specifically pursue the same obligations.

Also, while the Kyoto Protocol calls for "[m]easures to limit and/or reduce emissions of greenhouse gases,"[48] only those counties listed as Annex B have commitments to specific emission reductions.[49] All other countries merely need to enact measures that in some form could be said to limit or reduce emissions. In such cases, legislation to promote new and renewable energy or legislation to promote energy efficiency might suffice.

5.4 UNFCCC requires and supports energy innovation

Thus, the basic policy obligations of the UNFCCC and related legal efforts can be summarized:

1 To reduce the emission of greenhouse gases by several means:
   a Energy efficiency;
   b Enhancements of sinks and reservoirs and carbon sequestration;
   c Development and promotion of new and renewable forms of energy;
   d Elimination of supports and subsidies for activities that enable greenhouse gas emissions; and
   e Prevention of methane venting from various activities;
2 To provide means, both legal and financial, to ensure all nations can undertake obligations under the UNFCCC;
3 To provide for broad technology transfer, including intellectual property; and
4 To provide for the transboundary coordination of the above efforts.

The role of both technology and innovations in energy technology to provide the solution is self-evident from the listing. The necessary energy technologies, and thus the needed alternative energy supplies, are not yet in hand, so the Convention called for the support of their development and promotion and the facilitation of their adoption by all parties. This was a broad request of scientific resources, financial capabilities, and legal coordination between the parties.

While political discourse has not yet solved the issues of reducing subsidies to carbon fuels and effective reductions in emissions, it is clear that all parties otherwise strongly support the development of green energy technologies.[50] Given the commitment of the parties to the positive development of the technologies underlying this call, it would be reasonable to expect green and renewable technologies to provide more energy supplies in the future.

5.5 Summary and conclusions

This chapter has presented evidence that green energy policies, and in particular the requirements of the UNFCCC, could induce increases in energy supplies from green sources of energy. This is a simple claim, that encouraging the development of green energy production from a variety of angles could lead to more energy supplies from green energy sources. It would seem the very goal of the UNFCCC and green energy policies, and indeed it is.

But the crux of this chapter is to be found in combining its findings with the results from the subsequent chapters, that if energy supplies are added without substantially reducing supplies from other sources, then surplus energy supplies will lead to market clearing mechanisms that will result in both larger supplies of fossil fuels and cheaper supplies of fossil fuels. If there are more fossil fuel volumes offered at cheaper prices, it is readily foreseeable that more greenhouse gases could become emitted from these fuel stocks.

This chapter began with an examination of the Jevons paradox, the original energy policy conundrum. Jevons's observation is simple to state, that increases in energy efficiency will not result in lower demands for energy production, but rather will see new marginal demand that still clears the pre-existing levels of energy supplies. It is also generally added that Jevons's observation extends to suggesting that energy efficiency leads to increased energy demand, and ultimately, to increased demands for energy production.

As stated by the Khazzoom-Brookes postulate, improvements in energy efficiency will increase energy consumption, *ceteris paribus*.[51] In examining the functional aspects of the Khazzoom-Brookes postulate, Greening, Greene, and Difiglio recognized four mechanisms in coordination:

i Direct rebound effects;
ii Secondary fuel usage effects;
iii Energy market clearing mechanism effects; and
iv Transformational effects.[52]

As stated earlier, energy efficiency and the Jevons paradox present market effects that appear functionally similar to consumers as competitive energy products versus fossil fuel products, at the same time that energy efficiency lowers energy prices and creates an effectively larger energy supply. Thus, green energy policies that naively pursue energy efficiency gains may find themselves achieving energy efficiency but not necessarily the green energy goals themselves.

Next, the chapter outlined the basic call of the UNFCCC, to define greenhouse gases and to support their removal from energy supplies and from industrial emissions. It reveals that the UNFCCC both requires policy changes and has been updated to require effects by certain deadlines; this recalls the delayed policy implementation of the previous discussions on green paradoxes.

There are certain duties on developed economies to both develop green technologies and enable the transfer of those novel green technologies to developing economies, so that the whole world can move away from fossil fuels towards green energy production. Financial mechanisms, clean development mechanisms, technology mechanisms, and emission counting frameworks are all developed to enable a more market-friendly approach to resolving the challenges of ensuring the efficient reduction of the greatest amount of carbon emissions possible, without regards to who reduces first or how. This would seem to be a rational path, but as we'll explore in subsequent chapters, it is indeed an insufficient set of conditions to actually ensure avoidance of green paradox results.

Whereas the observations of interspatial and intertemporal models of leakage might suggest a consistent approach to rule setting on how and when to abate emissions, the UNFCCC and its associated agreements recognize a concept called 'common but differentiated obligations,' which recognizes that each country has its own history, technologies, and comparative advantages and disadvantages, especially with regards to developed and developing economies, so the legal duties for each state may be differently implemented. And while those different pathways of carbon planning could be coordinated to prevent forms of leakage, there is presently little in the way of international legal tools to accomplish that in any form other than by diplomacy.

This chapter has begun a presentation, to be continued in the subsequent chapters, that efforts to stimulate energy production from green energy sources will result in additional energy supplies with predictable market consequences. Even energy efficiency is suspected of creating market consequences very similar to increased supplies of energy while also stimulating additional energy demand. If the rest of the energy markets, and their corresponding policies and legal rules, are left unchanged while there is dramatic innovation on the side of green energy production and supply, then the market consequences for energy production and consumption, and corresponding levels of carbon emissions, could be far different than the explicit goals of those aspirationally green energy policies.

The next several chapters will explore in more detail how uncoordinated energy policies, contemporaneously promoted with the prioritized green energy policies, could lead to great policy frustration and inefficient use of policy resources.

Notes

1 195 countries have ratified the UNFCCC as of March 24, 2014; contrast that total against the 193 members of the United Nations. *See* First Steps to a Safer Future: Introducing The United Nations Framework Convention on Climate Change, *UNFCCC* (Jan. 11, 2015, 7:00 PM), https://unfccc.int/essential_background/

convention/items/6036.php; *See also* Member States of the United Nations, *UN* (Jan. 11, 2015, 7:00 PM), www.un.org/en/members/.

2 192 nations and regional organizations have ratified the Kyoto Protocol. *See* Status of Ratification of the Kyoto Protocol, *UNFCCC* (Aug. 31, 12:35 PM), https://unfccc.int/kyoto_protocol/status_of_ratification/items/2613.php; further, with regards to the ratification of the Paris Agreements, "To this date, 185 Parties have ratified of 197 Parties to the Convention." See Paris Agreement: Status of Ratification, *UNFCCC* (Aug. 31, 12:35 PM), https://unfccc.int/process/the-paris-agreement/status-of-ratification.

3 See section 2.4 and Chapter 3 for more discussion on points.

4 This example was the seminal green paradox example proposed by Sinn; Sinn (2008).

5 A rising tax rate is mathematically similar to a delayed higher tax rate and is thus analog to asynchronous implementation of the climate change policies across multiple countries.

6 Albeit, these results are differentiable from international carbon leakage or conventional green paradoxes in that the model focuses on the simultaneous application of divergent legal measures.

7 "It is wholly a confusion of ideas to suppose that the economical use of fuel is equivalent to a diminished consumption. The very contrary is the truth. . . . [E]very . . . improvement of the engine, when effected, does but accelerate anew the consumption of coal." Alcott (2005), 12.

8 See a recent monograph on the subject matter; Polimeni (2007).

9 In economics literature this has been described as the rebound effect of efficiency gains or as the backfire effect when policy goals of efficiency were to enable budget maintenance or reduction.

10 Assuming a Pareto distribution of income would suffice, that every level of wealth has fewer members than the level immediately below it.

11 Also known as the Khazzoom-Brookes postulate. Khazzoom and Brookes, separately, provided a series of articles on the variations of this concept, e.g., in 1978, 1980, 1982, 1987, and 1989. Greening, Greeneb, & Difiglio (2000) 389–390.

12 Greening, Greeneb, & Difiglio (2000), 390.

13 The postulate specifically assumes fixed real energy prices. Greening, Greeneb, & Difiglio (2000), 389.

14 Greening, Greeneb, & Difiglio (2000), 390. The authors noted that their typology took the perspective that demand for energy *cum* fuels was actually demand for a services product instead of a stock product, but for the purposes of this present research the nuance causes no significant difference.

15 Greening, Greeneb, & Difiglio (2000), 390. A more technical description is that energy products are assumed to have cross-price elasticities; the higher that elasticity the more one energy product will become substituted for a different energy product facing rising or higher prices. Energy efficiency gains will make certain energy products cheaper and will encourage consumers to buy more of the cheaper energy as a substitute against other more expensive but substitutable energy products.

16 Greening, Greeneb, & Difiglio (2000), 391.

17 Technically speaking, the firms need to display either constant returns or decreasing returns to scale with regards to energy-related inputs. This is normal for competitive firms and can be demonstrated for monopolistic firms. *See* note 5. The main exceptions to this behavioral standard would be firms experiencing endogenous increases in output, not unlike a Paul Romer perspective on endogenous growth. Greening, Greeneb, & Difiglio (2000), 391. For a reference to Romer's endogenous growth models, *see* the seminal article Romer (1990); and for perspective on the development of the model, *see* Romer (1994).

18 Greening, Greeneb, & Difiglio (2000), 390.
19 *See infra* section 5.2.
20 UNFCCC, Art. 2. While both the UNFCCC and the Kyoto Protocol have extensive language on the support of climate science and scientific monitoring, these topics do not appear to have substantial bearing on the green paradox concerns, so they have been omitted from the current review framework.
21 UNFCCC, art. 4. sec. 5.
22 *See* "anthropogenic emissions of carbon dioxide and other greenhouse gases." UNFCCC, art. 4, sec. 2(a).
23 UNFCCC, art. 4, sec. 1(b).
24 UNFCCC, art. 4, sec. 1(b).
25 Kyoto Protocol, art. 2, sec. 1(a).
26 Kyoto Protocol, art. 2, sec. 1(a)(i).
27 Kyoto Protocol, art. 2, sec. 1(a)(ii) and (iv).
28 Kyoto Protocol, art. 2, sec. 1(a)(iv).
29 Kyoto Protocol, art. 2, sec. 1(a)(v). This concerns the green paradox research directly in that by reducing the tax credits or deductions available to energy producers the requirement effectively requires a net increase on carbon-related taxes. Depending on how those changes are implemented, they could fit well within established areas of green paradox concerns.
30 Kyoto Protocol, art. 2, sec. 1(a)(vii) and (viii).
31 Kyoto Protocol, *Annex A. List of Greenhouse Gases*, http://unfccc.int/kyoto_protocol/items/3145.php.
32 Doha Amendment to the Kyoto Protocol, art. 1, sec. B.
33 *Id.* at art. 3, sec. 1. The targets are to be attained by 2012. The Doha Amendment to the Kyoto Protocol would extend that timeline to 2020 and deepen the emission cuts to be achieved. *See Doha Amendment to the Kyoto Protocol*, art. 1, C, "Article 2, paragraph 1 bis."
34 UNFCCC, art. 4, sec. 1(c).
35 This is a consistent sustainable development principle applied throughout both the UNFCCC and the Kyoto Protocol. *See* UNFCCC, art. 3, sec. 1 and 2. *See generally* UNFCCC, art. 4, sec. 2. *See also* UNFCCC art. 4, sec. 2(1) (noting that developed countries need to demonstrate that they are taking the lead in mitigating climate change).
36 UNFCCC, art. 4, sec. 3, 5.
37 *See* Kyoto Protocol, art. 10.
38 Kyoto Protocol, art. 11, sec. 2.
39 Kyoto Protocol, art. 12.
40 Kyoto Protocol, art. 6.
41 Conference of the Parties, Report of the Conference of the Parties on its eighteenth session, held in Doha from 26 November to 8 December 2012, FCCC/CP/2012/8/Add.2 (Nov. 26 to Dec. 8, 2012).
42 UNFCCC, art. 4, sec. 7.
43 UNFCCC, art. 4, sec. 6.
44 UNFCCC, art. 4, sec. 8. *See* Sec. 8(h).
45 UNFCCC, art. 4, sec. 9.
46 UNFCCC, art. 4, sec. 2(a).
47 UNFCCC, art. 4, sec. 2(e)(i).
48 Kyoto Protocol, art. 2, sec. 1(a)(vii).
49 Kyoto Protocol, Annex B. Also, Annex B's list of countries has seen some variation of included countries since its enactment.
50 While few might doubt the EU's and its member states, commitments to renewable energy, others might doubt China or the US; however, such concerns are largely

unmerited. China is the world's largest consumer of coal, but it also led investment in carbon-free energy in 2013 by funding $61,300 million in research, develop, and installation. Richard J. Campbell, Cong. Research Serv., RL41748, China and the United States: A Comparison of Green Energy Programs and Policies, 1 and 4, Respectively (2014). For a discussion on the US's efforts to support carbon-free energy technologies, *see infra* Chapter 6. Even OPEC has reaffirmed its commitments to supporting the Conventions goals, *see infra* section 7.2.

51 The postulate specifically assumes fixed real energy prices. Greening, Greeneb, & Difiglio (2000), 389.

52 Greening, Greeneb, & Difiglio (2000), 390. The authors noted that their typology took the perspective that demand for energy *cum* fuels was actually demand for a services product instead of a stock product, but for the purposes of this present research the nuance causes no significant difference.

6 Impact of domestic energy security policy laws

The United States supports innovations in energy resources through multiple measures and toolsets. While the United States is not the only nation to seek energy security, it is perhaps both the largest and most obvious example and can be used to highlight the theoretical problem examined in this chapter, that of multi-vectored energy policies to frustrate the reduction of greenhouse gas emissions.

The Department of Energy (DOE) is charged with leading civilian efforts and the Department of Defense (DOD) with military efforts; however, both departments are dwarfed in spending and are influenced by the effect of tax policies embedded within the United States' federal income tax code. These three actors need not necessarily be at odds with each other; instead, they could coordinate to achieve the energy policy goals as determined by the Congress, and, given the combined fiscal power of these three approaches, the effects to attain a focused energy policy would be stunning.

But the United States' overall policy is not to pursue a well-clarified energy goal but to pursue all directions at once: green energy, conventional hydrocarbons, and innovative nuclear technology are all encouraged by the DOE, the DOD, and by the Internal Revenue Code. Perhaps the only consistency in the overall energy policy is to ensure ample supplies of energy from all potential sources, to better ensure oversupply than face the consequences of undersupply.

The following sections provide a review of all three approaches to demonstrate that the promotion of energy security provides for innovations and future production of both fossil fuel resources and renewable energy resources that subsequently would lead to strong supplies from multiple sources, eventually leading to price competition and higher levels of consumption of all forms of energy, including fossil fuels.

6.1 Federal research programs

The United States maintains extensive support for the research and development of energy innovations. This support can be compared in terms of scale to the research programs that supported the development of the atomic bomb and the Apollo moon landings.[1] Whereas the Manhattan Project spent $22 billion over five years and the greater NASA/Apollo program spent $98 billion over fourteen years, the broader federal energy innovation projects spent more than $118 billion over thirty-five years prior to 2009; the annual rates of expenditure for energy innovation fell between the annual expenditures for the previous two programs.[2]

However, the United States has supported energy innovation for longer than suggested by the previous narrative. Arguably, the Hoover Dam Project and the Manhattan Project were energy research projects in that they provided new forms or scales of energy production.[3] Nonetheless, earnest energy innovation support began under the shadow of the 1970s' oil supply shocks.[4] This support occurred in two steps. First, the United States government increased coordination on energy innovation oversight by coalescing multiple energy research groups into the Energy Research and Development Administration (ERDA) and the Nuclear Regulatory Commission (NRC).[5] A second focusing of energy innovation efforts resulted in the creation of the DOE by merging the ERDA with fifty other energy offices and programs across the federal government.[6] In the first five years of those focused efforts to drive energy innovations, the federal government spent over $40 billion.[7]

The DOE has faced declining budgetary support from Congress in recent years; it received $10 billion in 1980 but only $3.4 billion in 2012.[8] Most of the DOE's research funding is driven to direct investment in research and development of energy innovations; its capacity for loans and loan guarantees has been effectively defunded by Congress.[9] The DOE supports research programs in fossil fuels, nuclear energy, energy efficiency, and renewable energy sources.[10] Approximately 27% of the DOE's research budget is allocated to renewable energy sources and another 27% is allocated to energy efficiency research.[11] Twenty-three percent of its funds are allocated to nuclear research.[12] Ten percent is aimed at fossil fuel research programs; primarily, programs that reduce greenhouse gas emissions.[13] The remainder is mostly spent on electrical delivery and reliability research.[14]

6.2 United States Department of Defense and energy innovations

While the DOE is the lead executive branch department tasked with stewarding energy innovations, the DOD actually spends more on energy products than any other section of the federal government, thus its policies and measures to impact energy innovation are noteworthy.[15] Reportedly, the DOD might be the world's largest energy consumer.[16] In 2010, the DOD's energy consumption represented 80% of the energy consumed by the federal government; it consumed an estimated 880 trillion BTUs that year.[17] It is also important to note that the legal aspects of these measures are primarily driven by budget requests and their integration in the budgetary measures approved by Congress.

The Defense Production Act provides authority for the DOD and its military branches to engage in support of energy technologies and resources.[18] First and foremost, energy is central to the act's concept of "national defense": "*[t]he term 'national defense' means programs for military and energy production* or construction, military or critical infrastructure assistance to any foreign nation, homeland security, stockpiling, space, and any directly related activity."[19]

The act establishes that the

> security of the United States is dependent on the ability of the domestic industrial base to supply materials and services for the national defense and to prepare for and respond to military conflicts, natural or man-caused disasters, or acts of terrorism within the United States,

and that "in order to ensure national defense preparedness, it is necessary and appropriate to *assure the availability of domestic energy supplies for national defense needs*."[20] The act requires that "to the maximum extent possible, domestic energy supplies should be augmented through reliance on *renewable energy sources (including solar, geothermal, wind, and biomass sources)*, more efficient energy storage and distribution technologies, and energy conservation measures."[21]

The DOD and the president of the United States are granted broad powers to economically support and encourage industrial activities under the act; purchase orders, federal loans, and federally backed loan guarantees are all made available. First, the DOD can move to provide industrial support via directed purchases, enabling private producers to obtain independent financing given secured sales or delivery contracts:[22]

To create, maintain, protect, expand, or restore domestic industrial base capabilities essential for the national defense, the president may make provision –

- A for purchases of or *commitments to purchase* an industrial resource or a *critical technology* item, for government use or resale;
- B for the encouragement of exploration, development, and mining of critical and strategic materials, and other materials;
- C for the development of production capabilities; and
- D *for the increased use of emerging technologies* in security program applications and the rapid transition of emerging technologies –
  - i from government-sponsored research and development to commercial applications; and
  - ii from commercial research and development to national defense applications.[23]

Second, energy resource providers can receive direct federal loans when necessary:

> [T]he President may make provision for loans to private business enterprises (including nonprofit research corporations and providers of critical infrastructure) for the creation, maintenance, expansion, protection, or restoration of capacity, the development of technological processes, or the production of essential materials, including the exploration, development, and mining of strategic and critical metals and minerals.[24]

Third, if the commercial producers need financial support to achieve production targets,

> [T]he President may authorize a guaranteeing agency to provide guarantees of loans by private institutions for the purpose of financing any contractor, subcontractor, provider of critical infrastructure, or other person in support of production capabilities or supplies that are deemed by the guaranteeing agency to be necessary to create, maintain, expedite, expand, protect, or restore production and deliveries or services essential to the national defense.[25]

When the United States provides support "to correct a domestic industrial base shortfall, the President should give consideration to the creation or maintenance of production *sources that will remain economically viable after such assistance has ended*."[26] Thus, to the extent that DOD measures under the act call for additional energy innovations, priority must be given to those technologies that would be economically feasible after establishment under the act. There are limits to the powers to provide economic incentives and supports for energy innovation under the Defense Production Act, but most of them are waived during periods of declared national emergency. Because the United States is currently in multiple states of declared emergency, those limits may not apply.[27] Thus the DOD, via the Defense Production Act, has extensive capacities to encourage and foster energy innovations outside of the civilian efforts at the DOE.

The primary fuels consumed by the DOD are products derived from petroleum.[28] The vast majority of that fuel is used to power aircraft.[29] This reliance on liquid fossil fuels is complicated by the fact that the DOD maintains fleets of aircraft and vessels that are expected to remain in service for long-term periods, so while the source of that liquid energy might be novel, e.g., green biodiesel, the need to combust that fuel in the in-place mechanical assets such as boat engines or jet engines will remain the same.[30] Thus, the DOD financially supports innovations in alternative liquid fuel sources. The United States Air Force (USAF) undertook obligations to acquire 50% of its domestic aviation fuels from alternative fuel blends by 2016.[31] Also notable in the USAF's approach is their apparent intent to drive the innovation by market demand, i.e., their procurement processes will be mandated to obtain such fuels instead of providing pre-market subsidies. This is best reflected in two elements: first, the USAF's primary expenditures on alternative fuels are to upgrade its engine assets to match new fuel blends,[32] and second, the USAF has pre-established a certification program to approve alternative fuels from biofuels, alcohol-derived aviation fuels, and Fischer-Tropsch-transformed natural gas stocks of aviation fuel.[33]

The United States Navy (USN) and the United States Marine Corps (USMC) have announced their goals to "lead the Nation in sustainable energy."[34] "[The Department of the Navy] will be protecting the environment with clean energy and lessening our dependence on foreign oil," by increasing reliance on alternative fuels, biofuels, solar energy systems, and geothermal energy systems.[35] By 2016, they intended to develop and deploy a "Green Strike Group," a cluster of ocean vessels and aircraft powered exclusively by biofuels, as a demonstration of the potential of biofuels.[36] They plan to ensure that 50% of USN and USMC fuel needs could be met with biofuels by 2020 by financially supporting innovations in biofuels, alongside the Departments of Agriculture and DOE, with over $500 million in committed funds.[37]

The net result of the DOD's powers to support innovation in energy sources, combined with its focus on replacing petroleum-derived aviation fuels, is that both additional capacity in alternative liquid fuels will be created at the same time that large quantities of petroleum-based fuels will no longer be consumed, thus the market will likely have increased quantities of both petroleum-derived and non-petroleum-based liquid fuels available for purchase.

6.3 Federal income tax incentives

The oil and gas sector has long received certain tax treatments from the United States tax code that are either obvious incentives for additional volumes of production, obvious incentives for technological enhancements that maintain the competitive cost structure of oil and gas investments, or are suspected incentives for increased levels of production, such as the depletion allowance. More recently, in 2006, the tax code added tax credits and other incentives for new and renewable energy sources.[38]

Combined, these tax incentives strongly facilitate energy innovations and aid in their commercial feasibility. The combined annual value of the tax code-driven incentives have been estimated at $20 billion, dwarfing the DOE's $3.5 billion in annual supports for the same targets.[39] As such, the tax code incentives represent the lion's share of the federal government's efforts to encourage energy innovation.

While support for energy has long been an area of focus within the tax code, it does not suggest that tax policymakers have slowed down their legislative efforts to provide for energy innovation supports. In the last decade, there have been eleven major enactments that addressed energy policy via tax code incentives.[40] Thus, the tax code remains a hot area of energy policy efforts.

6.3.1 Tax incentives for hydrocarbon energy production

Reportedly, tax credits and deductions have provided $470 billion in benefits to petroleum producers since the United States' federal income system began.[41] That estimate includes the forecasted $4.8 billion in annual benefits in recent years.[42] The scale of these benefits has led to calls for their repeal, including President Obama's recent budget proposal for fiscal year 2014.[43] Repeal of these tax incentives has been estimated to potentially provide $3.1 billion to $4.3 billion a year in additional tax revenues.[44]

The Internal Revenue Code (IRC) provides a range of tax credits uniquely applicable to oil and gas producers.[45] IRC § 43 provides tax credits for costs associated with enhanced oil recovery (EOR) methods; EOR methods are used to produce oil from fields where primary production has peaked and begun to decline. Primary production for oil wells is gravity driven and requires little beyond the well and pumps to extract crude oil from the well. EOR techniques enable enhanced recovery and rely on chemical injectants, gaseous pressure-injections, steam, and other means of heat injections into the well bed to stimulate additional production levels. Previously, this credit package sustained production when oil prices were low, but under current pricing levels, the credit is not available. A similar story can be told for IRC § 45(I), wherein wells with substantially low volumes of production were encouraged to remain in production; current pricing prevents the credit from being applicable.[46] The credits would otherwise be $3 per barrel of crude oil or per 1,000 standard cubic feet (scf) of natural gas.[47]

IRC § 45(K) allows for a nonconventional source production credit for qualified fuels; the credit is set at $3 per barrel-of-oil equivalent.[48] Qualified fuels include oil produced from shale and tar sands, gas produced from geo-pressured brine, Devonian shale, coal seams, a tight formation, or biomass, and liquid, gaseous, or solid synthetic fuels produced from coal (including lignite).[49]

IRC § 45Q(a)(2) provides tax credits for carbon capture and storage (CCS) facilities that are affiliated with oil and gas production activities.[50] The carbon dioxide sequestration credit is $10 per metric ton of qualified carbon dioxide, which is captured by the taxpayer at a qualified facility and disposed of by the taxpayer in secure geological storage.[51] The oil and gas production activities need to qualify under the same qualifications as the EOR tax credits.[52]

IRC § 907 provides tax credits for taxes paid on combined foreign oil and gas income derived outside of the United States.[53] Such income is recognized as the sum of both incomes related to oil and gas extraction and to other processing, marketing, and distribution incomes derived from oil and gas activities.[54] It is estimated that this allowance returns over $1 billion a year to petroleum producers.[55]

There are also a variety of unique income tax deductions allowed for fossil fuel producers. IRC § 167(h) enables the geological and geophysical costs of oil and gas exploration and development to be depreciated on a quicker time schedule than the ordinary rules.[56] It is estimated that this allowance returns $612 million to $1.1 billion a year to petroleum producers.[57]

IRC § 263(c) provides for the expensing of the intangible drilling and development costs associated with the development stage of an oil and gas project; this deduction allowance accelerates cost recovery on the investment.[58] It is estimated that this allowance returns $700 million to $3.5 billion a year to petroleum producers.[59]

IRC § 193 Tertiary Injectants enables the same-year cost recovery of the chemicals used to increase and facilitate production.[60] The injectants must be injectants that are not recoverable hydrocarbons.[61] The costs of this program are relatively small, estimated at $50 million over the five-year period beginning in 2013.[62]

IRC § 199 allows a specific deduction of up to 9% of the costs or incomes resulting from domestic production activities.[63] While the deduction is available to many industries beyond oil and gas, there are specific provisions for oil and gas producers that reduce the deduction by 3%.[64] The production, refining, processing, transportation, or distribution of oil, gas, or any primary product is included as domestic production.[65] It is estimated that this allowance returns $574 million to $1.4 billion a year to petroleum producers.[66]

6.3.2 Tax incentives for alternative energy production

While the IRC provides a larger economic boost to the fossil fuel industry, it also provides incentives for renewable energy programs; the expected costs of support for renewable energy innovations is estimated at $39.5 billion for the five-year period beginning in 2013.[67] The dominant focus within renewable energy incentives is on the development of technologies to produce electricity from renewable resources and the development of renewable transportation fuels.[68]

IRC § 40 and IRC § 40A provide tax credits for producers of alternative liquid fuels such as alcohol-based fuels,[69] biodiesels, and renewable diesel fuels.[70] Biodiesel,[71] agri-diesel,[72] and renewable diesel producers can receive $1 per gallon of produced fuels.[73] The cost of this program of tax credits is estimated to be $2.2 billion a year, with the alcohol component being comparatively small at $200 million annually.[74]

IRC § 45 enables a renewable electricity production credit to be earned by such producers; it returns $0.015 per kilowatt-hour produced.[75] The qualified resources are enumerated: wind, closed-loop biomass, open-loop biomass, geothermal energy, solar energy, small irrigation power, municipal solid waste, qualified hydropower production, and marine and hydrokinetic renewable energy.[76] It is estimated that this allowance could return $1.7 billion a year to producers of electricity from renewable resources.[77]

IRC § 45J enables an advanced nuclear power facility production credit; it returns $0.015 per kilowatt-hour produced by such facilities.[78] The dates of the design and intent to construct are key determinants of qualifying as an advanced nuclear power facility.[79]

IRC § 45Q(a)(1) provides tax credits for CCS facilities that are not affiliated with oil and gas production activities.[80] The carbon dioxide sequestration credit is $20 per metric ton of qualified carbon dioxide, which is captured by the taxpayer at a qualified facility and disposed of by the taxpayer in secure geological storage.[81]

IRC § 48 Energy Credits, or investment tax credits (ITC), are available to investments in energy production that utilize geothermal sources, micro-turbine sources, or combined heat and power solutions. The ITC may be up to 10% of the investment in the energy project.[82] The value of the credit program to investors has been estimated at $500 million annually.[83]

IRC § 25D provides a 30% tax credit for the purchases and installations of a variety home-based solar and wind power systems.[84] The value of those credits has been estimated to be close to $900 million a year.[85]

The impacts of tax code incentives for renewable energy might best be perceived from an "effective tax rate" (ETR) perspective instead of a bulk dollar perspective. An ETR is the tax rate as experienced after the various incentives have been included within the final tax calculation. Renewable energy projects show stunningly low ETR. Producers of electricity from solar thermal projects benefit from an ETR of -244.7 and wind projects benefit from their ETR of -163.8;[86] the minus sign denotes an effective net tax payment to the producers from the government. Nuclear power producers also benefit from an ETR of -99.5,[87] effectively reducing their tax incidence to incidental levels. Oil and gas producers range in ETR; integrated companies face an ETR of 15.2 while non-integrated operations benefit from an ETR of -13.5.[88] Producers of electricity from natural gas pay the highest ETR of 34.4.[89] Thus, it could be argued that renewable energy projects face more favorable net ETR under the tax code.

6.4 Summary and conclusions

It is often claimed that what America needs is a 'moon shot' approach to green energy. That if the federal government really put its fiscal powers to the task, that the necessary breakthroughs could occur and enable the emissions controls envisioned by the Paris Agreements. (Albeit, the Trump administration has 'removed' the US from those agreements, so such a federal mandate likely doesn't align with their policy agenda.)

However, as explored in this chapter, that argument doesn't quite hold water, as the Department of Energy has already made that fiscal commitment. To review from earlier,

> Whereas the Manhattan Project spent *$22 billion* over five years and the greater NASA/Apollo program spent *$98 billion* over fourteen years, the broader federal energy innovation projects spent more than *$118 billion* over thirty-five years prior to 2009; the *annual rates of expenditure for energy innovation fell between the annual expenditures for the previous two programs.*[90] (Emphasis added.)

Of course, this is chump change in contrast to the $16.3 trillion recently proposed by presidential candidate Bernie Sanders,[91] but $3 to $4 billion a year, sustained for decades, remains a substantial research budget allocation, one in alignment with other large government projects.

The Department of Defense plays a unique role in the American mission to develop technology and industrial capacities, one that is equally present in energy policy and related technological innovations. The DOD may also be one of the world's largest energy consumers, enabling it to play an outsized role in determining which products survive or thrive on the market.

Much of its authority to engage in energy policy stems from the Defense Production Act, which provides authority for the DOD and its military branches to engage in support of energy technologies and resources.[92] The act requires that the DOD ensure the security of energy supplies to enable the DOD and the US Armed Forces with all the energy that they might need to accomplish their various missions, and further, that the DOD should extend its base of domestic energy supplies by supporting research and use of renewable energy sources (including solar, geothermal, wind, and biomass sources), more efficient energy storage and distribution technologies, and energy conservation measures. It is very clear that the DOD is deeply engaged in energy policy, in both conventional domestic energy resources and in innovative green energy approaches to energy supplies.

It remains true that the main energy resource of the US military is crude oil and natural gas, to fuel the multitudes of vehicles and vessels in their many divisions and fleets. Jets fly on kerosene, Navy vessels need heavy diesels and oils to move, and the cars, trucks, and tanks of the Army need various diesel and gasoline products. And of course, lubricating oils are needed across this whole set of machinery. Thus, the DOD remains very engaged in supporting its access to hydrocarbon fuels. Yet, being so tied to fossil fuels is also identified as a potential weakness that an enemy could exploit, especially in cutting fuel supplies lines and convoys, so the DOD is very interested in the development of alternative energy resources. Its hopes to create a Green Fleet speak directly to that goal, as do their efforts to enable forward bases to utilize solar power and other forms of energy free of fossil fuel deliveries, or at least enabling those bases to survive on fewer and smaller shipments.

This first focus, to always have a sufficient supply of energy, dictates its own corollary, that it should be able to source energy needs from multiple pathways in case any particular mode of energy becomes inaccessible during combat or crisis, and necessarily implies a world of oversupply based in supplies from both fossil fuels and a diverse group of non-fossil fuel alternatives.

The IRS, via the tax code developed by Congress, oversees approximately $20 billion in tax subsidies and incentives for energy policy purposes. There are a wide variety of tax deductions and credits available, and also a range of favorable accounting methodologies, all of which stimulate investment in all of the various energy sectors. Fossil fuels have long benefited from specific tax rules to encourage production from both new fields and older or weaker fields. There are even special tax rules for taxes paid to other national governments by American oil and gas companies operating overseas.

However, the IRS also oversees tax credits and deductions for green and renewable energy resources too. As discussed previously, the interesting impact of those rules is to often reverse the tax system into a purely subsidizing role, and not to merely reduce the incidence of taxation. The ETRs of green energy producers is often negative, meaning that the government pays them to operate. Free money is sure to encourage additional investments in energy supplies, and one could foreseeably expect an increase of energy supplies to result.

The conclusion has to be that the US government, in the interest of energy security, has established a broad array of economic and strategic measures to ensure a strong and robust energy supply for the US. Both conventional fossil fuels and green energy supplies are heavily encouraged across a wide array of policies and agendas. This is likely to result in increased volumes of energy production from each sector and to also reduce the market price of each energy supply as the electricity from solar and crude oil are the same to the customer. Thus, in the near to medium term, barring any shocking infrastructure change, more fossil fuels are likely to be priced to be attractive to consumers both private and industrial and will be consumed at higher quantities, if these policy habits are not changed.

Notes

1 Solemn Declaration III 2009, *en passim.*
2 Solemn Declaration III 2009, 6, *see also* Table I.
3 The Hoover Dam began as a federally funded development with the Boulder Canyon Project Act, 43 U.S.C. § 617 (1928). The Manhattan Project was supported by the issuance of Exec. Order No. 8807, 3 CFR 3207 (1941), which created the Office of Scientific Research and Development, a war-time predecessor to today's Defense Advanced Research Projects Agency (DARPA).
4 Stine, Cong. Research Serv., RL34645, (2009).
5 Stine, Cong. Research Serv., RL34645, (2009); the legislative measure was the Energy Reorganization Act of 1974 (P.L. 93–438).
6 Stine, Cong. Research Serv., RL34645, (2009); the legislative measure was the Department of Energy Organization Act of 1977 (P.L. 95–91).
7 Stine, Cong. Research Serv., RL34645, (2009), 6 (taking note particularly of Table I).
8 In annualized 2011 dollars. Terry Dinan & Philip Webre, Cong. Budget Office, *Federal Financial Support for the Development and Production of Fuels and Energy Technologies* 1, 5 (Mar. 2012), www.cbo.gov/sites/default/files/03-12-Energy Technologies.pdf.
9 Philip Webre and Terry Dinan Federal Financial Support for the Development and Production of Fuels and Energy Technologies Congressional Budget Office (CBO), Issue Brief, released in March 2012; pages 1–10. http://www.cbo.gov/sites/default/files/cbofiles/attachments/03-06-FuelsandEnergy_Brief.pdf
10 Philip Webre and Terry Dinan Federal Financial Support for the Development and Production of Fuels and Energy Technologies Congressional Budget Office (CBO), Issue Brief, released in March 2012; pages 1–10. http://www.cbo.gov/sites/default/files/cbofiles/attachments/03-06-FuelsandEnergy_Brief.pdf
11 Philip Webre and Terry Dinan Federal Financial Support for the Development and Production of Fuels and Energy Technologies Congressional Budget Office (CBO), Issue Brief, released in March 2012; pages 1–10. http://www.cbo.gov/sites/default/files/cbofiles/attachments/03-06-FuelsandEnergy_Brief.pdf
12 Philip Webre and Terry Dinan Federal Financial Support for the Development and Production of Fuels and Energy Technologies Congressional Budget Office (CBO), Issue Brief, released in March 2012; pages 1–10. http://www.cbo.gov/sites/default/files/cbofiles/attachments/03-06-FuelsandEnergy_Brief.pdf
13 Philip Webre and Terry Dinan Federal Financial Support for the Development and Production of Fuels and Energy Technologies Congressional Budget Office (CBO), Issue Brief, released in March 2012; pages 1–10. http://www.cbo.gov/sites/default/files/cbofiles/attachments/03-06-FuelsandEnergy_Brief.pdf
14 Philip Webre and Terry Dinan Federal Financial Support for the Development and Production of Fuels and Energy Technologies Congressional Budget Office (CBO), Issue Brief, released in March 2012; pages 1–10. http://www.cbo.gov/sites/default/files/cbofiles/attachments/03-06-FuelsandEnergy_Brief.pdf
15 Schwartz, Blakeley, & O'Rourke (2012). For a recent article on the US military's climate change measures and responsive planning, *see* Sarah E. Light, The Military-

Environmental Complex, 55 *B.C. L. Rev.* 879 (2014). E.g., in the United States, its military is the largest consumer of energy products and services, and thus its internal planning with regards to energy products and services would have spillover impact on the United States' broader efforts to mitigate climate change.

16 Schwartz, Blakeley, & O'Rourke (2012), 1.

17 Schwartz, Blakeley, & O'Rourke (2012), 2. Reporting that after the DOD's 80% share of energy, the next largest user of energy was the postal service which used only 4% of the energy budget. The obvious disparity of the DOD's role on energy planning is stunning yet not generally recognized by the general public.

18 The Defense Production Act of 1950, as amended, is enacted at 50 U.S.C. App. § 2061 (2012).

19 50 U.S.C. § 2152(14) (emphasis added).

20 50 U.S.C. § 2062(a)(1) and (a)(5) (emphasis added). *See also id.* at § 2076, "[f]or purposes of this Act, 'energy' shall be designated as a 'strategic and critical material.'"

21 50 U.S.C. § 2062(a)(6) (emphasis added).

22 50 U.S.C. § 2093(a)(1).

23 50 U.S.C. § 2093(a)(1). (emphasis added).

24 50 U.S.C. § 2092(A) (2012) (emphasis added).

25 50 U.S.C. § 2091(a)(1).

26 50 U.S.C. § 2062(b)(4) (emphasis added).

27 E.g., in 2013, there were currently over twenty officially declared national states of emergency extent, *see* Patrick Thronson, Toward Comprehensive Reform of America's Emergency Law Regime, 46(2) *U. Mich. J. L. Reform* 737, 754, Table I (2013). As of 2019, a publicly edited and monitored list at Wikipedia lists thirty-three extant 'emergencies' (Aug. 31, 2019 12:30 PM), https://en.wikipedia.org/wiki/List_of_national_emergencies_in_the_United_States.

28 Schwartz, Blakeley, & O'Rourke (2012), 2.

29 Schwartz, Blakeley, & O'Rourke (2012), 3–4. The USAF consumes 53% of the DOD's energy budget and 90% of that is spent on aviation fuels. The USN similarly maintains flight lines in addition to boats; the Navy consumes 28% of the DOD's energy budget and 54% of their energy needs are met by petroleum-derived fuels. The United States Army relies on the USAF and USN to provide the bulk of its heavy lift and transportation needs, so the Army requires less energy overall; it consumes only about 18% of the DOD's energy budget.

30 Schwartz, Blakeley, & O'Rourke (2012), 15.

31 Schwartz, Blakeley, & O'Rourke (2012), 16 (citing to a US Air Force Briefing, "*Air Force Energy Consumption*," Mar. 6, 2012. The primary target is a 50:50 blend of traditional petroleum sources and non-petroleum-based fuels.).

32 Schwartz, Blakeley, & O'Rourke (2012), 17. Over $800 million in funding over the 2013–2017 fiscal years.

33 Schwartz, Blakeley, & O'Rourke (2012). The Fischer-Tropsch transformation enables natural gas, or other sources of hydrogen, to be converted into a liquid hydrocarbon; it is industrially known as the "gas-to-liquids" process (GTL).

34 Schwartz, Blakeley, & O'Rourke (2012), 18 (citing to Highlights of the Department of Navy FY 2013 Budget, *Dep't of the Navy*, Feb. 2012, 1–8).

35 Schwartz, Blakeley, & O'Rourke (2012), 18.

36 Schwartz, Blakeley, & O'Rourke (2012), 18 (citing to USN, *The Department of the Navy's Energy Goals*, www.navy.mil/features/Navy_EnergySecurity.pdf.

37 Schwartz, Blakeley, & O'Rourke (2012), 18.

38 Philip Webre and Terry Dinan Federal Financial Support for the Development and Production of Fuels and Energy Technologies Congressional Budget Office (CBO), Issue Brief, released in March 2012; pages 1–10. http://www.cbo.gov/sites/default/files/cbofiles/attachments/03-06-FuelsandEnergy_Brief.pdf

39 Philip Webre and Terry Dinan Federal Financial Support for the Development and Production of Fuels and Energy Technologies Congressional Budget Office

(CBO), Issue Brief, released in March 2012; pages 1–10. http://www.cbo.gov/sites/default/files/cbofiles/attachments/03-06-FuelsandEnergy_Brief.pdf

40 Sherlock provided a detailed listing and account of the various measures adopted during the 108th, 109th, 110th, 111th, and 112th Congresses. Sherlock, Cong. Research Serv., RL43206 (2013).

41 Andy Kroll, et al., Triumph of the Drill: How Big Oil Clings to Billions in Government Giveaways, *Mother Jones* (Apr. 14, 2014), www.motherjones.com/print/249086.

42 Kroll (2014).

43 Pirog, Cong. Research Serv., RL42374 (2013), 1.

44 Pirog, Cong. Research Serv., RL42374 (2013), 1.

45 The I.R.C. is enacted as the 26th volume of the United States Code, thus a citation to I.R.C. § 43 is identical to a citation to 26 U.S.C. § 43.

46 I.R.C. § 45I(a).

47 I.R.C. § 45I(b)(1)(A), (B). "Scf" is the industry standard reference for standard cubic feet, implying certain air pressure and temperature conditions.

48 I.R.C. § 45K(a)(1), (2). *See also*, "The term 'barrel-of-oil equivalent' with respect to any fuel means that amount of such fuel which has a Btu content of 5.8 million" I.R.C. § 45K(d)(5).

49 I.R.C. § 45K(c)(1).

50 I.R.C. § 45Q(a)(2).

51 I.R.C. § 45Q(a)(2)(A), (B).

52 I.R.C. § 45Q(d)(4). "The term 'qualified enhanced oil or natural gas recovery project' has the meaning given the term 'qualified enhanced oil recovery project' by § 43 (c)(2), by substituting 'crude oil or natural gas' for 'crude oil' in subparagraph (A)(i) thereof."

53 I.R.C. § 907(a), (b).

54 I.R.C. § 907(b)(1)(A). "[F]oreign oil gas extraction incomes" and (B) "foreign oil related incomes."

55 Pirog reported that the elimination of these credits could increase annual tax revenues by up to $11 billion over the tax decade of FY2014 to FY2023. Pirog, Cong. Research Serv., RL42374 (2013), 9. *See also* Weiss & Peterson (2014).

56 I.R.C. § 167(h)(1) allows for a 24-month recovery of the costs and I.R.C. § 167(h)(5) allows certain major integrated oil companies seven years to recover the costs.

57 Park, Kroll, Gilson, & Hansen-Bundy (2014).

58 This treatment is in contrast to the regular requirement to capitalize certain investments. Contrast I.R.C. § 263(a) and (c); "(a) General rule: No deduction shall be allowed for [a]ny amount paid out for new buildings or for permanent improvements or betterments made to increase the value of any property or estate[;]" and "(c) regulations shall be prescribed by the Secretary … which granted the option to deduct as expenses intangible drilling and development costs in the case of oil and gas wells."

59 Park, Kroll, Gilson, & Hansen-Bundy (2014). Pirog reported a potential increase in tax revenues of $1 billion a year from the repeal of this provision. Pirog, *supra* note 173, 4. In 2013, the deduction was seen as a $1.3 billion cost to tax revenues. Sherlock, *supra* note 170, 8.

60 I.R.C. § 193(a).

61 I.R.C. § § 193(b)(1) and (2).

62 Sherlock, Cong. Research Serv., RL43206 (2013), 14.

63 I.R.C. § 199(a)(1).

64 I.R.C. § § 199(c)(4)(A) and (d)(9).

65 I.R.C. § § 199(d)(9)(B).

66 Park, Kroll, Gilson, & Hansen-Bundy (2014). *See also* Weiss & Peterson, *supra* note 185. Pirog reported that the elimination of this allowance for domestic oil and gas producers could increase annual tax revenues by up to $17.4 billion over the tax decade of FY2014 to FY2024. Pirog, *supra* note 173, 5.
67 Sherlock, Cong. Research Serv., RL43206 (2013), 14.
68 Sherlock, Cong. Research Serv., RL43206 (2013), 15.
69 I.R.C. § 40(b)(2)(A). "The alcohol credit of any taxpayer for any taxable year is 60 cents for each gallon of alcohol which is not in a mixture with gasoline or a special fuel."
70 I.R.C. § 40A(b)(1)(A). "The biodiesel mixture credit of any taxpayer for any taxable year is $1.00 for each gallon of biodiesel used by the taxpayer in the production of a qualified biodiesel mixture." *See also* Sherlock, *supra* note 170, 11.
71 I.R.C. § 40A(d)(1). "The term 'biodiesel' means the monoalkyl esters of long chain fatty acids derived from plant or animal matter which meet – (A) the registration requirements for fuels and fuel additives established by the Environmental Protection Agency under section 211 of the Clean Air Act (42 U.S.C. 7545), and (B) the requirements of the American Society of Testing and Materials D6751."
72 I.R.C. § 40A(d)(2). "The term 'agri-biodiesel' means biodiesel derived solely from virgin oils, including esters derived from virgin vegetable oils from corn, soybeans, sunflower seeds, cottonseeds, canola, crambe, rapeseeds, safflowers, flaxseeds, rice bran, mustard seeds, and camelina and from animal fats."
73 Sherlock, Cong. Research Serv., RL43206 (2013), 11.
74 Sherlock, Cong. Research Serv., RL43206 (2013), 11. *See also* Molly F. Sherlock, Cong. Research Serv., RL31953, Energy Tax Incentives: Measuring Value Across Different Types of Energy Resources 7 (2012).
75 I.R.C. § 45(a)(1) and (2).
76 I.R.C. § 45(c)(1).
77 Sherlock, Cong. Research Serv., RL43206 (2013), 9.
78 I.R.C. § 45J(a).
79 I.R.C. § 45J(d)(2). "[T]he term 'advanced nuclear facility' means any nuclear facility the reactor design for which is approved after December 31, 1993, by the Nuclear Regulatory Commission (and such design or a substantially similar design of comparable capacity was not approved on or before such date)."
80 I.R.C. § 45Q(a)(1).
81 I.R.C. § 45Q(a)(1)(A) and (B).
82 Sherlock, Cong. Research Serv., RL43206 (2013), 10.
83 Sherlock, Cong. Research Serv., RL43206 (2013), 7 and 10.
84 I.R.C. § 25D. *See also* Sherlock, *supra* note 206, 10–11.
85 Sherlock, Cong. Research Serv., RL43206 (2013), 10.
86 Sherlock, Cong. Research Serv., RL43206 (2013), 22.
87 Sherlock, Cong. Research Serv., RL43206 (2013), 22.
88 Sherlock, Cong. Research Serv., RL43206 (2013), 22.
89 Sherlock, Cong. Research Serv., RL43206 (2013), 22.
90 Solemn Declaration III, *supra* note 114, 6, *see also* Table I.
91 "Directly invest an historic $16.3 trillion public investment toward these efforts, in line with the mobilization of resources made during the New Deal and WWII, but with an explicit choice to include black, indigenous and other minority communities who were systematically excluded in the past." Bernie Sanders, 'The Green New Deal' Issues, Bernie 2020, https://berniesanders.com/issues/the-green-new-deal/
92 The Defense Production Act of 1950, as amended, is enacted at 50 U.S.C. App. § 2061 (2012).

7 Impact of international energy conventions

While the previous chapter focused on one nation and its efforts to achieve energy security, this chapter examines two international trade agreements that encourage, *inter alia*, innovation in energy technologies, across many countries. Again energy security is the central topic, but in this chapter, the question is what happens to energy prices, energy supply, and ultimately, what happens to carbon emission levels when many countries attempt to coordinate on energy security.

The first agreement is the Energy Charter Treaty (ECT) that originally was intended to facilitate the interchange of energy products and investments between Europe and countries emerging from a Soviet era. The second agreement is OPEC, the collective of certain major petroleum-producing countries.

However, contrary to the intent of the UNFCCC, these international conventions attempt to secure the future of petroleum and other fossil fuels and immediately raise concerns of carbon emissions. While both efforts do acknowledge their recognition and support of the UNFCCC, they remain steadfastly committed to protecting and promoting the commercial feasibility of carbon-based fuels to compete alongside renewable energy resources.

Both of these arrangements are primarily, if not exclusively, focused on petroleum and natural gas. Both of them also require their contracting parties or member states to provide for research and development to secure future fossil fuel supplies at competitive prices. As such, both agreements oblige their members to provide for innovation in fossil fuel energy technologies to enable continued production, higher rates of production, and competitively priced production.

In short, these agreements call for energy innovations to provide sustained high levels of production of low-cost fossil fuels at prices competitive to market alternatives. Should they remain in effect, it is reasonably foreseeable that petroleum and other fossil fuels would remain in production at a potentially increasing level of output and thus sustain the provision of large supplies of competitively priced fuels for the global market.

It is also key to note that if global policies, led by the vision of the UNFCCC, aim at creating green and renewable energy supplies at greater volume and at lower unit prices, then the goals of the ECT and of OPEC are to ensure that their fossil fuels remains competitively priced in the market. Without additional steps of analysis, that means that successful implementation of green energy goals would result in cheaper fossil fuels, too, which would likely lead to more combustion and carbon emissions from those fossil fuels.

7.1 The Energy Charter Treaty

The ECT was originally drafted to facilitate trade in energy supplies and services.[1] It includes within its definition of "energy materials and products" items related to nuclear energy, coal power, various petroleum resources and products, natural gas energy, electrical energy, and certain forms of charcoal.[2] It supports a broad range of energy activities, including exploration, extraction, production, refining, storage, transport, distribution, and marketing.[3] Given this coverage, the whole of upstream, midstream, and downstream fossil fuels are addressed by the ECT.[4]

The ECT establishes state sovereignty and that the states have sovereign rights over the energy resources within their jurisdictions.[5] Thus, each state is empowered to decide what areas within its sovereign control are to be "made available for exploration and development."[6] They may also determine at what rates their resources may be depleted or extracted.[7] Environmental and other safety concerns remain similarly within the sovereign control of the states.[8]

The ECT sought to "develop an open and competitive market, for Energy Materials and Products."[9] However, many of the signatory parties were not members of the World Trade Organization's General Agreement on Tariffs and Trade (WTO/GATT) systems regulating international trade; therefore, the ECT references the WTO/GATT agreements as guidelines for its own implementation.[10] For instance, all parties to the ECT may not apply any trade-related investment measures inconsistent with Article III or XI of the GATT.[11] Each contracting party is required to alleviate market distortions and barriers to trade.[12] Further, transit and transportation of products and services covered by the ECT are to be governed by the principle of freedom of transit without distinction to origin, destination, or ownership.[13]

The ECT facilitates innovation in fossil fuel energy industries, as well as in other energy sectors. The transfer of energy technology between contracting parties is to be facilitated.[14] Investment in energy sectors of the contracting parties is to be encouraged,[15] which may be facilitated by programs and measures of the contracting parties.[16]

The ECT provides clarity on how environmental impact (EI) should be addressed by the contracting parties.[17] EIs are defined to include any given effect on the environment without particular reference to beneficial or harmful impacts.[18] EI might include such factors as human health and safety, air, water, and climate impacts; it may also include a wide range of impacts on socioeconomic conditions.[19] Each contracting party is obligated to minimize the range of potential EIs in economically efficient manners.[20] Such measures to minimize impacts should consider areas both within and without the specific state and consider the whole energy cycle of the relevant energy source.[21] Each contracting party is to undertake precautionary measures to prevent or minimize environmental degradation.[22] When uncertainty exists over the interpretation of the environmental provisions of the ECT, the primary resort should be to other appropriate international forums prior to taking ECT-based environmental disputes to review by the Charter Conference.[23]

Perhaps most importantly for the purposes of this discussion, the contracting parties have obligations to promote innovation and adoption of:[24]

i Energy efficiency technologies;
ii Renewable energy resources; and
iii Promotion of the use of cleaner greenhouse gas emitting fuels.

Such technologies and energy innovations must be shared;[25] furthermore, the contracting parties are required to promote and cooperate in the research, development, and application of those technologies.[26] Finally, the contracting parties are obligated to promote public awareness of these new energy technologies.[27] Thus, it is clear that the ECT promotes multiple forms of energy innovations, including fossil fuels and renewable energy sources.

There are specific provisions for losses and expropriations.[28] Investments in energy sectors are not to be nationalized, expropriated, or subjected to measures having similar effects unless four tests are met.[29] First, the only approved purpose for an expropriatory act is one whose purpose is in the public interest.[30] Second, the act of expropriation may not be discriminatory in character.[31] Third, any act of expropriation must be conducted under due process of law.[32] Finally, any such act must be accompanied by the payment of prompt, adequate, and effective compensation; such compensation must be for the fair market value of the asset.[33]

Thus, the ECT provides for the ongoing research, development, and investment into energy technologies across a spectrum of energy alternatives, but it primarily attempts to provide a legal framework to integrate the energy markets of the contracting parties. As such, the primary energy innovations would be in the fossil fuels and nuclear energy sectors.

7.2 Conventions of the Organization of the Petroleum Exporting Countries

Five countries established OPEC in 1960: Iran, Iraq, Kuwait, Saudi Arabia, and Venezuela.[34] Presently, it has one dozen members, including Qatar, Libya, the United Arab Emirates, Algeria, Nigeria, Ecuador, Gabon, and Angola.[35]

7.2.1 The OPEC Statute

OPEC is primarily governed by the OPEC Statute.[36] The "principal aim of the Organization shall be the coordination and unification of the petroleum policies of the Member Countries."[37] Further, the statute requires OPEC to determine the best means to protect the member countries' individual and collective interests.[38] Thus, OPEC has an active duty to provide for the coordinated planning of the interests of oil exporting countries.

A member state can be either one of the original five founder countries or any other country that possesses a "substantial net export of crude petroleum" and is otherwise well aligned with the pre-existing members of OPEC.[39] If a country has net exports of petroleum, but not 'substantial net exports,' then it is entitled to join OPEC as an Associate Member but not as a Full Member.[40] This means that the voting membership of OPEC is limited to countries that are substantial net exporters of petroleum.[41]

One of the organization's primary goals is to ensure the economic viability of petroleum products and investments. OPEC is required to stabilize prices for petroleum products and to eliminate price fluctuations to promote petroleum's role in international markets.[42] Further, the organization is tasked with securing steady income for its member countries, securing efficient, economic, and regular petroleum supplies for consuming nations, and securing fair returns on investments in the petroleum industry.[43] The organization is overseen by a secretary general who must meet certain prerequisites for service, including a minimum of a decade in the 'oil industry,' while ministry service or oversight of international business operations are seen as preferable.[44] These requirements have not been amended since the original enactment of the statute.[45]

The secretary general of OPEC is assisted in his duties by the Division of Research.[46] The Division of Research is required to research, forecast, and monitor the petro-energy and petro-chemical industries for hydrocarbons and derived products, including non-energy products.[47] The Division of Research is also tasked with maintaining research on economic and financial factors associated with the previously mentioned industries and products.[48] The division has a duty to advance data sharing across member countries.[49]

Similarly, the secretary general is assisted by the Division of Support Services.[50] One of the division's duties is to keep the secretary general abreast of policy changes in the international petroleum industry, which could affect OPEC or its member countries.[51] Further, when OPEC's own resources are insufficient to fulfill the previously mentioned duties, the secretary general is to commission consultants as necessary.[52]

7.2.2 OPEC Solemn Declaration II of 2000

OPEC may convene summits to bring together the collected heads of state of the member countries to further refine and clarify the policies and agendas of the organization.[53] There have been three such summits: in 1975, in 2000, and in 2007.[54] The second summit of 2000 was convened against the backdrop of global negotiations on climate change.[55] The third summit was drawn to support and re-affirm the centrality of natural resources and the sovereign rights of the member countries to govern their own resources.[56] The Solemn Declarations are the work products of those summits; they enhance but do not amend the OPEC Statute.[57]

The Solemn Declaration II is a brief but dense four-page document containing twenty resolutions.[58] The declaration charges OPEC to continue to preserve and enhance the role of crude oil and natural gas in world energy markets. It calls for a cessation in efforts to discriminate against petroleum products and for the reduction of petroleum or carbon taxes that cause similar trade effects. It also delimits OPEC's support of the UNFCCC's goals; it starkly confronts the global community to recognize poverty and not climate change as the premier environmental tragedy. As such, the declaration supports the expansion of petroleum consumption as a means to end global poverty; OPEC is to remain on path to provide technological innovations to ensure the supply and affordability of petroleum products and industries.

The declaration reaffirms the role of OPEC to preserve and enhance the "role oil would play in meeting future energy demand."[59] OPEC has a duty to steward and optimize the economic value recoverable from the member countrie' petroleum assets.[60] In particular, OPEC is to protect the OPEC member countries' share of petroleum revenues *vis-à-vis* other oil exporting countries.[61]

OPEC has a duty to ensure that petroleum products remain remunerative for its owners and investors, stable in supply, and competitive with other energy sources for consumers.[62] Additionally, the Solemn Declaration II calls for increased consumption of crude oil and natural gas when "other fuels are recognized as being damaging to the global environment."[63] The declaration calls on consuming countries to prevent discrimination against crude oil consumption, stating that they should "adopt fair and equitable treatment of oil in world energy markets."[64] Key among those forms of discrimination are differing forms of petroleum taxes and potential carbon taxes; the declaration calls these taxes a burden that prevents just and equitable terms of trade.[65]

The Solemn Declaration II delimits OPEC support of the UNFCCC. It does recognize and support OPEC's engagement with the UNFCCC, but it requires special attention to two policies that would limit the overall impact on petroleum producers and certain potential petroleum consumers.[66] First, the UNFCCC should be guided by recognition of the "principle of common but differentiated responsibility," that not all countries should face identical consequences for industrialization and resultant carbon emissions, as many countries have not yet benefitted from such industrialization and did not yet emit such volumes of greenhouse gases.[67] Additionally, the declaration urges the countries listed in Annex I of the UNFCCC to promote measures to minimize the adverse social and economic impacts that would occur to countries whose economies are highly dependent on the production and export of fossil fuels.[68]

Additionally, the declaration warns that OPEC will retain the eradication of poverty, not climate change, as its premier target for economic and social development and sustainability.[69] In fact, the declaration explicitly challenges the Annex I nations to "recognize that the premier environmental tragedy facing the globe is human poverty," and not anthropogenic climate change.[70] It states that OPEC will continue to engage in the UNFCCC processes but that OPEC will also continue its advocacy on poverty issues within other UN forums.[71]

7.2.3 OPEC Solemn Declaration III of 2007

The Solemn Declaration III[72] follows and extends the principles of the previous declaration by developing three themes: stability of energy markets, energy for sustainable development, and energy and the environment.[73]

Under the theme of stability for energy markets, the declaration promotes increases in investment in both upstream and downstream capacities to enable greater supplies of petroleum to reach the market.[74] The instability of petroleum supplies, petroleum demand, and short-term energy prices are to be improved for the benefit of both producers and consumers.[75] The roles of both technology and innovation in efficiency and sustainability of petroleum production are to be promoted.[76] Finally, the declaration calls for the adoption of transparent, non-discriminatory, and predictable trade, fiscal, environmental, and energy policies to better enable free trade access to markets. Clearly, this section expects petroleum production to be sustained and expanded upon by support from technology and innovation and rewarded with access to markets without limits posed by environmental or trade barriers.

Within the topic of energy for sustainable development, the declaration reasserts that the eradication of poverty should be the "first and overriding global priority."[77] Developed countries are urged to promote the diffusion of technology, especially environmentally friendly technologies, to developing countries.[78] The declaration announces a plan to eradicate what it refers to as "energy poverty" in the developing world.[79] As a part of that plan, OPEC is called to develop financial tools and measures to ensure that financial cooperation among OPEC members enables those developing countries to obtain the energy products they need.[80]

Under its discussion on energy and environment, the declaration calls for OPEC to provide "clean, affordable and competitive petroleum resources for global prosperity."[81] It calls for cost-effective measures to address global environmental problems.[82] It calls for the support of forests and reforestation as a means to sink greenhouse gases.[83]

Yet, the discussion re-addresses the "common but differentiated" paradigm of the previous declaration.[84] Within the same set of resolutions, it calls for the OPEC countries to promote innovation in petroleum technology with the "objective of increasing the petroleum resource base."[85] It also calls for technological innovations to reduce the costs of production.[86] The declaration calls for policies based on the UNFCCC to take into account the special needs of countries heavily dependent on the production and export of fossil fuels.[87] Finally, the declaration calls for two fields of technological innovation: (i) the transformation of petroleum products into clean energy products and (ii) the development of technologies that address climate change.[88]

7.3 Summary and conclusions

The results spelled out in this chapter are essentially a study of a game theory model called the 'game of chicken,' wherein two players commit to strategies to collide, hoping that the other player 'chickens out' first; e.g., player one hopes to reach the goal point by so believably pursuing that goal at all costs, including risk of collision with player two, that player two will quit before player two reaches the foreseeable point of collision, leaving the goal and its payoffs solely to the benefit of player one.

There is no way for both green energy and fossil fuel energy to win in this game. Either green energy wins and climate change is averted, or fossil fuels remain a major fuel source and carbon emissions reflect that level of consumption and combustion.

In some ways, the ECT was built with the intent to secure the new opportunities for peace and trans-Eurasian harmony in the wake of the dissolution of the Soviet Union. Economic benefits could flow into areas in need of financial support and reciprocally states could receive energy supply deliveries to alleviate their own energy security policies, reducing their reliance on petroleum from other locations, such as from the Persian Gulf. And to that end, it was successful.

Not to be too clever about it all, the ECT was and is primarily about petroleum; particularly how to connect resources from areas associated with the former Soviet Union and countries both east and west of there, to benefit all parties and to thus build a better sense of interconnectivity and future cooperation. It is, in a nutshell, inspired to some degree by the 1951 Treaty of Paris that established the European Coal and Steel Community (ECSC),[89] perhaps the most successful 'peace' treaty of the 20th century.

Despite the strong focus on petroleum and other forms of fossil fuels, the ECT does provide for the support of green energy supplies. Apart from the ECT's call for environmental impact assessments, which are not *per se* green energy related, the ECT provides obligations to promote innovation and adoption of (i) energy efficiency technologies, (ii) renewable energy resources, and (iii) the promotion of cleaner greenhouse gas emitting fuels.

Energy efficiency, as discussed in Chapter 5, does not necessarily equate to green energy or decreased carbon emissions. There is absolutely nothing illogical about increasing energy efficiency while expanding a carbon-based energy system; Jevons developed his hypothesis on energy efficiency, that it would not save the day as claimed, during the coal era of early 19th-century England ... that is pre-Drake crude oil, pre-Einstein photovoltaic, and pre-Fermi-Szilárd nuclear fission. What does appear to occur with energy efficiency is that it expands the number of individuals who have access to power, as they need to purchase less energy to achieve tasks that previously may have been outside of their budget; this is an expansion of demand for energy supplies.

Skipping to the obligation to encourage 'cleaner fossil fuels,' it is a *prima facie* case that this strategy is not green, as it supports continued emission of carbon from fossil fuels. Is there as an argument that by burning less carbon-rich fuels fewer emissions will be emitted, and thereby achieve a green result? No, we cannot obtain that result with this limited set of assumptions, as policymakers and consumers might consider such a fuel 'safe enough' and continue to use it and thus extend the period or increase the volume of carbon emissions.

Also, *arguendo*, capital is limited, both in terms of financial capital and energy technology human capital, and thus to invest in one prevents investment in the other, even at the marginal edge of investment. The logic here is there are opportunity costs to investments; you can invest in alpha at the cost of not being able to invest that capital in beta.

One might reasonably understand that the promotion or encouragement of cleaner greenhouse gas emitting fuels is tantamount to increasing the supply and the demand for these fuels. Although there might be many ways to accomplish that, the classical way taught in basic economics is to expand supplies while dropping market prices. One can also add marketing and education to change the preference structures of the consumers, to increase their demand for cleaner greenhouse gas emitting fuels. This all leads to both more folks burning more fossil fuels, and to renewable energy sources facing stiffer price competition on the market.

And then, the ECT requires promoting innovation and adoption of renewable energy resources. Against the previous two obligations, which increased demand and supply of fossil fuels, while also likely working to suppress market prices of fossil fuels to further expand consumption, this requirement to support renewable energy supplies appears hopeful, much like the final gift in Pandora's *pithos*.[90]

Yet, here too, the effect of financially supporting above a natural level, to better ensure its uptake and adoption, is quintessentially a subsidy with the foreseeable results of increased supply and lowered costs. As fossil fuel options remain in the same market space as renewable energies, more abundant and cheaper renewable energy is likely to put competitive pressure on the prices and supply of fossil fuels. It is far from obvious how this might result in a reduction of fossil fuel consumption, although it might well cause price reductions that hurt profitability of fossil fuel producers. Nevertheless, one might reasonably assume that in most scenarios, that competition of energy supply choices will result in price competition and likely reduce the market price of fossil fuels, at least in the short run.

Thus, the ECT is a strong and effective framework to support its original goals, to support both producers and consumers of petroleum, but much less so for supporting the transition to reduced carbon emissions, including even when it takes efforts to support green energy pathways.

OPEC clearly exists to support the revenues obtained by petroleum producer nations, and as such, strongly prioritizes the ongoing and future production of petroleum. That is not a green paradox, that is simply straightforward purpose, to increase the sales and revenues of their primary products.

Perhaps most interesting, OPEC squarely rejects the UNFCCC's core assumption that anthropogenic climate change is the greatest threat to humanity, outside of war itself. OPEC counters that global poverty is a much more severe threat. And following that logic, efforts to improve human welfare, especially economic welfare and health, are to be prioritized over efforts to reduce carbon emissions. In its Solemn Declarations II, OPEC commits to prioritizing poverty eradication while it also promises to support UNFCCC, albeit not where these goals conflict.

In two very different treaties, energy security is provided for by very different means and with very different goals. The ECT builds on the vision of the ECSC, hoping to both provide immediate energy and economic benefits to its parties while also hoping to build for a more integrated and peaceful future. The ECT yields to and coordinates with the UNFCCC, accepting both as functional and operative international law. OPEC, created out of a struggle for certain oil-producing countries to assert control over their own petroleum resources from reservoir to consumer, has taken a different path to energy security. For OPEC, energy security operates at two ends – comfortable for the consumer, reliable revenues for the producer. OPEC resists the UNFCCC, supporting its goals but placing preference with its own Solemn Declarations, seeing human poverty as a more urgent crisis than climate change.

Yet, both strongly promote the continued use of fossil fuels. Even where they place some effort on green energy policy, the strategies engaged are risky at also encouraging additional greenhouse gas emissions.

Much as was seen in Chapter Six, wherein the US's multi-vectored approach to energy security, including its efforts to support green energy projects, put the US on a path to likely increased carbon emissions in the short run, here too, we find that the ECT and OPEC are similarly pursuing strategies to ensure energy security but perhaps at the risk of encouraging higher levels of carbon emissions. In these cases, fossil fuels may win these rounds of the chicken game.

In the next chapter, a study is made of international trade laws that were not drafted to address climate change issues; indeed, they were designed to support trade, investment, and in some places, accelerated economic development. Yet, these rules will have surprising effects on carbon emissions. The causes and effects of those trade rules are examined in detail.

Notes

1 The Energy Charter Treaty [hereinafter ECT] Annex I to the Final Act of the European Energy Charter Conference, Dec. 17, 1994. *See also* ECT, art. 2, "This Treaty establishes a legal framework in order to promote long-term cooperation in the energy field." Its membership includes, broadly, European countries, Eurasian/post-Soviet countries, Japan, and Australia. Its observers include Canada, China, the US, and others. *See* Members and Observers, *Energy Charter* (Oct. 20, 2014), www.encharter.org/index.php?id=61.

2 ECT, art. 1, sec. 4, which references the Harmonized System of the Customs Co-operation Council and the Combined Nomenclature of the European Communities. See the listings at ECT, Annex EM, for a complete listing of the various energy resources included within the ECT. The nuclear energy options under Annex EM do not include traditional fusion nuclear energy supplies but only fissile energy supplies and stocks. See Annex EM, sec. 26.12 and 28.44.

3 ECT, art. 1, sec. 5.

4 However, not to the exclusion of other energy sources, such as nuclear energy.

5 ECT, art. 18, sec. 1. This recognition is tempered in a subsidiary requirement, also at sec. 1, that such sovereign rights are subject to the rules of international law.

6 ECT, art. 18, sec. 3.

7 ECT, art. 18, sec. 3.
8 ECT, art. 18, sec. 3.
9 ECT, art. 18, art. 3.
10 ECT, art. 18, art. 4 and 5.
11 ECT, art. 5(1).
12 ECT, art. 18, art. 6.
13 ECT, art. 18, art. 7.
14 ECT, art. 18, art. 8.
15 ECT, art. 18, art. 10, sec. 1.
16 ECT, art. 18, art. 9.
17 ECT, art. 19.
18 ECT, art. 18, sec. 3(b).
19 ECT, art. 18, sec. 3(b). From such a broad perspective on potential EI, the effects of anthropogenic climate change are reasonably includable as EI.
20 ECT, pt. 4, art. 19, sec. 1. Energy cycle is defined to be the full set of activities associated with a given type of energy resource over the complete life-span of the resource from extraction to final consumption and emissions. *Id.* at sec. 3(a).
21 *See* Energy Charter Treaty, art. 19(1), *opened for signature* Dec. 17, 1994, 2080 U.N.T.S. 95 (entered into force Apr. 16, 1998). Such measures to include the full energy cycle should promote market-oriented prices but also provide for the inclusion of more complete environmental costs from that full energy cycle. *See id.* at art. 19(1)(b).
22 ECT, art. 19(1).
23 ECT, art.19(2).
24 ECT, art.19(1)(d).
25 ECT, art.19(1)(e).
26 ECT, art.19(1)(g).
27 ECT, art.19(1)(f).
28 ECT, arts. 12 and 13.
29 ECT, art. 13(1).
30 ECT, art.13(1)(a). Measures undertaken to limit anthropogenic climate change might reasonably be construed as in the public interest, so a reasonable reader might wonder if climate change policies that limited property rights or infringed on free trade principles might be accepted hereunder as in the 'public interest.' While art. 11 is safe from the application of art. 24, it is of note that art. 24, generally speaking, allows for any contracting party to preclude application of any section of the ECT if a contracting party deems it "necessary to protect human, animal, or plant life or health." *Id.* art. 24(b)(i). Thus, if climate change were found to cause such forms of harm, then it could well be deemed necessary to limit application of the ECT under 24–2(b)(i) or under 13–1(a).
31 ECT, art. 13(1)(b). Following the discussion, *supra* at note 30, if climate change measures were to be introduced in alignment with the ECT, then such measures would need to also be non-discriminatory, even if otherwise allowable as a form of expropriation. Similarly, *see id.* at art. 24(2), for limits on disguised restriction or certain forms of trade discrimination.
32 ECT, art. 13(1)(c).
33 ECT, art. 13(1)(d).
34 Member Countries, *Org. of the Petroleum Exporting Countries* (Jan. 10, 2015), www.opec.org/opec_web/en/about_us/25.htm.
35 Member Countries, 2015.
36 OPEC Statute, art. 1, Jan. 1961, 443 U.N.T.S. 247.
37 OPEC Statute, art. 2(A).
38 OPEC Statute, art. 2(A).
39 OPEC Statute, art. 7(A)–(C).

40 OPEC Statute, art. 7(D).
41 Indonesia was once a Full Member, but it has not only lost its Full Member status it has also lost Associate Member status as well due to its change from a net exporter to a net importer of petroleum. It terminated its membership in 2009. *See Member Countries*, OPEC.
42 OPEC Statute, art. 2(B).
43 OPEC Statute, art. 2(C).
44 OPEC Statute, art. 28(A)(c).
45 *See generally* OPEC Statute, *Org. of the Petroleum Exporting Countries*, www.opec.org/opec_web/en/publications/345.htm. *See also* OPEC Statue, Amendments to the Statue.
46 OPEC Statute, art. 32(A).
47 OPEC Statute, art. 33(A)(2).
48 OPEC Statute, art. 33(A)(3).
49 OPEC Statute, art. 33(A)(4).
50 OPEC Statute, art. 32(A).
51 OPEC Statute, art. 33(B)(3).
52 OPEC Statute, art. 34(A).
53 *See* Solemn Declarations, *Org. of the Petroleum Exporting Countries* 1 (2009), www.opec.org/opec_web/static_files_project/media/downloads/publications/Solemn_Declaration_I-III.pdf.
54 Solemn Declarations, 2009.
55 Solemn Declarations, 2009.
56 Solemn Declarations, 2009.
57 Solemn Declarations, 2009.
58 *See* Solemn Declaration II, The Second Summit of Heads of State and Government of OPEC Member Countries, *Org. of the Petroleum Exporting Countries*, 13 (2009), www.opec.org/opec_web/static_files_project/media/downloads/publications/Solemn_Declaration_I-III.pdf.
59 Solemn Declarations II 2009, Resol. 1.
60 Solemn Declarations II 2009, Resol. 2.
61 Solemn Declarations II 2009, Resol. 4.
62 Solemn Declarations II 2009.
63 Solemn Declarations II 2009, Resol. 11. The declaration does not explicitly state what kinds of fuels these might be, but one might reasonably assume that fuels based in fission nuclear technologies, as seen at Chernobyl or Fukushima, might be such fuels. Additionally, concerns that ecological disturbances might be caused by wind turbines or by wave turbines could similarly be classified in this manner.
64 Solemn Declarations II 2009, Resol. 14.
65 Solemn Declarations II 2009, Resol. 15.
66 Solemn Declarations II 2009, Resol. 10.
67 Solemn Declarations II 2009, Resol. 10.
68 Solemn Declarations II 2009, Resol. 11. Broadly speaking, those countries are highly correlated to the membership listing of the G-20; they include the member states of the EU and the EU itself, the Russian Federation, Canada, Australia, New Zealand, the US, Japan, and other countries in or very close to Europe. *See* List of Annex I Parties to the Convention, *United Nations*, http://unfccc.int/parties_and_observers/parties/annex_i/items/2774.php.
69 Solemn Declarations II 2009, Resol. 12.
70 Solemn Declarations II 2009, Resol. 12.
71 Solemn Declarations II 2009, Resol. 12.

72 Solemn Declaration III, Conference of Sovereigns and Heads of State of OPEC Member Countries. Riyadh, Saudi Arabia, *Org. of the Petroleum Exporting Countries*, 17 (2009), www.opec.org/opec_web/static_files_project/media/downloads/publications/Solemn_Declaration_I-III.pdf.
73 Solemn Declaration III 2009, 17.
74 Solemn Declaration III 2009, 18, Resol. 5.
75 Solemn Declaration III 2009, Resol. 6 and 7.
76 Solemn Declaration III 2009, Resol. 8.
77 Solemn Declaration III 2009, Resol. 8. Energy for Sustainable Development, Resol. 1. In contrast to climate change or other agendas, one might reasonably assume is the intended ranking preference.
78 Solemn Declaration III 2009, Resol. 4.
79 Solemn Declaration III 2009, Resol. 6.
80 Solemn Declaration III 2009, Resol. 7.
81 Solemn Declaration III 2009, 21.
82 Solemn Declaration III 2009, Resol. 1.
83 Solemn Declaration III 2009, Resol. 3. Obviously the primary intent here is to reabsorb released carbon dioxide, as forests are not particulary suited to reabsorb methane or other greenhouse gases.
84 Solemn Declaration III 2009, Resol. 4. *Per se* the resolution addresses the UNFCCC to suggest that while OPEC and its member countries endorse the UNFCCC and its apirations, they distinguish between the duties and obligations of developed and developing economies.
85 Solemn Declaration III 2009, Resol. 2.
86 Solemn Declaration III 2009, Resol. 2.
87 Solemn Declaration III 2009, Resol. 5. The declaration suggests that a balanced agenda is needed between those nations emitting greenhouse gases and those in earlier stages of economic development.
88 Solemn Declaration III 2009, Resol. 7. However, the example of such a climate change technology is carbon capture and sequestration and not a new or renewable energy source.
89 ESCS Treaty or Paris Treaty: Treaty Establishing the European Coal and Steel Community, 18 April 1951, 261 U.N.T.S. 140. By its terms, the treaty expired July 23, 2002.
90 Pandora's box is apparently a misnomer, as it is believed that Erasmus substituted πυξίς (pyxis) for πίθος (pithos); a pithos being a large storage vase and pyxis being a circular box for make-up and minor beauty accessories. See Meagher 1995, 56, where he discusses this event while reconstructing the importance of the symbolism of the pithos within this story. The pithos was sometimes used as a coffin, and as such, was a rich metaphor for Pandora opening something best left unopened.

8 International trade laws could frustrate green policies

The global trading system, as exemplified by the WTO, works to secure the free trade of goods and services without discriminatory tariffs or barriers. The WTO is not the only such effort, as there are many regional trade zones that either provide broad economic alignments, such as the EU, or provide zones of expedited free trade, such as the Association of South East Asian Nations (ASEAN) and the North America Free Trade Agreement (NAFTA). These organizations strive to provide protection to equal terms of trade and open markets with limited exceptions to protect certain national interests.

To the extent that energy resources, their products, and the services that sustain their use are covered by the WTO and its agreements, and similarly by other free trade groups, those energy products and services are likely to benefit from the application of the free trade regimes established by such organizations. As such, the various existing energy products, both fossil fuel and renewables, would benefit from free trade and removal of restraints and discriminations to their flow in the global marketplace. Without other environmental trade agreements to the contrary, this would enable various energy products and services to compete with each other directly on energy content and price structures, fostering additional competition in the energy sector.

And in this light, free trade and open competition sounds ideal, "let the best ideas win!" However, in the short run, such competition may place too many goods, new green energy sources, and already-on-the-market fossil energy supplies into the market as the market searches to learn what it wants and doesn't want, as it seeks to learn its new optimal equilibrium in the face of new options and new knowledge.

This chapter explores the potential impact of international trade law on efforts to promote green energy policies. It will focus on the World Trade Organization's (WTO's) General Agreement on Trade and Tariffs (GATT) and its General Agreements on Trade in Services (GATS). This chapter will reveal that there are foreseeable risks from these legal frameworks that could lead to frustration in implementing green energy policies.

8.1 General Agreement on Trade and Tariffs (GATT)

The GATT[1] provides a legal framework for the WTO's efforts to reduce barriers to trade and the elimination of discriminatory treatment in international commerce.[2]

8.1.1 The GATT attempts to achieve the free flow and free trade of goods

The GATT begins by requiring each contracting party to provide "most favored nation" treatment to all other contracting parties;[3] this treatment enables each contracting party to set its own unique custom or tariff measures while simultaneously enabling all other parties to receive as-good-as terms. Each contracting party is also required to maintain "schedules of concessions" of their measures.[4] Domestic taxes and similar levies are likewise required to offer no benefit to domestic production nor discrimination against foreign production.[5] Freedom of transit, of several varieties, is guaranteed under the GATT.[6]

No quantitative prohibitions or restrictions may be imposed on the importation of goods between contracting parties, other than by duties, taxes, and the like.[7] If a quantitative prohibition or restriction is imposed, then the GATT requires those measures to be equally applied against all third parties.[8] The GATT prohibits domestic regulations of contracting parties from requiring domestic production content and prohibits domestic regulations from setting guidelines for foreign production content.[9]

Temporary shocks to the free trade system can be accommodated under the GATT. Subsidies to increase exports or reduce imports can be permitted under the GATT, but not without a substantial review of the circumstances.[10] Dumping of products below comparable prices is prohibited and may be responded to by assessment of levies to 'correct' for the market price of the dumped goods.[11] Similarly, when unforeseen developments place domestic products at risk of serious injury, then contracting parties may take certain liberties with their GATT obligations with regard to their schedule of concessions.[12]

8.1.2 The GATT particularly promotes exports of fossil fuels from developing parties

The GATT recognizes that the attainment of its trade policy goals would be best achieved coincident with the progressive development of those contracting parties whose economies can only support low standards of living and are in early stages of development.[13] Such developing contracting parties may apply flexibility to their tariff structures to support a nascent industry, or they may apply quantitative measures to similarly support development.[14]

Contracting parties that qualify as both "low standards of living" and "in early stages of development" shall be free to temporarily deviate from the GATT's terms under specific requirements.[15] For those countries that depend heavily on exports of a small number of primary commodities[16] such as oil, when those exports are seriously reduced, then those contracting parties may seek consultation for sympathetic consideration for flexibility under the GATT requirements.[17]

In order to help less-developed contracting parties develop their economies and improve their standards of living, the GATT supports the rapid and sustained expansion of those parties' export earnings.[18] Since most of those parties rely heavily on the export of primary products such as crude oil or natural gas,[19] the GATT supports recognition of the need to provide favorable and acceptable access to world markets "in the largest possible measure."[20] Stable, equitable, and remunerative prices are to be achieved by the WTO's policies and the efforts of contracting parties to support these primary products through expanding their demand on the world market and increasing the level of trade in these primary resources.[21] Thus, the GATT recognizes an obligation to support the sustained and competitive export of primary products, including fossil fuels, for the social and welfare needs of its lesser-developed contracting parties.

However, this support of primary product exports is to be accompanied with ancillary developments in industrial diversification;[22] this might be in converting primary products to secondary products or developing industry unrelated to the primary products. Thus, Section 5 could be satisfied in a variety of ways related to energy products; for instance, (i) crude oil sales could be diversified to include refinery products; (ii) fossil fuel revenues could be used to acquire renewable energy technology and sources; or (iii) separate sources of financing could support acquisition of alternative energy sources. In all manners, the path of diversification could foreseeably result in additional energy products, potentially requiring increased levels of domestic primary production to support the diversified export product lines.

To further support the lesser-developed contracting parties, the developed parties under the GATT agree to certain "commitments," or obligations.[23] Key among these obligations is to refrain from the introduction of non-tariff import barriers that might frustrate the export of primary products targeted in the previous discussions.[24] Another obligation is to improve the access to world markets for those primary products of lesser-developed parties.[25] Developed parties are obligated to undertake action to achieve international arrangements to facilitate such results if necessary; parties are encouraged to collaborate to achieve concrete measures to support long-run profitable export of those primary products.[26]

While the original intent of these terms may not have foreseen the needs of climate change mitigation efforts, it appears that the developed countries do bear commitments to protect those critical primary product exports or, under Article XXXVI, to financially support the replacement of those revenues through some means of industrial diversification.

While certain WTO parties are both developed and rich in fossil fuel resources,[27] many countries rich in such assets remain lesser-developed contracting parties to the GATT. To the extent that those countries need the revenues from the exports of their natural resources, the developed parties of the WTO have undertaken obligations to not only allow but to foster and encourage the development of such fossil fuel exports into the global markets. Given the number of lesser-developed states requiring such fossil fuel export revenues and the broader challenges of advancing their economies and standards of living, it is foreseeable that the WTO will need to continue the sustained support of expanding and ensuring the profitability of fossil fuel exports. Given those requirements, it is also reasonably foreseeable that the WTO would continue to ensure that larger supplies of fossil fuels remain on the market and that such products would be priced to remain sustainably competitive.

8.1.3 Exceptions for other situations

Article XX allows for the imposition of certain critical or necessary measures, so long as the measures themselves are not arbitrary or unjustifiable forms of trade restrictions or trade discrimination.[28] There are several measures that might apply to the export of primary products and to the energy industries.

First, if the imposed measure is necessary for the protection of human, animal, or plant life, then such a measure would not be prevented by the GATT.[29] Given the multitude of concerns about the potential impacts of climate change, it would be reasonable for some parties to present arguments that they need to implement certain measures to mitigate the overall hazards to human life, animal life, and plant life within their jurisdictions. However, while such measures might be applied internally, it appears that no power exists under the GATT to impose such measures on other contracting parties; thus, if one party was concerned about the impact of fossil fuel consumption, it might be able to reduce fossil fuel consumption within its own jurisdiction but have no ability to impose a similar measure on a third contracting party. So, if that third party wanted to produce and export fossil fuel primary products or derivative products, then the GATT would not avail a power to limit that party's choice of production; indeed, as discussed,[30] the GATT might require the first party to support that export of fossil fuel if the first party was developed and the exporting party was a lesser-developed party.

Second, if the measures are necessary to accommodate compliance with other treaties or regulations then the measures would not be prevented by the GATT, so long as those requirements and measures are not otherwise inconsistent with the requirements of the GATT.[31] Similar to the key logic in the preceding paragraph, this section would allow parties to enable their own compliance with climate change agreements or energy market agreements, but it would not enable them to expand those measures onto other unwilling parties under the GATT. This section might allow multiple parties to engage in the development and construction of coordinated climate change measures and enable their own reduction of carbon emissions, but again, such measures would first need to be not inconsistent with the goals of the GATT, and second be limited to those volitionally so motivated and not beyond. Given that the GATT requires support of primary product exports from developing parties, climate change management efforts would need to accommodate those needs as well. Indeed, the UNFCCC does call for such assistance, and the technology mechanism is an instance of such assistance,[32] but the broader requirement to improve the economic development and to improve the standard of living for those lesser-developed parties remains; it is unclear if the UNFCCC measures will result in such changes.[33]

The third and fourth measures are closely related. Third, if the measures are related to the conservation of exhaustible natural resources, then such measures would be allowed so long as they are implemented alongside similar restrictions on domestic production or consumption.[34] Fourth, if a measure is undertaken to comply with any intergovernmental commodity agreement and is not otherwise inconsistent with the requirements of the GATT, then such a measure would be allowed.[35] This is interesting in that a variety of such agreements, such as the ECT and OPEC, do exist for fossil fuel type commodities. OPEC and the ECT clearly call for larger supplies of fossil fuels at sustainable and competitive prices, goals that appear very much in line with the broader goals of the GATT. Also, while commodity exporters might be prevented from dumping oil products on other contracting parties,[36] the GATT does not appear to prevent them from self-constraining their own domestic production.[37] Broadly speaking, it is foreseeable that intergovernmental agreements on commodities, particularly commodities drawn from primary products, would be designed to increase the level of trade and export parties' revenues; thus, it is foreseeable that Article XX(h) may lead to higher levels of fossil fuel production, not less.

Ergo, while the GATT itself enables parties to undertake certain measures as general exceptions to the broader requirement of the GATT's obligations, it appears that on balance such exceptions would do little to reduce fossil fuel production, *sans* volitional agreements by the relevant parties, and foreseeably its Article XX rules could lead to increased levels of such production.

8.2 General Agreement on Trade in Services (GATS)

Energy is not only physical products; energy as an industry also includes a range of service products. This section examines the character of the General Agreements on Trade in Services for its influence on international and transboundary trade of energy products and services.

The GATS's rules apply to services rendered by a party in one member to a customer in another member.[38] It supports the efforts of members to create and enter into agreements of economic integration; such economic integration agreements both provide substantial sectorial coverage and provide for the absence or elimination of trade discrimination.[39]

Domestic regulation of service industries must be reasonable, objective, and impartial.[40] Technical standards or regulations must be based on objective and transparent criteria,[41] not be more burdensome than necessary,[42] and for licensing procedures, not be themselves a restriction on trade.[43] Also, the GATS provides for the recognition that certain business practices of service suppliers may also restrain competition that results in restrictions in trade of services.[44]

The members are obligated to support the growth and development of the domestic service capacity of developing members.[45] Key among these obligations are the requirements to liberalize market access and to liberalize the modes of supply of export interest to the developing members.[46] Due to the special economic situations, special priority is to be given to the support of least-developed members.[47] Their development, trade, and financial needs are to be taken account of in the setting of their obligations within the GATS.[48] When developing members are parties to agreements on economic integration, flexibility shall be allowed to them to support their development.[49]

Article XIV "Security Exceptions" provides for members to potentially take certain actions to support their obligations under the United Nations Charter for the maintenance of international peace and security;[50] further, members may take measures to provision a military establishment or to act in time of war or for emergencies in international relations.[51] *Arguendo*, the impacts of climate change are expected to affect international peace and security, and most members of the GATS are signatories to the UNFCCC and its subsequent accords, thus members of the GATS might reasonably be allowed to deviate from the GATS's rules to ameliorate anthropogenic climate change. Additionally, militaries are becoming increasingly responsive to imminent climate change impacts as part of their near-term planning,[52] and as such, such measures might be well permitted under the GATS.

Nothing within the GATS prevents members from adopting domestic measures to address the causes of anthropogenic climate change, but it would limit the manner in which said measures were designed; the measures must remain in support of the goals of the GATS to enable free trade in services free from trade discrimination.

8.3 Summary and tentative conclusions

There are several initial conclusions to be drawn from the last two sections and the above three chapters on the policy impacts from encouraging the development of multiple vectors of energy supply and energy security policies.

First, legal measures intended to alleviate causes of anthropogenic climate change are providing incentives to stimulate innovation and production of energy from new and renewable energy sources. It is reasonable to expect at least some progress on this front, and if so, then energy supplies will increase. Anecdotal evidence supports the hopes that green energy might soon be abundant and affordable.[53]

Second, international legal conventions exist that support the sustained production and marketing of fossil fuels. As a part of their efforts, they also provide incentives for innovations to sustain, extend, and expand the current levels of hydrocarbon production. As seen in the recent shale ('frac'ing') oil developments, and in potential offshore methane hydrates developments, it is reasonably foreseeable that these efforts will result in additional and sustained hydrocarbon energy supplies; again, anecdotal evidence reinforces this conclusion.[54]

Third, nations are pursuing energy security targets, as modern industrial nations are dependent on energy sources to sustain the scale of their economies. For example, the United States is pursuing innovation on all fronts: renewables, hydrocarbons, and nuclear energy. Very large subsidies and other incentives are provided to attain these goals; again, it is reasonably foreseeable that energy security needs will result in greater energy supplies. Anecdotal reports support that progress is being made to further develop energy supplies for security.[55]

Fourth, most of the world's economies are connected via international trade law conventions that support free trade, trade without unfair tariffs, and discrimination-free trade. Thus, it would be very difficult to control the flow of energy products for contracting parties of those conventions. Further, the WTO has certain obligations to support the export of primary products and to ensure the growth of economic development and raise the standard of living for its contracting parties, especially its lesser-developed members. As such, these legal conventions will advance the competitive markets of energy products and provide the economic mechanisms that enable market forces to regulate market results.

Clearly, the foreseeable result is the possibility that energy supplies will be expanded on a variety of fronts and that these energy products will face a fairly competitive marketplace. Given the nature of the market and the demand for energy from a growing and developing population, it is likely that more energy will be consumed; *ergo*, there is a risk that higher levels of fossil fuels will also be consumed.

8.3.1 International energy laws are driving a cornucopia of energy innovations

The previously discussed studies have shown that three major clusters of energy law or energy conventions provide incentives for energy innovations. Those energy innovations include all areas of energy sources: fossil fuels, renewable fuels, and other non-green energy sources such as nuclear fuel. Those measures are all aimed at increasing the potential amount of energy supply from targeted energy sources and ensuring that the resultant energy supplies are market competitive with other existing or emerging energy supplies.

The UNFCCC provided a framework of strategies to reduce greenhouse gas emissions by multiple approaches.[56] Energy efficiency was called for; however, energy efficiency leaves surplus energy on the market if not consumed, and the Jevons paradox has long raised doubts of whether energy efficiency ever reduced consumption.[57] Innovations in new and renewable energy sources were called for. With success, the world might soon have abundant supplies of green energy. But those energy products will be fungible and competitive with existing electrical supplies and transportation fuels; global competitive energy supplies will be increased. The prevention of methane emissions and the capture of carbon in sinks and reservoirs is laudable, but the presence of carbon sinks might serve to justify arguments that fossil fuels can be consumed safely. Many sinks and reservoirs, such as forests and wetlands, would not be directly connected to the energy user and would remain somewhat of a public good. Thus, many might claim to use what might only sustain a few in carbon absorption and storage.

The role of the ECT and of OPEC to promote hydrocarbon resources is clearly laid out.[58] Both organizations have contracting parties committed to the sustained development, production, and marketing of their petroleum and natural gas assets. They endeavor to ensure that their products remain price competitive

with substitutable goods and that their industries continue to provide reasonable returns on capital investment. They further seek to support their products in international trade. As such, it is reasonable to expect that these states will endeavor to provide continued and expanded levels of energy supplies from fossil resources.

Energy security laws are designed to provide secure sources of energy in a world of instability; it is in the nature of such provisional planning to plan for redundancy – in short to plan and provide for surplus energy supply capacity. The United States has multiple strategies that each support divergent energy sourcing options. The DOE is charged with energy innovation and reliability and provides programmatic incentives to achieve those goals.[59] The DOD has distinguishable energy security needs and operates primarily from the Defense Production Act; still, the DOD remains committed to a variety of energy innovation projects.[60] The United States' broader energy agenda, as enunciated by Congress through the tax code, provides a hodgepodge of economic incentives to petroleum energy resources, new and renewable energy sources, and alternative energy sources.[61] Given the scale of the programs and incentives, it is reasonable to expect that additional energy supplies could result.

The WTO's particular support of primary products from lesser-developed parties is of additional note, that a body ostensibly aiming for even and fair trade has taken concern to ensure that lesser-developed countries are able to export their primary products in a manner that leads to their further economic development.[62] As petroleum is a key primary product for certain lesser-developed countries, in addition to being a primary export for certain countries, the WTO system supports the growth of fossil fuels in a manner that it likely would be unable to support new and renewable energy supplies *sans* additional growth in the scope of the WTO.

Thus, the variety of energy laws reviewed demonstrates that their policy goals are to increase levels of energy supplies available to the global market and to ensure that those energy supplies are affordable to consumers. Additionally, to the extent that the consumption of most energy products is path-dependent on the installed machine base, energy source alternatives will remain compatible to current electrical and transportation fuel norms of production.[63] Thus, if the goals of those legal measures are attained, it is reasonably foreseeable that consumers would be presented with increased levels of energy supplies, that those energy supplies will be competitive goods in character and usage, and that the costs of those energy products and services would likely be competitive with one another.

8.3.2 International trade laws and market forces could result in higher consumption

International trade regimes, as exemplified by the WTO, strive to enable idealized conditions for trade: free transit of goods and services, tariff-free marketing, and the absence of market discrimination. Commodities and services can freely enter into a variety of markets; indeed, the concept of a global market is correlated with the success of the GATT parties to reach to such a high percentage of the world's states.

When all other things stay the same,[64] additional quantities of otherwise "competitive products"[65] into a common market should result in lower prices if the overall demand function also remains unchanged.[66] That lower price enables the market to clear and to consume all of the products. In this case, the products would be the whole mix of energy products, including fossil fuels and renewable energy sources. If the market did clear all of the energy products placed into it, that clearing would require the purchase and expected consumption of the fossil fuel products; such consumption would result in greenhouse gas emissions, as the fossil fuels are combusted for energy release.

8.3.3 Higher energy consumption could lead to increased greenhouse gas emissions

If only the legal measures that address the support and sustained production and future remunerative nature of fossil fuel industries are successful in their efforts, the world would likely encounter increased quantities of hydrocarbon production, at least for the next several decades, or potentially much longer.[67]

Increased consumption of those fossil fuels could result from several scenarios. First, if the global population continues to increase its standard of living,[68] it will likely have higher demands for energy. Second, if the world's population continues to increase in size, and at least maintains its current standard of living, then the additional humans would require additional energy consumption. Third, if the increased supplies were subject to traditional supply and demand analysis, then even when no increases in the demand function were to be observed, we would expect the prices of such fuels to drop until they were all purchased.[69] It is likely that standard of living will continue to improve; it is likely that the world's population will continue to increase in count, and it is likely that prices will be adjusted to ensure that the products are consumed.

Green energy innovations might not be sufficient to cure this result. First, the creation and production of highly substitutable energy sources, biofuels to replace conventional diesel, and solar plants to replace coal power plants, does not ensure the elimination of fossil fuel consumption globally but does reduce the previous consumption of those fuels, effectively rendering more fossil fuels into the marketplace, i.e., avoiding the consumption of fossil fuels effectively increases their supply for other consumers.

8.3.4 Gains in efficiency might not help

One might expect gains in energy efficiency to reduce overall energy demand by technologically requiring less energy for each task, as mandated by the UNFCCC.[70] However, gains in energy efficiency seldom result in lower levels of energy consumption. The UNFCCC and related regulatory efforts encourage the promotion of energy-efficient technologies as a complement to encouraging renewable and carbon-free energy sources.[71] The basic concept is that if engines and machines needed less energy, then less conventional fossil fuels would be consumed.

However, as Jevons first wrote nearly two centuries ago, energy efficiency does not necessarily lead to a reduction in energy demand and may well encourage increased energy demand.[72] There are several motivations for the traditional Jevons paradox and the related theories of "rebound effects."[73] While the economic phenomena related to energy efficiency, Jevons paradox, and the potential for energy efficiency to increase energy could engage very lengthy discussions,[74] the following is a quick sketch of several known related phenomena.

The inelasticity of demand plays a key role; if a market is able to absorb all of the energy provided to it at high prices, then it will likely absorb greater supplies of energy at lower prices.

Efficiency gains can create a virtual increase in supply. Considered from a unitized perspective:[75] assume a task originally took two parts of energy to complete and then was made more efficient to require only one part of energy; although the overall supply of energy was left unchanged, the user of the machine will observe twice as much supply *vis-à-vis* their operational needs. From the perspective of the consumer, energy efficiency would make the supply of energy appear increased.

Reducing the necessary energy for any particular task brings that task in range of more numerous populated but smaller energy budgets; energy efficiency puts more tasks in range of more people.[76] By enabling more people to consume energy, it is possible that energy efficiency can lead to additional economic activity and potentially economic growth.[77]

Lower prices, increases in effective supply, and reduced scale of energy needs per activity all could lead to sustained or higher levels of energy consumption. Higher energy consumption could lead to higher levels of greenhouse gas emissions.

Notes

1 General Agreement on Tariffs and Trade, Oct. 30, 1947, 61 Stat. A-11, 55 U.N.T.S. 194 [hereinafter GATT].
2 GATT, Preamble.
3 GATT, pt. I, art. I.
4 GATT, art. II.
5 GATT, pt. II, art. III, sec. 1 and 2. E.g., imposition of carbon taxes would be allowed so long as they did not provide for discriminatory effects, among other issues.
6 GATT, art. V.
7 GATT, art. XI, sec. 1.
8 GATT, art. XIII, sec. 1.
9 GATT, art. III, sec. 5–7.
10 GATT, art. XVI.
11 GATT, art. VI, sec. 1–2. Valuation of products is set out in art. VII, wherein it is set at the "actual value"; actual value is a defined term meaning the value of "like merchandise ... sold or offered for sale in the ordinary course of trade under fully competitive conditions."

12 GATT, art. XIX, sec. 1(a).
13 GATT, art. XVIII, sec. 1. *See also* GATT Annex I, Ad. art. XVIII, wherein it is clarified that the process of market correction to cure overreliance on primary production can also merit an economy as "in the early stages of development."
14 GATT, pt. II, art. XVIII, sec. 2.
15 GATT, sec. 4(a) (referencing Sections A, B, and C of art. XVIII). Many energy exporting nations are arguably such states, such as Chad.
16 Primary products include fuels and mining products, coal, crude oil, and natural gas. *See* Standard International Trade Classifications, sec. 3, div. 27, 28, 32, 33, 34, and 68, http://unstats.un.org/unsd/trade/sitcrev4.htm. *See also* World Trade Organization, *International Trade Statistics* 2011, 188–190 (2011).
17 GATT, pt. II, art. XVIII, sec. 5, with reference to art. 22.
18 GATT, pt. IV, art. XXXVI, sec. 1 and 2.
19 Crude oil, natural gas, and coal are considered primary products. WTO, *supra* note 238, 190. *See also* U.N. Dep't of Econ. & Soc. Affairs, Standard International Trade Classification, Revision 4, U.N. Doc. ST/ESA/STAT/SER.M/34/Rev.4, U.N. Sales No. E.06.XVII.10 (2006), http://unstats.un.org/unsd/publication/SeriesM/SeriesM_34rev4e.pdf (crude oil is listed at Division 33, natural gas at Division 34, and coal at Division 32).
20 GATT, pt. IV, art. XXXVI, sec. 4.
21 GATT, pt. IV, art. XXXVI, sec. 4.
22 GATT, pt. IV, art. XXXVI, sec. 5.
23 GATT, pt. IV, art. XXXVII.
24 GATT, pt. IV, art. XXXVII, sec. 1(b).
25 GATT, pt. IV, art. XXXVIII, sec. 2(a).
26 GATT, sec. 2(a) and (c).
27 E.g., Norway and the United States.
28 GATT, pt. IV.
29 GATT, pt. IV, sec.(b).
30 *See supra* section 8.1.2 (discussion on GATT's role to support development of lesser-developed primary product exporting parties).
31 GATT, pt. II, art. XX, sec.(d).
32 *See supra* section 5.3.
33 Arguably, this is the crux of OPEC's concerns on global poverty and not climate change as the premier global environmental crisis. *See supra* Part II.B.3 (discussion on OPEC's concern on global poverty).
34 GATT, pt. II, art. XX, sec.(g).
35 GATT, pt. II, art. XX, sec.(h).
36 GATT, I, art. VI.
37 On the other hand, to the extent that such Art. XX(g) "conservation efforts" measures were to be found to be adverse to the economic development of those lesser-developed parties, then the GATT might actually require the developed parties to reach out in collaboration to resolve the situation in a manner that led to greater exports and to more sustainable prices. *See* GATT, pt. IV, art. XXXVI.
38 GATS, pt. I, art. I, secs. 1 and 2.
39 GATS, pt. II, art. V, sec. 1.
40 GATS, pt. II, art. VI, sec. 1.
41 GATS, pt. II, art. VI, sec. 4(a).
42 GATS, pt. II, art. VI, sec. 4(b).
43 GATS, pt. II, art. VI, sec. 4(c).
44 GATS, pt. II, art. IX, sec. 1.
45 GATS, pt. II, art. IV, secs. 1(a), (b), and (c).
46 GATS, pt. II, art. IV, sec. 1(c).

47 GATS, pt. II, art. IV, sec. 3.
48 GATS, pt. II, art. IV, sec. 3.
49 GATS, pt. II, art. IV, art. 5, sec. 3(a).
50 GATS, pt. II, art. XIV *bis*, sec. 1(c).
51 GATS, pt. II, art. XIV *bis*, secs. 1(b)(i) and (iii).
52 *See supra* section 6.2, for discussion on the US DOD's climate change planning.
53 Researchers at Stanford University and University of California at Davis have provided an excellent review of the "feasibility of providing worldwide energy for all purposes" from wind power, solar power, and water power sources by 2030. *See* Jacobson & Delucchi (2011); *see also* Delucchi & Jacobson (2011).
54 Shale oil continues to play a substantial role in the reassessment of potential fossil fuel reserves. The largest shale oil deposit in the United States is the Green River Formation near Wyoming, Colorado, and Utah. It is estimated to contain a very large volume of recoverable petroleum. As a Rand Corporation study stated, "the midpoint in our estimate range [for the Green River Formation], 800 billion barrels, is more than triple the proven oil reserves of Saudi Arabia. Present US demand for petroleum products is about 20 million barrels per day. If oil shale could be used to meet a quarter of that demand, 800 billion barrels of recoverable resources would last for more than 400 years." Bartis et al. (2005). Similarly, the potential volumes of offshore methane hydrates range nearly 100-fold that of current conventional natural gas reserves. *See* Partain (2017).
55 For the official perspective on the "Great Green Fleet" at the core of the USN's climate change policies and its progress to achieve a fleet running on new and renewable fuels, *see* Energy, Environment and Climate Change, *US Navy*, http://greenfleet.dodlive.mil/energy/great-green-fleet/. Prior to its full-time deployment set to begin in 2016, the Great Green Fleet participated in the 2012 Rim of the Pacific (RIMPAC) offshore naval exercise, "the world's largest international maritime exercise." *Id.* For a report from progressive media on the recent developments, including coverage of that debut of the fleet in 2012, *see* Whitty (2013).
56 *See supra* sections 2.1 and 5.4.
57 For an in-depth review of the Jevons paradox and its nexus with climate change concerns, *see* Polimeni, Kozo, Giampietro, & Alcott (2009).
58 *See supra* sections 7.1 and 7.2.
59 *See supra* section 6.2.
60 *See supra* section 6.2.
61 *See supra* section 6.3.
62 *See supra* section 8.1.
63 This problem is most clearly revealed in the DOD's green energy planning. *See supra* section 6.2.
64 The economic modeling phrase of *ceteris paribus* is the targeted meaning herein.
65 The economic parlance would be 'similarly priced, highly substitutable (or *close* substitutes) goods' in lieu of 'competitive goods.'
66 Mankiw (2009), 82, *see* Table 4. *See also* Frank (2010), 37–41. In more formal terms, *see* Mas-Colell, Whinston, & Green (1995). The references here are to several popular textbooks at the undergraduate and post-graduate level of economics courses. The original concept(s) was pioneered by Alfred Marshall, who called it "scissors analysis," building on its previous discovery of "supply and demand" theory by Antoine Augustin Cournot.
67 While many might expect that hydrocarbons are running into short supply, such is not the actual case. While arguments could be presented that the costs to explore and develop crude oil assets are increasing, technology has continued to develop, and certain costs of previously unproducible hydrocarbon assets have come in

recent range. The development of the shale oil industry, colloquially referred to as "frack oil" or as "frac'ing," has dramatically reset the global markets in crude oil. Another potential hydrocarbon resource, offshore methane hydrates, were only recently the subject of pure research; however, Japanese researchers demonstrated the production potential of those resources in 2013. For an in-depth discussion on the centuries-long potential production profile of offshore methane hydrates, *see* Partain (2017).

68 A *per se* requirement of GATT and its contracting parties, *see* section 5.1.

69 This discussion is a gross simplification of the underlying economic processes required, but it makes the effort to suggest that such results and events are potential outcomes of current legal policies. It does not make an effort to prove or extensively demonstrate any sense of specific likelihoods, but instead, it merely posits that such scenarios might be feasible under current legal measures. To the extent that they are potential future risks or hazards is sufficient for the present legal analysis, no demonstration of proof or certainty is made herein.

70 *See supra* section 5.2.

71 *See supra* section 5.4.

72 "It is wholly a confusion of ideas to suppose that the economical use of fuel is equivalent to a diminished consumption. The very contrary is the truth.... [E]very ... improvement of the engine, when effected, does but accelerate anew the consumption of coal." Alcott (2005), 12.

73 The Khazzoom-Brookes postulate states that improvements in energy efficiency will increase energy consumption, *ceteris paribus*; the postulate specifically assumes fixed real energy prices. Greening, Greeneb, & Difiglio (2000), 389. As the postulate assumes no change in energy prices, the quantity demanded necessarily reflects a new demand function for energy after the achievement of energy efficiency. Greening, Greene, and Difiglio proposed a four-part typology to separate the various mechanisms responsible for the effects postulated by Khazzoom-Brookes. *Id.* at 390. They recognized the four mechanisms as (i) direct rebound effects, (ii) secondary fuel usage effects, (iii) energy market clearing mechanism effects, and (iv) transformational effects. *Id.* at 390. The authors noted that their typology took the perspective that demand for energy *cum* fuels was actually demand for a services product instead of a stock product, but for the purposes of this comment, the nuance causes no significant difference.

74 *See* Polimeni 2007.

75 In economics literature this has been described as the rebound effect of efficiency gains or as the backfire effect when policy goals of efficiency were to enable budget maintenance or reduction.

76 Assuming a Pareto distribution of income would suffice, that every level of wealth has fewer members than the level immediately below it.

77 Also known as the Khazzoom-Brookes postulate. Khazzoom and Brookes, separately and not as co-authors, provided a series of articles on the variations of this concept, e.g. in 1978, 1980, 1982, 1987, and 1989. *See* Greening, Greeneb, & Difiglio (2000), 390.

9 Choosing better policies

This chapter attempts to bring together the multiple findings presented in the last four chapters to both highlight the discovered risks and the potential policy pathways to avoid these hazards.

As will be discussed in detail later it has been recognized that certain elements of international climate change conventions have the potential to provide economic incentives that could, at least in certain time periods, lead to increases in greenhouse gas (GHG) emissions and thus worsen the likelihood of those climate change hazards. Thus, their moniker of 'green paradoxes'; that is, that climate change laws contain a potential outcome that worsen climate change conditions such as in increased greenhouse gas emissions.

If the risks of green paradoxes are considered from a perspective of international environmental law, their existence could provide foundations for the invocation of the precautionary principle to restrain the development of climate change laws to prevent the threat of climate change laws to the environment. To the extent that new international trade law conventions were to be drafted, and to the extent that such conventions might operate to worsen climate change via green paradox pathways, the precautionary principle might similarly be of concern. This is a very odd result, and again, this is a call for additional research to ensure that such risks are well understood.

Indeed, these concerns bear further research; the research challenge lies in that the consideration of green paradox models for environmental law researchers is concatenated by the addition of international trade laws to their already complex green paradox model problem sets.

International trade law has served to attain "raising standards of living, ensuring full employment ... developing the full use of the resources of the world and expanding the production and exchange of goods."[1] At the same time, the UNFCCC and similar regional and domestic enactments of legal policies have provided legal measures to prevent the anthropogenic climate risks posed by emissions of GHGs. Free trade and green energy policy; all aiming for a better tomorrow.

It appears from the models that most if not all of the drivers leading to the paradoxical policy results stem from a group of economic incentives. As such, it is in the economic marketplace that green paradoxes can best be resisted, but also best accelerated. Thus, it is important for future research to look into the complexity and confusion that would need to be managed in order to ensure that green policies actually result in green impacts. And to accomplish that, the arena of international trade law is central to providing a global response.

This chapter proceeds by first examining Sinn's own recommendations for addressing the green paradoxes that he had identified. Each one of these recommendations will be critically assessed in turn. Then, the chapter will look at the larger picture, how might policymakers engaged in energy policy, international trade policy, all with focus on supporting green energy planning, best proceed to avoid accidentally increasing the emissions of greenhouse gases; can it be achieved within the numerous legal frameworks already in place?

The chapter will conclude with a finding that green energy policies can lead to increased greenhouse emissions, but there is certainly no Hardinian "Tragedy of the Green Paradox" to speak of, that by carefully examining the complexity of the regulatory space and by keeping in mind the action-reaction systems of economic mechanisms, policymakers can hope to create new green energy policies that can fully achieve their goals of renewable and sustainable energy production.

9.1 Sinn's proposals to mitigate carbon emissions

The developing awareness of anthropogenic climate change led to the adoption of the United Nations Framework Convention on Climate Change (UNFCCC) and its Kyoto Protocol during the 1990s.[2] In 2008, Sinn took notice that under certain conditions, the legal requirements of green energy policies, when evaluated within a Hotelling-based model, could lead to increased emissions of anthropogenic greenhouse gases.[3] Sinn's forecasted effects, of increased greenhouse gas emissions due to green energy policies, have been labeled as 'green paradox' phenomena.[4] Since his seminal observations, many researchers have developed other economic models of potential green paradox phenomena.[5]

As a result of those discussions, Sinn enumerated several policies that he thought might achieve some form of GHG emissions reductions and avoid the onset of green paradox results.[6]

His policy ideas can be clustered into four basic groups: command and control policies, subsidies to fossil fuel producers, alternative tax mechanisms, and what might be called *rescued by technology* solutions.

9.1.1 Command and control of emitted carbon quantities

Sinn states that regulated quantity constraints could reduce GHG emissions without initiating green paradox problems.[7] The argument is that by explicitly delimiting the overall volumes of emitted GHG,[8] the fundamental concern of green paradoxes is addressed head-on; thus, no paradoxical accident of increased emissions. Such an approach would clearly require a sufficient scale, both transboundary and cross-temporally, to effectively limit and constrain such emissions on a global basis.[9] Also, such measures would be expected to necessitate traditional command-and-control-type regulatory powers; again, in an unusual extent of transboundary and cross-temporal application and enforcement.[10] Within this discussion, Sinn assumed the market-based allocation of tradable emission permits *cum* carbon credits to be an integral component of this approach to mitigating emissions without backfiring policy.[11]

Arguendo, carbon or other emissions are not generally perceived of as products or goods and thus might not directly fall under GATT's provisions. However, to the extent that the manufacture or transport of any other goods or products would come under rules impacted by quantitative carbon emission limits, those rules would need to comply with national treatment rules on regulation.[12] Similarly, if subsidies of one contracting party to attain production of certain goods were to enable that party to place those goods so produced at prices at odds with the anti-dumping and countervailing duties rules,[13] then such efforts to support quantitative carbon limits could be impacted by the GATT rules, and thus effect the likelihood of green paradox events. The interactions could be complex, and it might be difficult to map the correlation and causation between quantitative limits on emissions, their interactions with GATT requirements, and the ultimate impact on green paradox models.

However, as discussed within section 8.3, this is ultimately an item of coordinated policy and could be implemented within GATT mechanisms. Similarly, the EU has enacted such controls under its Kyoto Protocol Obligations;[14] thus, *arguendo*, the GATT or other large free trade zones could implement their own conventions in support of enforcing quantitative limits to GHG emissions, so long as those agreements remained in alignment with the underlying trade agreements.

9.1.2 Subsidies to fossil fuel producers

There are two ideas clustered within this group; subsidies to *not produce* fossil fuels and to enhance property rights to fossil fuel assets.[15] By providing economic subsidies to the fossil fuel producers to not produce fossil fuels,[16] the argument runs that the fossil fuel producers could be provided incentives to reduce their overall level of production and thus limit emissions of GHGs.[17]

Next, the potential to avoid a panic by fossil fuel producers to produce more quickly while they still retain control over those assets could be furthered by improvements to their property rights in those assets,[18] including the rights to future economic values if otherwise diminished by green emission policies. *Arguendo*, Sinn is recognizing that green policies might effect a 'takings' in property rights from the fossil fuel asset owners. By better securing their economic rights, the fossil fuel producers would not face certain economic incentives to produce and deplete prior to such green 'takings' or other forms of asset loss.[19]

Clearly, certain subsidies are *per se* controlled under GATT.[20] Subsidies that operate to directly or indirectly increase exports or reduce imports of any product or good are required to be reported to the contracting parties.[21] Should those reported subsidies be found to create 'serious prejudice,' then the parties are advised to limit the subsidization.[22]

Prima facie, it would not appear that Article XVI rules would prevent subsidies to fossil fuel producers if the subsidies were effectively targeted at reducing exports of those fuels. *Arguendo*, if the subsidies were created as property acquisitions, such as national acquisitions of the minerals in place, the policy effects might not even be properly characterized as subsidies.[23] Thus, if sufficient international alignment enabled falling petroleum prices as fossil fuels were banned, then domestic subsidies to prevent a 'property rights taking' from those producers could arguably be enabled under GATT.

Also, nothing within GATT would appear to prevent nations or other parties without a specific contracting party from acquiring those in-place mineral rights or from subsidizing such fossil fuel producers by contracting with those producers in exchange for monetary payments.

9.1.3 Alternative tax mechanisms

Sinn's original green paradox model was built on rising carbon taxes that provided the economic incentive to produce fossil fuels in an earlier time period of lower taxes;[24] by reversing the model to implementing decreasing carbon taxes, the incentives work to defer fossil fuel production into future time periods.[25] This particular model makes near-term fossil fuels expensive *vis-à-vis* future time periods and putatively provides price-competitive incentives for near-term green energy producers, but one wonders if those incentives would not also be akin to the concerns raised earlier under the topic of energy substitutes for fossil fuels.[26]

Partially because Sinn was concerned that a decreasing carbon tax would be difficult to implement,[27] he also noted that a unit tax on carbon mass would also suppress carbon production without providing incentives in support of green paradox models. However, the correct calculation of such a unit tax to avoid green paradox incentives requires an accurate internalization of the externalities of climate change harms,[28] which might be difficult to define politically and economically.

Finally, Sinn presented an argument to close tax havens, to tax "man-made" capital gains, but to leave the capital gains of natural resource owners untaxed.[29] But Sinn conceded that it would "not be easy to calculate such a tax in practice."[30] Also, given Sinn's precautionary advice on easing the fossil fuel owners' concerns on property rights to future income,[31] one wonders how that might square *vis-à-vis* the proposed action on tax havens.

GATT's focus on tax policy is to ensure that domestic tax regulations do not provide unfair advantages to domestic products or unfair disadvantages against imported products.[32] Imported goods should not be taxed in excess of domestic products.[33] But nothing would appear to prevent the implementation of domestic production taxes against domestically produced fossil fuels; further, such practices are currently in place within contracting parties without dispute. Within the US, many oil and natural gas producing states have a variety of production tax systems.[34] Nor would GATT appear to bear on the manner of domestic taxation on domestic production, so any of the earlier-proposed schemes would be equally of no consequence under GATT rules.

To avoid a repetition on the potential to coordinate the domestic policies of contracting parties via the GATT or other trade organizations, reference is encouraged to the discussions earlier.

9.1.4 Rescued by technology

If strategies to reduce GHG emissions are not available, then various technologies to otherwise absorb and prevent the continued presence of atmospheric carbon could be employed to prevent green paradox events.

Sinn described carbon capture and sequestration (CCS) and afforestation as a "unique opportunity" to delink the levels of fossil fuel production and resultant GHG emissions,[35] as such, they represent a 'magic bullet' for preventing green paradox phenomena. However, due to the technological challenges and potential risk associated with CCS, Sinn did not pin much hope on CCS to ameliorate green paradox hazards.[36] Other scholars would disagree with Sinn, holding that CCS is closely related to technologies already employed in the petroleum sector for decades and that has been found to readily absorb CO_2 when injected.[37]

Similarly, Sinn recognized that then-current trends suggested that forests were shrinking and not enlarging, limiting the likely potential of afforestation to provide relief against carbon emissions.[38]

Nevertheless, despite Sinn's caveats, the argument remains accurate, if technologies such as CCS or afforestation could be widely and sufficiently implemented, then green paradox results could be averted. This is perhaps the most viable recommendation made by Sinn, although he himself placed less reliance on it.

9.2 Could international trade law govern green paradox phenomena?

To grapple with green paradox models and their potential interactions with international trade law, it would be critical to first capture and describe in less mathematical terms what causes such results, what might avoid such results, and concerns on their inevitability.

Most simply stated, green paradox phenomena occur when green climate policies provide economic incentives for fossil fuel producers to increase production volumes and to thus enable higher levels of GHG emissions.

As a means to avoid green paradox pathways, a policymaker could avoid the seminal causes that lead to those counterproductive incentives, could implement alternative green climate policies that *a priori* do not provide such perverse incentives, and could take consideration of whether those strategies are in fact implementable. These options are reviewed later in the chapter.

While the roots of the models developed by the environmental economists appear highly nuanced and mathematically motivated, the collection of models can be made approachable for policymakers by identifying the quintessential concerns of the underlying assumptions of those models.

From the discussions in earlier chapters, the seminal causes of green paradox phenomena can be identified; thus identified they might be avoided by careful trade law policies. There are broadly three main concerns that give rise to increased GHG emissions: competitive pressure on fossil fuel products, lack of policy coordination, and attainment of energy-efficient technologies.

Hereunder is a review of how international trade laws might be engaged to resist or prevent increases in carbon emissions.

9.2.1 Competitive pressure on fossil fuels

First, increased GHG emissions are expected when fossil fuel products face pressure from competitive substitutable energy products. The logic herein is that given a limited time frame and the existence of impending or increasing competition from other energy products, the producers of fossil fuels would act to increase production and sales before they are displaced from the market. These forms of competitive and displacing energy products could be from clean backstops such as solar voltaic products or wind power products. They might include gray backstops such as fissile nuclear energy, which has minimal GHG emissions but presents other environmental concerns. They might also include, as noted by Heal, a variety of dirty backstop technologies such as tar sands or shale oils.

Generally speaking, the General Agreement on Trade and Tariffs (GATT) agreements have served to promote the free trade of goods and products free of various impediments or restraints to trade.[39] For example, all members are to receive 'most favored nation status' once becoming contracting parties;[40] products and goods are to be treated equivalently to domestic products and goods;[41] goods, products, and even transportation equipment are to be availed of free transit;[42] among a host of other rules to protect and facilitate free trade. Thus, should any contracting party possess products or goods that could serve as substitutes or as competitive alternatives to fossil fuels, then those alternative energy products should benefit from the free trade rules afforded under the GATT. As discussed earlier, additional competition against fossil fuels from alternative energy products would increase the likelihood of increased GHG emissions; thus, the free trade rules of GATT could facilitate the problems expected from the green paradox models.

In what might seem at first a bit like "through the looking-glass"[43] to readers familiar with the existing literature on the interface of climate change laws and international trade laws, efforts to mitigate the effects of a green paradox model look to GATT to determine when GATT could support the suppression of free trade in green energy products to prevent green paradoxical increased GHG emissions.

Thus, traditional strategies to coordinate green industrial policies with GATT rules can read upside down when addressing green paradox concerns. For example, recalling that the models suggest that additional competitive pressure on fossil fuels could lead to pathways that increase GHG emissions, Article XX strategies could be suggested to limit the application of GATT rules to green energy products.[44]

If green paradox results are worthy of precautionary principle concerns,[45] then perhaps Article XX(b) could be invoked to address the needs of "human, animal, or plant life or health."[46] Article XX(d) could provide an argument that if contracting parties of GATT were also bound by climate change conventions, such as the UNFCCC, and if those two sets of rules were not inconsistent in purpose, then the contracting parties could accommodate the climate change conventions in restricting the application of GATT.[47] Article XX(g), relating to the conservation of exhaustible resources, could be invoked if policies to limit trade of green energy products were to be coordinated with other domestic policies to restrict domestic production or consumption of similar resources.[48]

Thus, while Article XX could be leveraged to mitigate the results of competitive green energy products within a green paradox model context, the overall legal approach is similar to pre-existing literature on coordinating green industrial policies with GATT rules, except that in the green paradox model context it is the results of green industrial policy that are the target of restricted trade and not the products of fossil fuels.

9.2.2 *Improve on transboundary and cross-temporal policy coordination*

Second, incoherent, incongruous, or inconsistent policies on limiting GHG emissions, either amidst multiple nations or across multiple time periods, provides incentives for emissions to relocate from one space to another space. When this movement is more geographical in character, it is often known as international carbon leakage;[49] when more temporal in nature, it tends to be identified as a green paradox.

Temporal instances of this concept include delayed policy models, raising carbon tax models, and general multi-period models. Delayed policy models examine the effects of announcing an emissions-limiting policy that is to be applied only in future time periods; thus, a fossil fuel producer would need to react by optimizing their sales, and thus increasing emissions, prior to the onset of those policies. Carbon taxes could be implemented to rise over time in order to provide increasing disincentives to produce fossil fuels; however, such taxes would provide economic incentives to reschedule production volumes of fossil fuels to earlier periods of lower tax rates. If taxes were set to rise to a point that would make the sales of fossil fuels infeasible, then the producers would be expected to produce as much as they could prior to that point; again, emissions would be expected to soar in the short term prior to that specific tax date. Multi-period models explore more complicated but similar paradigms to the two prior explanations and find that later-period policies that frustrate fossil fuel producers provide incentives for those producers to bring forward in time production volumes; again, if those frustrations might eliminate the economic value of their investments in fossil fuel production assets, then those producers might be faced with a rush to produce as much as they can prior to some termination date.

GATT provides for the coordination and publication of a variety of trade-related policies.[50] GATT also enables coordinated policy responses to respond to the needs of its lesser-developed contracting parties.[51] Joint action is required of the contracting parties and can enable the GATT agreements to evolve by amendment or otherwise.[52] Such amendments need not be accepted by all existing contracting parties, as a two-thirds majority of the contracting parties suffice to enact an amendment for those parties agreeing to it;[53] such flexibility could enable concerned parties to move forward and avoid stagnation on the central issues. Thus, the GATT does enable its contracting parties to adopt measures that could both exacerbate and relieve scenarios associated with green paradox models.

Somewhat at odds with the traditional idea of green industrial policies, the GATT has certain provisions aimed at assisting the development of lesser-developed contracting parties, which in turn might *arguendo* be useful in the protection of primary products such as fossil fuel exports.[54] Yet, these requirements are complex to interpret in the face of green paradox models, as the ultimate requirement is to facilitate the economic development away from such simple reliance on limited numbers of primary products[55] and thus could portend a variety of industrial options to develop more integrated products, both fossil fuel and alternative energy related. For example, the GATT requirements could be met by integrating crude primary fossil fuel products into more sophisticated products, such as plastics, or by assisting the development of alternative production structures such as photovoltaic plants.[56]

9.2.3 Cautious implementation of energy efficiency

Third, energy efficiency can lead to green paradox results by effectively increasing the supply of all energy stocks,[57] because less are needed by the new efficient technologies, and placing economic pressure on fossil fuels to be more price competitive.[58] Additionally, energy efficiency itself could be seen as a competitive substitute to the fossil fuels already scheduled to reach the marketplace and thus could repeat the analysis of the first argument.

To the extent that energy efficiency is embodied in a good or product, similar arguments can be made, as in the case of fossil fuel substitute products, that the fundamental purpose of GATT is to facilitate the potential of free trade and as such could lead to the exacerbation of green model scenarios.[59]

Thus, the encouragement and/or subsidization of energy efficiency policies should be handled with a similar approach to handling surplus green energy supplies that could result in price competition with fossil fuels to better prevent increased levels of fossil fuel combustion from resultant gains in energy efficiency. Such measures might include *per se* quantity limits on fossil fuel energy supplies as efficiency gains are measured, or to otherwise require that any reported gains in energy efficiency are tracked for potentially correlated increases in carbon emissions with complementary requirements to carbon offset any such detected emissions.

9.3 Green paradox models bowed but not broken

Sinn was clearly convinced that both green paradox models demonstrated the potential for increased GHG emissions and that those effects were likely inevitable. However, recent research, including this book, has made his first assumption less secure and thus provided a measure of skepticism of whether green paradox models are accurate models of real-world GHG emissions scenarios.[60]

The results of that research suggested that many, potentially a majority, of the recently published green paradox models relied on unrealistic assumptions or assumptions counter to the original underlying models of exhaustible resources as developed by Hotelling, Dasgupta, and Heal.[61]

Thus, those models of green paradox phenomena cannot be relied upon; other models need to be developed to more effectively provide testable or falsifiable results to ascertain the actual pathways for increased GHG emissions from green climate policies.

Let it be clearly stated that the findings of the aforementioned research did not conclude that models of green paradoxes were disproven, far from it; rather, they concluded that a subset of current models were unlikely to be able to prove the existence of green paradox phenomena.[62] And as such, better models are needed.[63]

Nevertheless, green-paradox-type results are a reasonably foreseeable set of consequences of current energy policies. By extending the paradigm of green paradox models to include other co-existing yet potentially contrary energy policies, the potential for green energy laws to adversely interact with other energy agendas to create green-paradox-like conditions can be demonstrated as fairly probable in likelihood.[64] The conflict of fossil fuel producers and consumers, with their international conventions, and of advocates of climate change mitigation, with their international conventions, alongside those countries with substantial energy security concerns and their domestic legislations, makes for a potent and wasteful brew of energy policies, one certain to increase energy supplies and offer pathways to increased GHG emissions.[65]

There is a reasonable likelihood that increased GHG emissions would result under the broader inclusion of multiple energy policies, and there are reasonable concerns that even climate change laws themselves may provide sufficient incentives to increase GHG emissions. It is time to recognize that complexity can bedevil even the best of intents. But it is also clear from the earlier discussions that the interactions of international trade laws on conditions conducive to emergent green paradox events may compound those concerns.

In summation, without improved alignment in energy agendas and more sophisticated understandings on the interactive results of climate change policies, increased GHG emissions will remain a foreseeable consequence of current policies.

9.4 Conclusion – better choices in innovation

What the world needs to avoid green paradox type results are better choices in innovation; as said by others, "the Stone Age did not end for a lack of stones."[66]

Thus, in the present situation, without some form of change in law and legal conventions, the world is faced with the imminent possibility of increased greenhouse gas emissions as additional energy supplies from both fossil fuels and new and renewable energy sources respond to the incentive to innovate. There are several ways to prevent this from happening.

First, the existing laws and legal conventions could be altered, and such efforts are indeed in progress. The UN hoped for a major update to the UNFCCC in 2015 at what was once referred to as Paris 2015.[67] However, it is already some three plus decades since the international legal negotiations have been underway, starting with the original talks that led to the UNFCCC itself. Major economies have recently reduced their engagement with certain UNFCCC/Kyoto targets, namely Australia and Canada. Another major economy, the United States, never joined in the Kyoto obligations, nor now, in the Paris Agreements.[68] The world remains without a united governance paradigm to achieve global reductions in greenhouse gases.

Second, failing to achieve coordinated measures, governments might attempt unilateral movements in domestic legal measures to try to cobble together movement towards reductions in greenhouse gas emissions. Such efforts have been undertaken, indeed much of the green policies in place – certainly those of the United States – have been undertaken from such a perspective. However, any effort to provide incentives for green energy innovation *sans* other acts of energy law coordination merely adds to global energy supplies as discussed in this book[69] and perhaps enables international carbon leakage problems.[70]

Third, the general public could be persuaded to shift their priorities and consumption preferences to create stronger market demand for new and renewable energy products. An example of such an effort is Al Gore's slideshow *cum* book *cum* movie *An Inconvenient Truth* and its worldwide media coverage, which ensured that most people today are aware to some extent of the issues.[71] However, as green energy products are designed as close substitutes for traditional energy products, their consumption might merely relocate the consumption of fossil fuels to those consumers either unaware or indifferent to the concerns of climate change, and indeed, some might be prioritizing purchases of green energy products; but nowhere are fossil fuels abandoned, nowhere are there piles of fuel abandoned for use.[72]

So the best answer is hidden in that simple term of 'perfect substitutes.' As long as the green energy innovations are designed and implemented as mere substitutes, they will not be effective at eliminating fossil fuels from the marketplace but will merely enable the continued means of fuel and energy delivery. As long as the systems remain similar, and as long as the relevant parties remain engaged in maintaining and sustaining price competitiveness, the price of fossil fuels will only face pressure to drop and thus become available for a greater range of consumption options.

Perfect substitutes lead to competition, which can only be won on pricing, *ceteris paribus.* And given the natural monopoly tendencies of most petroleum fields, with decreasing average costs of production, those green substitutes will likely also need to feature similar characteristics to the model of natural monopolies.

Ergo, the innovations that are needed are either those innovations that so transform the cost structure of new and renewable energy sources as to make them consistently preferable to the substantial totality of global customers, i.e., likely those technologies that enable natural monopoly type costs of energy supplies, and those innovations that would make the character of new and renewable energy sources so sufficiently superior that few would want to consume fossil fuels.

Instead of simply attempting to encourage all new and renewable energy alternatives, energy policies that encourage innovation should be focused on these two agendas: (i) dominant cost superiority and (ii) dominant energy character. More energy, more readily accessed, at lower costs, all while providing superior environmental and climate protection.

Focusing on those policies that seek to squeeze fossil energy out from one area will only encourage its consumption elsewhere. Policies that attempt to deny the property rights of those that currently own and derive their livelihoods from those resources is also ethically and practically fraught with complexity and other hazards.[73] New technologies that accomplish the task better and at cheaper costs displace the old technologies. The world needs those innovations in energy; legal measures to suppress fossil fuels likely will not work.

Does the world need an era of *fossil fuel prohibitionism*? Or, should the world seek better choices? The answer lies in better choices.

The goal for green energy policies should be to help green and renewable energy options to outcompete fossil fuels on attributes of use and on costs to consumers. Just as cars displaced horse-drawn buggies, some consumers may still prefer the 'elegance of a gas lit fire' for some purposes, but with superior market choices, the market will simply move on from fossil fuels to green and renewable energy choices.

The best green energy choices will pull us into the future, and not the other way around.

Notes

1 GATT Preamble.
2 The Framework Convention was a direct result of the first assessment report on climate change from the Intergovernmental Panel on Climate Change ("IPCC"). See *Background on the UNFCCC: The International Response to Climate Change*, United Nations Framework Convention on Climate Change, http://unfccc.int/essential_background/items/6031.php (last visited Nov. 6, 2014).
3 Sinn (2008), 366–369, 389–392.
4 Sinn provides the earliest description of green paradox results in Sinn (2008). Section 2, 364, and in Section 4 he provided Figure 1 labeling a pathway as a 'green paradox.' *See id.* at 375. However, it is in Section 5 that he provided the nomenclature of 'green policy paradoxes' and explained its meaning. Sinn (2008), 377–382.
5 For a discussion of a variety of green paradox models, *see supra* section 2.4 and Chapter 3.

6 Sinn lists four strategies under his section 6 but breaks out six strategies in his concluding remarks. Sinn (2008), 382 and 388.
7 Sinn (2008), 385 and 388.
8 Sinn signals that his suggestion herein follows the model of the Kyoto Protocol. Sinn (2008), 385.
9 "This can best be done with a complete system of emissions license trading … that spans the world and incorporates all countries." Sinn (2008), 385.
10 "The big problem is the completeness of the trading system." Sinn (2008), 385. Sinn detailed that the then-in-place Kyoto Protocol addressed only 29% of the annual global carbon supply. Sinn (2008), 386.
11 Sinn (2008), 385–387.
12 *See* GATT Pt. II, Art. III, sec. 1 and 4.
13 *See* GATT Pt. II, Art. IV, sec. 1 (a)–(b).
14 For adoption of the UNFCCC, *see* 94/69/EC: Council Decision of 15 December 1993 concerning the conclusion of the United Nations Framework Convention on Climate Change. O.J. (L 33), 11. For adoption of the Kyoto Protocol, *see* 2002/358/EC: Council Decision of 25 April 2002 concerning the approval, on behalf of the EC, of the Kyoto Protocol to the United Nations Framework Convention on Climate Change and the joint fulfillment of commitments thereunder, O.J. (L 130), 1. *See also* Decision No 280/2004/EC of the European Parliament and of the Council of 11 February 2004 concerning a mechanism for monitoring Community GHG emissions and for implementing the Kyoto Protocol. O.J. (L 49). 1. See also Decision No 280/2004/EC of the European Parliament and of the Council of 11 February 2004 concerning a mechanism for monitoring Community GHG emissions and for implementing the Kyoto Protocol, O.J. (L 49). 1.
15 *See* Sinn's sections 6.1.3 and 6.2. Sinn (2008), 383–385.
16 Sinn (2008), 383–384.
17 A similar notion, not stated by Sinn, is that nations could simply begin to acquire fossil assets in place as a form of strategic assets. In this application, the asset is the prevention of climate change in addition to potential extraction in energy emergencies.
18 Sinn (2008), 385.
19 Sinn (2008), 385.
20 Most notably at GATT Pt. II, Art. XVI, sec. 1; however, subsidy effects could be in play within Pt. II. Art. III and Pt. II, Art. VI.
21 GATT Pt. II, Art. XVI, sec. 1.
22 GATT Pt. II, Art. XVI, sec. 1.
23 *See* GATT Annex I, Ad Art. XVI, para. 3 enables a contracting party to stabilize a domestic price or return for domestic producers of a primary product without application of the subsidy rules under certain limited exceptions. There is a reasonable argument that if the contracting party provided assistance to secure returns to domestic producers as the international price of a primary mineral product (ad Art. XVI, sec. B.2.) sank below domestic prices, that such subsidy supports could be allowed under GATT.
24 *See supra* in section 3.1.
25 Sinn refers to a "decreasing ad valorem tax rate." Sinn (2008), 382.
26 *See supra* in section 3.2.
27 He actually described the unit tax as a "better way to achieve a similar result." For the present purposes, it is not necessary to investigate the validity of that claim; it suffices to note that the unit tax suppresses carbon production *sans* creation of green paradox incentives. Sinn (2008), 383.
28 *See* Sinn's third paragraph of section 6.1.2. Sinn (2008), 383.
29 Sinn (2008), 384–385.

30 Sinn (2008), 384.
31 *See* discussion above in section 4.2.2.
32 GATT Pt. II, Art. III, sec. 1.
33 GATT Pt. II, Art. III, sec. 2.
34 See Alaska's production tax system at AS 43.55 and 15 AAC 55; see Texas's production tax systems at Title II, "State Taxation," sec. 202 et seq. for crude oil, and at sec. 201 et seq. for natural gas.
35 Sinn (2008), 387.
36 Sinn provided four concerns that could frustrate the implementation of CCS to prevent green paradox results. Sinn (2008), 387.
37 Notably, the author of this book has written extensively on this topic. *See* Faure & Partain (2017), Partain & Faure (2017), and Partain (2019).
38 He notes that the world loses forest coverage roughly equivalent to an Ireland and a half every year. Sinn (2008), 387.
39 GATT, *en passim*. *See* its Preamble, *see* also Pt. IV, Art. XXXVI, sec. 1(a), and (d)–(e) as to the basic objectives of the GATT.
40 GATT, Pt. I, Art. I.
41 GATT, Pt. I, Art. III.
42 GATT, Pt. I, Art. V.
43 Lewis Carrol, *Through the Looking-Glass, and What Alice Found There* (1871), which was the sequel to Carrol's *Alice's Adventures in Wonderland* (1865).
44 GATT, Pt. II, Art. XX.
45 *See* the discussion below on Sinn's concerns that not only are the results of green paradox models possible but likely inevitable, section 4.2. If green paradox events merit that level of concern then *arguendo* a nation might be justified in applying the precautionary principle to those acts that facilitate green paradox events, such as the trade of fossil fuel substitutes as evaluated here.
46 GATT, Pt. II, Art. XX(b).
47 GATT, Pt. II. Art. XX(d).
48 GATT, Pt. II, Art. XX(g).
49 International carbon leakage was identified a couple decades prior to the broader pattern of green paradoxes by Sinn, and as such, those models often retain their earlier moniker of international carbon leakage.
50 For example, the trading terms that enable the evaluation of receipt of Art. I Most-Favored Nation treatment, of Art. II's Schedule of Concessions, or of Art. III's National Treatment all require substantial disclosures to the body of contracting parties to enable coordination under the GATT.
51 GATT, Pt. II, Art. XVIII and Pt. IV, Art. XXXVI.
52 GATT, Pt. III, Art. XXV "Joint Action by the Contracting Parties" and Art. XXX, "Amendments".
53 GATT, Pt. III, Art. XXX(1).
54 GATT pt II, Art. XVIII, sec. 5, and see also Pt. IV, Art. XXXVI, sec. 4.
55 The economic health of such states being facilitated by the "avoidance of excessive dependence on export of primary products" and the "diversification of the structure of their economies." *See* Pt. IV, Art. XXXVI, sec. 5.
56 GATT, Pt. IV, Art. XXXVI, sec. 5.
57 *See* the discussion on the Jevons paradox, *supra* section 5.2.
58 In no way does this book suggest the avoidance of energy-efficient technologies; there are sound policy justifications for energy efficiency apart from emissions abatement strategies, e.g., energy efficiency leads to greater public welfare, *ceteris paribus* and *sans souci* for emission concerns. However, this study does evaluate the potential impact of such policies on the generation of green paradox phenomena.

59 *See* the discussion on competitive pressure applied on fossil fuels, *supra* section 3.2.
60 *See supra*, section 4.6.
61 *See supra*, sections 4.4 and 4.5.
62 *See supra*, section 4.6.
63 *See supra*, section 4.6.
64 For a study on how international trade laws (such as GATT), energy trade laws (such as OPEC or the Energy Charter), energy security laws (such as the US's Defense Production Act, 50 U.S.C. App. § 2061 et seq.), and climate change laws (such as required under the Kyoto Protocol), see Partain, at note 136.
65 *See supra*, section 8.3.
66 "The Stone Age did not end for lack of stone, and the Oil Age will end long before the world runs out of oil." Often attributed to Sheikh Zaki Yamani. *See* The End of the Oil Age, *The Economist* (Oct. 23, 2003), www.economist.com/node/2155717.
67 See 21st Conference of the Parties on Climate Change 2015, *France Diplomatie* (July 14, 2014), www.diplomatie.gouv.fr/en/french-foreign-policy-1/climate-7436/2015-paris-climate-conference/. *See also* Nick Nuttall, Negotiations towards New Universal Climate Agreement in 2015 Get Underway, *UNFCCC* (Mar. 14, 2014), http://unfccc.int/files/press/press_releases_advisories/application/pdf/20141403_adpclose.pdf.
68 For an earlier assessment on the limits of the American government to agree to international climate accords, *see* Partain & Lee (2013).
69 *See supra* Chapter 5.
70 For a discussion on international carbon leakage, *see* section 3.4.
71 *See* Al Gore, *An Inconvenient Truth: The Planetary Emergency of Global Warming and What We Can Do about It* (Rodale Press, Emmaus, PA, 2006). *See also* Kakutani's review of the book, Michiko Kakutani, Al Gore Revisits Global Warming, With Passionate Warnings and Pictures, *N.Y Times* (May 23, 2006), www.nytimes.com/2006/05/23/books/23kaku.html?pagewanted=all&_r=0.
72 Details on the potential for oil prices to drop much further and remain above their marginal costs of production are discussed in section 4.3.6.
73 Sinn was very concerned with this topic of property rights and their impact on accelerated depletion rates. Sinn (2008), 385.

References

10.1 A

Adelman, Morris A. “Mineral depletion, with special reference to petroleum.” *The Review of Economics and Statistics* (1990): 1–10.

Adelman, Morris Albert & Gordon Campbell Watkins, Reserve Prices and Mineral Resource Theory, 29 *The Energy Journal* 1, 5–6 (2008).

Alcott, B., Jevons’ Paradox, 54(1) *Ecological Econ.* 9, 12 (2005).

Arrow, Kenneth, Partha Dasgupta, Lawrence Goulder, Gretchen Daily, Paul Ehrlich, Geoffrey Heal, Simon Levin, Karl-Göran Mäler, Stephen Schneider, David Starrett, & Brian Walker, Are We Consuming Too Much?, 18 *J. Econ. Persp.* 147, 168 (2004).

10.2 B

Bartis, James T., et al., *Oil Shale Development in the United States: Prospects and Policy Issues ix* Rand Corporation (2005).

Bengtsson, Lennart, et al., Pontifical Academy of Sciences, *Fate of Mountain Glaciers in the Anthropocene* 7 (2011).

Burniaux, Jean-Marc & Joaquim Oliveira Martins, Carbon Leakages: A General Equilibrium View, 49 *Econ. Theory* 473 (2012).

10.3 C

Cairns, Robert D., The Green Paradox of the Economics of Exhaustible Resources, 65 *Energy Pol’y* 78, 80 (2014).

Campbell, Richard J., Cong. Research Serv., RL41748, China and the United States: A Comparison of Green Energy Programs and Policies (2014).

Carrol, Lewis, *Alice’s Adventures in Wonderland* (1865).

Carrol, Lewis, *Through the Looking-Glass, and What Alice Found There* (1871).

10.4 D

Dasgupta, Partha & Geoffrey Heal, The Optimal Depletion of Exhaustible Resources, 41 *Rev. Econ. Stud.* 3, 5–6 (1974).

Delucchi, Mark A. & Mark Z. Jacobson, Providing All Global Energy with Wind, Water, and Solar Power, Part II: Reliability, System and Transmission Costs, and Policies, 39 *Energy Policy* 1170 (2011).

Devarajan, Shantayanan & Anthony C. Fisher, Hotelling's "Economics of Exhaustible Resources": Fifty Years Later, 19 *J. Econ. Literature* 65 (1981).

Di Maria, Corrado, Sjak Smulders, & Edwin van der Werf, Absolute Abundance and Relative Scarcity: Environmental Policy with Implementation Lags, 74 *Ecological Econ.* 104 (2012).

10.5 E

Eichner, Thomas & Rüdiger Pethig, Carbon Leakage, the Green Paradox, and Perfect Future Markets, 52 *Int'l Econ. Rev.* 767 (2011).

The End of the Oil Age, *The Economist* (Oct. 23, 2003), www.economist.com/node/2155717

10.6 F

Faure, Michael G. & Roy A. Partain, *Carbon Capture and Storage: Efficient Legal Policies for Risk Governance and Compensation* Cambridge, Massachusetts, USA (MIT Press, Mar. 2017).

Fischer, Carolyn & Stephen W. Salant, *Limits to Limiting Greenhouse Gases: Intertemporal Leakage, Spatial Leakage, and Negative Leakage* 2–5 (May 9, 2013) (unpublished paper), http://citeseerx.ist.psu.edu/viewdoc/summary?doi=10.1.1.384.1648

Frank, Robert H., *Microeconomics and Behavior*, Eighth Edition (New York: McGraw-Hill, 2010).

10.7 G

Gaudet, Gérard, Natural Resource Economics under the Rule of Hotelling, 40 *Can. J. Econ.* 1033, 1037 (2007).

Gerlagh, Reyer, Too Much Oil, 57 *CESifo Econ. Stud.* 79 (2011).

Gore, Al, An Inconvenient Truth: The Planetary Emergency of Global Warming and What We Can Do about It (2006).

Grafton, R. Quentin, Tom Kompas, & Ngo Van Long, Substitution between Biofuels and Fossil Fuels: Is There a Green Paradox?, 64 *J. Envtl. Econ. & Mgmt.* 328 (2012).

Greening, Lorna A., David L. Greeneb, & Carmen Difiglio, Energy Efficiency and Consumption: The Rebound Effect: A Survey, 28(6–7) *Energy Pol.* 389, 389 (2000).

Gronwald, Marc, A Characterization of Oil Price Behavior: Evidence from Jump Models, 34 *Energy Econ.* 1310, 1314–1316 (2012).

10.8 H

Habermacher, Florian & Gebhard Kirchgässner, *Climate Effects of Carbon Taxes, Taking into Account Possible Other Future Climate Measures* (CESifo Working Paper No. 3404, 2011).

Halvorsen, Robert & Tim R. Smith, A Test of the Theory of Exhaustible Resources, 106 *Q. J. Econ.* 123, 126–128 (1991).

Hardin, Garrett, The Tragedy of the Commons, 162(3859) *Science* 1243–1248 (1968).

Harstad, Bård, Buy Coal! A Case for Supply-Side Environmental Policy, 120 *J. Pol. Econ.* 77 (2012).

Heal, Geoffrey, The Relationship between Price and Extraction Cost for a Resource with a Backstop Technology, 7 *Bell J. Econ.* 371, 372–377 (1976).

Heal, Geoffrey, Reflections: The Economics of Renewable Energy in the United States, 4 *Rev. Envtl. Econ. & Pol'y* 139, 140 (2010).

Hidalgo, César A. & Ricardo Hausmann, The Building Blocks of Economic Complexity, 106 *Proc. Nat'l Acad. Sci.* 10570 (2009).

Hoel, Michael, Global Environmental Problems: The Effects of Unilateral Actions Taken by One Country, 20 *J. Envtl. Econ. & Mgmt.* 55 (1991).

Hoel, Michael, The Green Paradox and Greenhouse Gas Reducing Investments, 5 *Int'l Rev. Envtl. & Resource Econ.* 353 (2011).

Hoel, Michael, The Supply Side of CO2 with Country Heterogeneity, 113 *Scandinavian J. Econ.* 846 (2011).

Hoel, Michael, Carbon Taxes and the Green Paradox, in *Climate Change and Common Sense: Essays in Honor of Tom Schelling* (R. W. Hahn & A. Ulph, eds., Oxford University Press, UK 2012).

Hoel, Michael & Svenn Jensen, Cutting Costs of Catching Carbon: Intertemporal Effects Under Imperfect Climate Policy, 34 *Resource & Energy Econ.* 680 (2012).

Hotelling, Harold, Stability in Competition, 41 *Econ. J.* 41 (1929).

Hotelling, Harold, The Economics of Exhaustible Resources, 39 *J. Pol. Econ.* 137, 138 (1931).

10.10 J

Jacobson, Mark Z. & Mark A. Delucchi, Providing All Global Energy with Wind, Water, and Solar Power, Part I: Technologies, Energy Resources, Quantities and Areas of Infrastructure, and Materials, 39 *Energy Policy* 1154 (2011).

Jakobsson, Kristopher, Roger Bentley, Bengt Söderbergh, & Kjell Aleklett, The End of Cheap Oil: Bottom-Up Economic and Geologic Modeling of Aggregate Oil Production Curves, 41 *Energy Pol'y* 860, 861 (2012).

10.11 K

Kakutani, Michiko, Al Gore Revisits Global Warming, with Passionate Warnings and Pictures, *N.Y Times* (May 23, 2006), www.nytimes.com/2006/05/23/books/23kaku.html?pagewanted=all&_r=0

Park, Alex, Andy Kroll, Dave Gilson, & Benjy Hansen-Bundy, Triumph of the Drill: How Big Oil Clings to Billions in Government Giveaways, *Mother Jones* (Apr. 14, 2014).

10.12 L

Levhari, David & Nissan Liviatan, Notes on Hotelling's Economics of Exhaustible Resources, 10 *Can. J. Econ.* 177, 178 (1977).

Light, Sarah E., The Military-Environmental Complex, 55 *B.C. L. Rev.* 879 (2014).

Meagher, Robert E., *The Meaning of Helen: In Search of an Ancient Icon* (Bolchazy-Carducci Publishers, Wauconda, Illinois, 1995).

10.13 M

Mankiw NG. *Principles of Economics*, 5th edition. South-Western Cengage Learning; Mason, Ohio, USA. 2011.

Mas-Colell, Andreu, Michael D. Whinston, & Jerry R. Green, *Microeconomic Theory* (Oxford University Press, New York, 1995).

Michielsen, Thomas, Brown Backstops Versus the Green Paradox, 68 *J. Envtl. Econ. & Mgmt.* 87, 87–88 (2014).

10.14 N

Nordhaus, William D., Hendrik Houthakker, and Robert Solow. "The allocation of energy resources." Brookings papers on economic activity 1973.3 (1973): 529–576.

Nordhaus, William D., *Managing the Global Commons: The Economics of Climate Change* (1994).

Nuttall, Nick, Negotiations Towards New Universal Climate Agreement in 2015 Get Underway, UNFCCC (Mar. 14, 2014).

10.16 P

Paltsev, Sergey V., The Kyoto Protocol: Regional and Sectoral Contributions to the Carbon Leakage, 22 *Energy J.* 59 (2001).

Partain, Roy A., Is a Green Paradox Spectre Haunting International Climate Change Laws and Conventions?, 33 *UCLA Journal of Environmental Law & Policy* 61 (2015).

Partain, Roy A., Gored by a Cornucopia: The Risks to Climate Change from Laws and Policies that Incentivize Competitive But Divergent Energy Innovations, 3(2) *LSU Journal of Energy Law & Resources* 433 (2015).

Partain, Roy A., Climate Change, Green Paradox Models, and International Trade Laws, in *Research Handbook on Climate Change and Trade Law* (Edward Elgar Publishing Ltd, Cheltenham, UK 2016).

Partain, Roy A., *Environmental Hazards from Offshore Methane Hydrate Operations: Civil Liability and Regulations for Efficient Governance* (Wolters Kluwers International, Zuidpoolsingel, Netherlands 2017).

Partain, Roy A., Efficient Development and Enforcement of a Regulatory Framework for Private Operators in South Korea's Offshore Carbon Capture and Storage Activities, in *Linking Climate Change Policies: Korean and Chinese Perspectives and Opportunities* (Stefan Weishaar, Eun-Jung Kim, & Fitsum Tiche, eds., Edward Elgar Publishing Ltd, Cheltenham, UK, 2020).

Partain, Roy A. & Michael Faure, Development of a Regulatory Framework for CDM-Enabled Offshore Carbon Capture and Storage (OCCS) in China, in *The Rise of the Regulatory State: The U.S., E.U. and China's Theory and Practice* (Stefan Weishaar & Niels Philipsen, eds., Edward Elgar Publishing Ltd, Cheltenham, UK, 2017).

Partain, Roy A. & Sanghyun "John" Lee, Article 20 Obligations under the KORUS FTA: The Deteriorating Environment for Climate Change Legislation in the U.S., 24 *Am. Const. Stud.* 441 (2013).

Pirog, Robert, Cong. Research Serv., RL42374, Oil and Natural Gas Industry Tax Issues in the FY2014 Budget Proposal (2013).

Polimeni, John M., Mayumi Kozo, Mario Giampietro, & Blake Alcott, *The Myth of Resource Efficiency* (Earthscan, London, 2009).

Polimeni, John M., *The Jevons Paradox and the Myth of Resource Efficiency Improvements* (Earthscan, London UK, 2007).

10.18 R

Ritter, Hendrik & Mark Schopf, *Unilateral Climate Policy: Harmful or Even Disastrous?* 1–4 (Otto von Guericke Universität Magdeburg Faculty of Econ. and Mgmt., Working Paper No. 10, 2013).

Romer, Paul M., Endogenous Technological Change, 98(5) *J. Pol. Econ.* S71–S102, (October 1990).

Romer, Paul M., The Origins of Endogenous Growth, 8(1) *J. Econ. Perspectives* 3-22 (1994).

10.19 S

Intergovernmental Panel on Climate Change [IPCC], Summary for Policymakers, in *Climate Change 2013: The Physical Science Basis. Contribution of Working Group I to the Fifth Assessment Report of the IPCC 17* (Thomas F. Stocker et al. eds., Cambridge University Press, New York, 2013).

Samuelson, Paul Anthony, *Foundations of Economic Analysis* (Harvard University Press Cambridge, Massachusetts 1947).

Schwartz, Moshe, Katherine Blakeley, & Ronald O'Rourke, Cong. Research Serv., R42558, Department of Defense Energy Initiatives: Background and Issues for Congress, (Dec. 10, 2012).

Sherlock, Molly F., Cong. Research Serv., RL31953, Energy Tax Incentives: Measuring Value Across Different Types of Energy Resources (2012).

Sherlock, Molly F., Cong. Research Serv., RL43206, Energy Tax Policy: Issues in the 113th Congress, Appendix (2013).

Sinn, Hans-Werner, Public Policies against Global Warming: A Supply Side Approach, 15 *Int'l Tax & Pub. Fin.* 360, 377–381 (2008).

Sinn, Hans-Werner, *The Green Paradox: A Supply-Side Approach to Global Warming* (MIT Press, Cambridge, Massachusetts 2012).

Slade, Margaret E. & Henry Thille, Whither Hotelling: Tests of the Theory of Exhaustible Resources, 1 *Ann. Rev. Resource Econ.* 239, 256 (2009).

Smulders, Sjak et al., Announcing Climate Policy: Can a Green Paradox Arise without Scarcity?, 64 *J. Envtl. Econ. & Mgmt.* 364 (2012).

Stern, Nicholas, *Stern Review: The Economics of Climate Change.* Vol. 30, 3 (HM Treasury, London, 2006).

Stiglitz, Joseph E., Monopoly and the Rate of Extraction of Exhaustible Resources, 66 *Am. Econ. Rev.* 655 (1976).

Stine, Deborah D., Cong. Research Serv., RL34645, the Manhattan Project, the Apollo Program, and Federal Energy technology R&D Programs: A Comparative Analysis 3 (2009).

Stocker, Thomas F. & Dahe Qin (eds.), *Climate Change 2013: The Physical Science Basis: Summary for Policymakers* (2013), Working Group I Contribution to the Fifth Assessment Report of the Intergovernmental Panel on Climate Change. Intergovernmental Panel on Climate Change, 3.

Stürmer, Martin & Gregor Schwerhoff, *Non-Renewable But Inexhaustible: Resources in an Endogenous Growth Model* (Max Planck Inst. for Research on Collective Goods, Paper No. Bonn 2012/09, 2012).

10.20 T

Thronson, Patrick, Toward Comprehensive Reform of America's Emergency Law Regime, 46(2) *U. Mich. J. L. Reform* 737, 754, at Table I (2013).

10.21 U

Background on the UNFCCC: The International Response to Climate Change, United Nations Framework Convention on Climate Change, http://unfccc.int/essential_background/items/6031.php (last visited Nov. 6, 2014).

10.22 V

van der Ploeg, Frederick & Cees Withagen, Is There Really a Green Paradox?, 64 *J. Envtl. Econ. & Mgmt.* 342 (2012).

van der Ploeg, Frederick & Cees Withagen, *On the Relevance of Green Paradoxes* 1–2 (Oxford Ctr. for the Analysis of Res. Rich Econ., Policy Paper No. 18, 2013).

van der Werf, Edwin & Corrado Di Maria, Imperfect Environmental Policy and Polluting Emissions: The Green Paradox and Beyond, 6 *Int'l Rev. Envtl. & Resource Econ.* 153 (2012).

van Veldhuizen, Roel & Joep Sonnemans, *Nonrenewable Resources, Strategic Behavior and the Hotelling Rule: An Experiment* 7–10 (WZB Berlin Soc. Sci. Ctr. Discussion Paper No. SP II 2014–203, 2014), http://bibliothek.wzb.eu/pdf/2014/ii14-203.pdf

10.23 W

Watkins, G. C., Oil Scarcity: What Have the Past Three Decades Revealed?, 34 *Energy Pol'y* 508, 510 (Gordon Campbell Watkins, 2006).

Weiss, Daniel J. & Miranda Peterson, With Only $93 Billion in Profits, the Big Five Oil Companies Demand to Keep Tax Breaks, *Energy & Enviro., Center for Am. Progress* (Feb. 10, 2014), www.americanprogress.org/issues/green/news/2014/02/10/83879/with-only-93-billion-in-profits-the-big-five-oil-companies-demand-to-keep-tax-breaks/

Whitty, Julia, My Heart-Stopping Ride Aboard the Navy's Great Green Fleet: With Washington Frozen Solid on Climate, the Navy is Breaking the Ice, *Mother Jones*, (Mar./Apr., 2013).

10.27 Legal Instruments

Council Directive 2001/42 of the European Parliament and of the Council of 27 June 2001 on the Assessment of the Effects of Certain Plans and Programmes on the Environment, 2001 O.J. (L 197) 30, 30–37 (EC).

The Energy Charter Treaty [hereinafter ECT] Annex I to the Final Act of the European Energy Charter Conference, Dec. 17, 1994.

Energy Charter Treaty, *opened for signature* Dec. 17, 1994, 2080 U.N.T.S. 95 (entered into force April 16, 1998).

General Agreement on Tariffs and Trade, Oct. 30, 1947, 61 Stat. A-11, 55 U.N.T.S. 194.
Kyoto Protocol to the United Nations Framework Convention on Climate Change, Dec. 10, 1997, U.N. Doc FCCC/CP/1997/7/Add.1, 37 I.L.M. 22 (1998).
Kyoto Protocol to the United Nations Framework Convention on Climate Change, Dec. 11, 1997, 2303 U.N.T.S. 148.
OPEC Statute, Org. of the Petroleum Exporting Countries (Jan. 10, 2015).
Solemn Declaration II, The Second Summit of Heads of State and Government of OPEC Member Countries, *Org. of the Petroleum Exporting Countries*, 13 (2009).
Solemn Declaration III, Conference of Sovereigns and Heads of State of OPEC Member Countries. Riyadh, Saudi Arabia, *Org. of the Petroleum Exporting Countries*, 17 (2009).
Solemn Declarations, *Org. of the Petroleum Exporting Countries* 1 (2009).
United Nations Framework Convention on Climate Change, May 9, 1992., U.N. Doc. FCCC/Informal/84; GE.05–62220 (E) 200705.
United Nations Framework Convention on Climate Change Conference, Doha, Qatar, Amendment to the Kyoto Protocol, U.N. Doc. C.N.718.2012.TREATIES-XXVII.7.c, Art. 1, Annex A (Dec. 8, 2012).

10.28 Governmental Documents and Archives

21st Conference of the Parties on Climate Change 2015, France Diplomatie (July 14, 2014), www.diplomatie.gouv.fr/en/french-foreign-policy-1/climate-7436/2015-paris-climate-conference/
2014 Orphan Well List, Cal. Dep't of Conservation, ftp://ftp.consrv.ca.gov/pub/oil/orphan/Current%20Orphan%20List.pdf (last visited Nov. 8, 2014).
Conference of the Parties, Report of the Conference of the Parties on Its Eighteenth Session, held in Doha from 26 November to 8 December 2012, FCCC/CP/2012/8/Add.2 (Nov. 26 to Dec. 8, 2012).
Idle and Orphan Well Program, Cal. Dep't of Conservation, www.conservation.ca.gov/dog/idle_well/Pages/idle_well.aspx (last visited Nov. 8, 2014).
Highlights of the Department of Navy FY 2013 Budget, Dep't of the Navy, Feb. 2012, at 1–8.
Two Severance Tax Incentives Extended the Two-Year Inactive Well Incentive for Oil Wells and Gas Wells and the High-Cost Gas Incentive, R.R. Comm'n of Tex., www.rrc.state.tx.us/oil-gas/publications-and-notices/notices-to-industry/notices-to-industry-1994-1999/two-severance-tax-incentives/ (last updated May 21, 2014).
U.N. Dep't of Econ. & Soc. Affairs, Standard International Trade Classification, Revision 4, U.N. Doc. ST/ESA/STAT/SER.M/34/Rev.4, U.N. Sales No. E.06.XVII.10 (2006).
USN, *The Department of the Navy's Energy Goals*, www.navy.mil/features/Navy_EnergySecurity.pdf
World Trade Organization, International Trade Statistics 2011, 188–190 (2011).

Index

For Product Safety Concerns and Information please contact our EU representative GPSR@taylorandfrancis.com
Taylor & Francis Verlag GmbH, Kaufingerstraße 24, 80331 München, Germany

www.ingramcontent.com/pod-product-compliance
Ingram Content Group UK Ltd.
Pitfield, Milton Keynes, MK11 3LW, UK
UKHW011018180926
475701UK00004B/819